THE COMPLETE
PIES & TARTS
COOKBOOK

THE COMPLETE
PIES & TARTS
COOKBOOK

bay books

Key Lime Pie, page 203

Vegetable Pie with Cheese Topping, page 88

Beef and Red Wine Pies, page 79

Contents

Real Lemon Pie, page 214

You will find the following cookery ratings on the recipes in this book:

A single pot symbol indicates a recipe that is simple and generally straightforward to make—perfect for beginners.

Two symbols indicate the need for just a little more care and a little more time.

Three symbols indicate special recipes that need more investment in time, care and patience—but the results are worth it.

Spinach and Feta Filo Roll, page 59

Thai Three Mushroom Tart, page 108

Tomato and Bacon Quiche, page 154

Salmon Pie, page 70

Perfect Pastry

What does 'rub in the butter' mean? How do you 'line the tin with pastry'? Why are some pastry cases baked blind before they are filled? These are some of the questions that can vex newcomers to pastry-making. Take a little time to read the following hints and all will be clear.

WHICH PASTRY?

For most of the recipes in this book, you can make your own pastry or buy ready-made. If we specify a home-made pastry it is because the taste is better in that particular pie.

We have used only a few types of pastry throughout this book. Beginners should probably choose recipes using the easiest pastries such as shortcrust or quick flaky. Puff pastry requires a lot more rolling and chilling and is a little less predictable when baked. Instead of, or as well as, butter, some pastries use olive oil and others lard. Some shortcrusts have sugar or an egg added—you could still use bought shortcrust, but the pastry won't be quite as rich. Plain shortcrust can be used for sweet pies but sweet pastry is most commonly used.

INGREDIENTS

Pastry at its simplest is flour mixed with half its weight in some form of fat, then bound with water.

Flour Plain white flour is the one most commonly used for pastry. For a slightly different texture, a combination of wholemeal plain and plain white flour is used. Store your flour in an airtight container.

Fat Butter is the most commonly used fat for making pastry and gives a wonderful colour to the pastry. Use real butter, not margarine or softened butter blends. Sometimes a mixture of butter and lard is used, sometimes all lard. Lard gives a good flaky texture. Butter and lard are usually chilled and cut into cubes to make it easier to incorporate them into the flour, keeping the pastry cooler and more manageable.

Generally, unsalted butter should be used for sweet and salted butter for savoury recipes. Olive oil is sometimes used to give pastries a different texture, for example in a traditional spinach pie.

Salt Salt can be added to both sweet and savoury pastry to add flavour.

Sugar Caster sugar is used in sweet shortcrust pastry as its fine texture ensures that it blends well.

Liquid The usual binding liquid in pastry-making is iced water, but sometimes an egg or an egg yolk will be used to enrich the dough. You will find that most pastry recipes only give an approximate liquid measure because the amount will vary according to the flour, the temperature, the altitude and the humidity. Add a little at a time and work it in until the pastry 'starts to come together' in clumps that can then be pressed together.

TOOLS OF THE TRADE

Food processor While not essential, a food processor can make pastry-making easy. Pastry should be kept cool and a processor means you don't need to touch the dough as you mix. The processor method is described on page 9. If you prefer, you can use the processor just to combine the butter and flour before continuing to mix by hand.

Marble pastry board Although not strictly necessary, marble boards are favoured by pastry-makers for their cool and hygienic surface. If you don't have one, place a roasting tin full of iced water on your work surface for a while to cool the surface before rolling your pastry.

Rolling pins are an essential tool in pastry-making. They are now available in traditional wood, marble, plastic and stainless steel. Lightly sprinkle your rolling pin with flour to prevent the pastry sticking. You can also use the rolling pin to lift the pastry into the tin and then trim away the excess pastry by rolling over the top.

Baking paper is very useful when rolling out pastry. The dough is rolled out between two sheets of paper, the top sheet is removed and the pastry is inverted into the tin before removing the other sheet. A crumpled sheet of baking paper is also used to line pastry shells when blind baking.

Baking beads Re-usable baking beads are spread in a layer over baking paper and used to weigh down pastry during blind baking. They are available in kitchenware shops and department stores. Dried beans or uncooked rice can also be used and stored in a jar for re-use.

Cutters are available in all shapes and sizes. They are used to cut bases and tops for small pies and to cut out pieces of dough to decorate the pie. Cutters may need to be dusted lightly with flour to prevent them from sticking to the pastry. If you don't have a pastry cutter, a fine-rimmed glass, turned upside-down, is a good substitute.

Pie tins and dishes are available in many styles. While testing the pies for this book we baked with metal, glass and ceramic pie dishes. We found the crispest base crusts were achieved in the metal tins.

Pastry brushes are used for glazing. A glaze gives the pastry crispness and colour. Pastry can also be sealed and joined by brushing the edges with milk or beaten egg. Use only a small amount of liquid or your pastry may become soggy.

PASTRY-MAKERS' TIPS

1 Dough must be kept cool. Work in a cool kitchen if possible. If you are baking in summer, chill your work surface by leaving a tin of iced water on it before you start rolling or shaping. Make sure all the ingredients are as cool as possible and that they stay cool during the preparation.

2 Because your hands are warm, try to handle the pastry as little as possible. Cool your hands under cold water. Good pastry-makers work quickly—too much handling will cause the cooked pastry to toughen and shrink.

3 Flours vary in their moisture content. Because of this variation, the liquid (usually iced water) is not added all at once. Test the dough by pinching a little piece together. If it holds together and doesn't crumble, you don't need more liquid. If the pastry is too dry, it will be difficult to put into tins; if too wet it will shrink when cooked.

4 Pastry should be wrapped in plastic and put in the fridge for 20–30 minutes before rolling or shaping. In hot weather, refrigerate the pastry for at least 30 minutes.

5 For ease of rolling, roll out dough between two sheets of baking paper.

6 Pies with a bottom crust benefit from being cooked on a heated metal baking tray. Put the tray in the oven as the oven warms up.

7 Pastry can be stored in the fridge for two days or frozen for up to three months. Ensure that it is well sealed in plastic wrap and clearly labelled and dated. Thaw on a wire rack to let the air circulate.

8 Pastry should always be cooked in a preheated oven, never one that is still warming up. It is a good idea to use an oven thermometer.

9 Pies can be frozen as long as the filling is suitable (don't freeze creamy, egg fillings) and the pastry has not already been frozen. For best results, a frozen pie should be reheated in a slow oven.

10 To test if a pie is cooked, poke a metal skewer into the centre. If the skewer is cold, the pie needs to be baked for longer.

SHORTCRUST PASTRY

This recipe makes 375 g (12 oz) of basic shortcrust pastry, which is enough to line the base of a 23 cm (9 inch) pie dish, or just the top. If you need 750 g (1¹/₂ lb) of pastry, simply double the quantity.

For 375 g (12 oz) shortcrust pastry, you will need 2 cups (250 g/8 oz) plain flour, 125 g (4 oz) chilled butter, chopped into small pieces, and 2–3 tablespoons iced water. If you want to line the top and base, you will need 600 g (1¹/₄ lb) and for this you need 400 g (13 oz) plain flour, 180 g (6 oz) chilled butter, chopped into small pieces, and 3–4 tablespoons iced water.

1 Remove the butter from the fridge 20 minutes before you make the pastry, except in hot weather. Sift the flour and ¹/₄ teaspoon of salt into a large bowl. Sifting the flour will aerate the dough and help make the finished pastry crisp and light.

2 Add the chopped butter and rub the pieces of butter into the flour with your fingertips—your palms will be too warm—until the mixture resembles fine crumbs. As you rub the butter into the flour, lift it up high and let it fall back into the bowl. If applicable, stir in other dry ingredients such as sugar or herbs.

3 Make a well in the centre, add nearly all the water and mix with a flat-bladed knife, using a cutting rather than a stirring action, turning the bowl with your free hand. The mixture will come together in small beads of dough. If necessary, add more water, a teaspoon at a time, until the dough comes together. Test the dough by pinching a little piece between your fingers. If it doesn't hold together, it needs more water. If the pastry is too dry, it will fall apart when rolled. If too wet, it will be sticky and shrink when baked.

4 Gather the dough together and lift out onto a lightly floured work surface or a sheet of baking paper. Press the dough together into a ball. The trick here is not to knead or handle the dough too much, but just to press it together into a ball. Refrigerate, wrapped in plastic or in a plastic bag for 20–30 minutes—this makes it easier

MAKING SHORTCRUST PASTRY

Add the chopped butter to the flour and rub it in until it resembles fine crumbs.

Mix in the water with a knife, using a cutting, rather than a stirring, action.

Roll out the pastry, from the centre outwards, rotating the dough.

to roll and helps prevent shrinkage during cooking. If the weather is hot, refrigerate for at least 30 minutes.

5 Roll out the pastry between two sheets of baking paper or plastic wrap or on a lightly floured surface to prevent sticking. Always roll from the centre outwards, rotating the dough, rather than backwards and forwards.

6 If you used baking paper to roll out the pastry, remove the top sheet and then carefully invert the pastry over the tin. Make sure you centre the pastry, as it can't be moved once in place, and then peel away the paper. If you rolled out on a floured surface, roll the pastry back over the rolling pin so it is hanging, then ease it into the tin.

7 Once the pastry is in the tin, quickly lift up the sides so they don't break over the sharp edges of the tin. Use a small ball of excess dough to press the pastry firmly into the base and side of the tin. Let the excess hang over the side and, if using a tart tin, roll the rolling pin over the top of the tin to cut off the excess pastry. If you are using a glass or ceramic pie dish, use a small sharp knife to trim the excess pastry.

8 However gently you handle dough, it is bound to shrink a little, so let it sit slightly above the side of the tin. If you

rolled off the excess pastry with a rolling pin, you may find it has bunched down the sides. Gently press the sides of the pastry with your thumbs to flatten and lift it. Now refrigerate the pastry-lined tin for 15 minutes to relax the pastry and prevent or minimise shrinkage.

SHORTCRUST VARIATIONS:

Herb pastry Add 2–3 tablespoons chopped fresh herbs to the flour.

Cheese pastry Add 60 g (2 oz) grated Parmesan to the flour.

Nut pastry Add 2–3 tablespoons ground nuts, such as almonds, walnuts or pecans, to the flour.

Seed pastry Add 2 teaspoons sesame or poppy seeds to the flour.

Mustard pastry Add 1 tablespoon wholegrain mustard to the flour.

Citrus pastry Add 2–3 teaspoons finely grated orange or lemon rind to the flour.

English shortcrust pastry Use half butter and half lard.

Rich shortcrust pastry This is often to give fruit pies, flans and tarts a richer, crisper crust. To transform a basic shortcrust into a rich one, gradually add a beaten egg yolk to

the flour with 2–3 tablespoons iced water as above in step 3. Mix with a flat-bladed knife.

Sweet shortcrust pastry This is a variation that can be used for sweet recipes. Follow the directions for rich shortcrust, adding 2 tablespoons caster or icing sugar after the butter has been rubbed into the flour.

Food processor shortcrust A food processor is a useful tool for pastry-making. Shortcrust pastry can be made quickly with a food processor and, because you don't handle the pastry much, it stays cooler than if made by hand. Process the flour and cold chopped butter in short bursts, using the pulse button if your machine has one, until the mixture resembles fine breadcrumbs. While the processor is running, add a teaspoon of water at a time until the dough holds together. Process in short bursts again—don't over-process or the pastry will toughen and shrink on cooking. You will know you have overworked the dough if it forms into a ball in the processor. It should just come together in clumps. Tip it out onto a lightly floured surface, gather into a ball and wrap in plastic wrap, then refrigerate it for 20–30 minutes.

PUFF PASTRY

Puff pastry is made by layering dough with butter and folding and rolling to create hundreds of layers. When baked, the butter melts and the dough produces steam, forcing the layers apart to make the pastry rise.

For perfect puff pastry that rises evenly, the edges must be cut cleanly with a sharp knife, not torn. Egg glazes give a shine but must be applied carefully—any drips down the side will glue the layers together and prevent them rising evenly.

Always bake puff pastry at a very high temperature—it should rise evenly so, if your oven has areas of uneven heat, turn during baking. When cooked, the top and base should be brown, with only a small amount of under-baked dough inside, and the layers visible.

Puff pastry is not always perfect—it may fall over or not rise to quite the heights you had imagined—but provided you don't burn it, and it is well cooked, it will still be delicious.

The recipe we have given below makes about 500 g (1 lb) of puff pastry. You will notice that we've given a range for the butter quantity. If you've never made puff pastry before, you'll find it easier to use the lower amount. You will need 200–250 g (6½–8 oz) unsalted butter, 2 cups (250 g/8 oz) plain flour, ½ teaspoon salt and ⅔ cup (170 ml/5½ fl oz) iced water.

1 Melt 30 g (1 oz) butter in a pan. Sift the flour and salt onto a work surface and make a well in the centre. Pour the melted butter and iced water into the well and blend with your fingertips, gradually drawing in the flour until you have a crumb mixture. If it seems a little dry, add a few extra drops of water before bringing it all roughly together with your hands to form a dough.

2 Cut the dough with a pastry scraper, using a downward cutting action, then turn the dough and repeat in the opposite direction. The dough should now come together in a soft ball. Score a cross in the top to prevent shrinkage, wrap in plastic and refrigerate for 15–20 minutes.

3 Soften the remaining butter by pounding it between two sheets of baking paper with a rolling pin. Then, still between the sheets of baking paper, roll it into a 10 cm (4 inch) square. The butter must be the same consistency as the dough or they will not roll out the same amount and the layers will not be even. If the butter is too soft it will squeeze out of the sides, and if it is too hard it will break through the dough and disturb the layers.

4 Put the pastry on a well-floured surface. Roll it out to form a cross, leaving the centre slightly thicker than the arms. Place the butter in the centre of the cross and fold over each of the arms to make a parcel. Tap and roll out the dough to form a 15 x 45 cm (6 x 18 inch) rectangle. Make this as neat as possible, squaring off the corners—otherwise, every time you fold, the edges will become less neat and the layers will not be even.

5 Fold the dough like a letter, the top third down and the bottom third up, brushing off any excess flour between the layers. Give the dough a quarter turn to your left and press the seam sides down with the rolling pin to seal them. Re-roll and fold as before to complete two turns and mark the dough by gently pressing into the corner with your fingertip for each turn—this will remind you where you're up to. Wrap the dough in plastic wrap and chill again for at least 30 minutes.

6 Re-roll and fold the pastry twice more and then chill, then roll again to complete six turns. If it is a very hot day, you may need to chill for 30 minutes after each turn, rather than doing a double. The pastry should now be an even yellow and is ready to use—if it looks streaky, roll and fold once more. The aim is to ensure that the butter is evenly distributed so that the pastry rises evenly. Chill the pastry for at least 30 minutes before baking to relax it.

MAKING PUFF PASTRY

Cut the dough with a pastry scraper, using a downward cutting motion.

Place the butter in the centre and fold over the arms to make a parcel.

Fold the top third of the pastry down and the bottom third up.

QUICK FLAKY PASTRY

Flaky pastry is a member of the puff pastry family. This is a very easy, quick version which will give you a crust with a nice flaky texture with some rise. It is important to use frozen butter and to handle the dough as little as possible. The butter is not worked into the dough at all but left in chunky grated pieces. If the butter starts to soften, it is absorbed into the flour and the flakiness is lost. This is why it is important to keep the pastry chilled. The amount of pastry given here will make enough to cover two pies. Any leftover pastry can be used for decoration, or refrigerated for up to two days, or wrapped in plastic wrap and frozen for up to three months. This recipe makes about 600 g (1¼ lb) pastry.

1 Sift 350 g (12 oz) plain flour and ½ teaspoon salt into a large bowl. Grate 220 g (7 oz) frozen unsalted butter into the bowl, using the largest holes on the grater. Mix the butter gently into the flour with a knife, making sure all the pieces are coated in flour. Add 3 tablespoons chilled water and mix with a metal spatula.
2 The pastry should come together in clumps. Test the dough by pinching a little piece between your fingers. If it doesn't hold together, mix in a teaspoon of iced water.
3 When the dough holds together, quickly gather it into a neat ball in the bowl. Cover and refrigerate the dough for 30 minutes, then roll out as required for your recipe.

READY-MADE PASTRY

For busy cooks, there is a large range of ready-made frozen or refrigerated pastries available at supermarkets. Standard puff and shortcrust pastries are available in blocks, and puff, butter puff and shortcrust pastries also come as ready-rolled sheets. The recipe will simply say '2 sheets puff pastry' or '250 g shortcrust pastry' and these should be thawed. Thaw frozen block pastry for 2 hours before using. Sheets only take 5–10 minutes to thaw at room temperature.

LINING THE TIN

Roll out the dough between two sheets of baking paper, or on a lightly floured surface. Always roll from the centre outwards, rotating the dough, rather than rolling backwards and forwards. Reduce the pressure towards the edges of the dough. If you used baking paper, remove the top sheet and invert the pastry over the tin, then peel away the other sheet. Centre the pastry as it can't be moved once in place. Quickly lift up the sides so they don't break over the edges of the tin. Use a small ball of dough to press the pastry into the side of the tin. Trim away the excess pastry with a small, sharp knife or by rolling the rolling pin over the top. However gently you handle the dough it is bound to shrink slightly, so let it sit a little above the side of the tin. Chill the pastry in the tin for 20 minutes to relax it and minimise shrinkage.

BLIND BAKING

If a pie or tart is to have a liquid filling, the pastry usually requires blind baking to partially cook it before filling. This prevents the base becoming soggy.

When blind baking, the pastry needs to be weighted down to prevent it rising. Cover the base and side with a crumpled piece of baking paper or greaseproof paper. Pour in a layer of baking beads (also called pie weights), dried beans or uncooked rice and spread out over the paper to cover the pastry base. Bake for the recommended time (usually about 10 minutes), then remove the paper and beads. The beads are re-usable and dried beans or rice can also be kept in a separate jar for re-use for blind baking (but they are not now suitable for eating). Return the pastry to the oven for 10–15 minutes, or as specified in the recipe, until the base is dry with no greasy patches. Let the pastry cool completely.

The filling should also be completely cooled before filling the shell—filling a cold shell with a hot mixture can also cause the pastry to become soggy.

MAKING QUICK FLAKY PASTRY

Using the large holes on the grater, grate the butter into the flour.

Mix the butter into the flour with a knife, making sure the butter is coated.

When the pastry comes together in clumps, form it into a ball.

Savoury Pies

CHICKEN AND LEEK PIE

Preparation time: 20 minutes
Total cooking time: 40 minutes
Serves 4

60 g (2 oz) butter
2 large leeks, finely sliced
4 spring onions, sliced
1 clove garlic, crushed
1/4 cup (30 g/1 oz) plain flour
1 1/2 cups (375 ml/12 fl oz) chicken
   stock
1/2 cup (125 ml/4 fl oz) cream
1 barbecued chicken, chopped
2 sheets puff pastry
1/4 cup (60 ml/2 fl oz) milk

1 Preheat the oven to 200°C (400°F/ Gas 6). In a pan, melt the butter and add the leek, spring onion and garlic. Cook over low heat for 6 minutes, or until the leek is soft but not browned. Sprinkle in the flour and mix well. Pour in the stock gradually and cook, stirring well, until thick and smooth. Stir in the cream and add the chicken.
2 Put the mixture in a shallow 20 cm (8 inch) pie dish and set aside to cool.
3 Cut a circle out of one of the sheets of pastry to cover the top of the pie.

Paint around the rim of the pie dish with a little milk. Put the pastry on top and seal around the edge firmly. Trim off any overhanging pastry and decorate the edge with a fork.
4 Cut the other sheet of pastry into 1 cm (1/2 inch) strips and roll each strip up loosely like a snail. Arrange the spirals on top of the pie, starting from the middle and leaving gaps between them. The spirals may not cover the whole surface of the pie. Make a few small holes between the spirals to let out any steam and brush the top of the pie lightly with milk. Bake for 25–30 minutes, or until the top is brown and crispy. Make sure the spirals look well cooked and are not raw in the middle.

NUTRITION PER SERVE
Protein 25 g; Fat 55 g; Carbohydrate 40 g; Dietary Fibre 3 g; Cholesterol 185 mg; 3105 kJ (740 cal)

VARIATION: Make small pies by putting the filling in four greased 1 1/4 cup (315 ml/10 fl oz) round ovenproof dishes. Cut the pastry into small rounds to fit the tops of the dishes. Bake for 15 minutes, or until the pastry is crisp.

Seal the edge firmly and trim off any overhanging pastry with a sharp knife.

Roll up the strips of pastry into spirals and arrange them on top of the pie.

OSSO BUCO PIE

Preparation time: 40 minutes
Total cooking time: 3 hours
Serves 4–6

1 kg (2 lb) veal shanks
plain flour, to coat
2 tablespoons olive oil
1 onion, finely chopped
1 carrot, finely chopped
1 celery stick, finely diced
2 cloves garlic, finely chopped
$^2/_3$ cup (170 ml/5$^1/_2$ fl oz) beef stock
400 g (13 oz) can chopped tomatoes
$^2/_3$ cup (170 ml/5$^1/_2$ fl oz) dry white
    wine
1 teaspoon dried oregano

GREMOLATA
4 tablespoons finely chopped
    fresh flat-leaf parsley
1–2 cloves garlic, finely chopped
1 tablespoon grated lemon rind

PARMESAN POLENTA
1 cup (150 g/5 oz) instant polenta
$^1/_2$ cup (125 ml/4 fl oz) cream
$^1/_2$ cup (60 g/2 oz) grated Parmesan

1 Cut the veal into six pieces, each about 3.5 cm (1$^1/_2$ inches) thick. Coat with flour. Heat 1 tablespoon of the oil in a large frying pan over high heat. Cook the veal, turning often, until brown, then set aside. Preheat the oven to 180°C (350°F/Gas 4).
2 Heat the remaining oil in a 2 litre flameproof casserole. Cook the onion, carrot, celery and garlic over low heat for 8 minutes, until soft but not brown.
3 Arrange the meat on top of the vegetables. Add the stock, tomato, wine and oregano and season well. Cover and bake for 1$^1/_2$–2 hours, or until the meat is falling off the bones and the liquid has thickened. Remove the bones from the veal with tongs. If

you like the marrow, spoon it out and return it to the casserole.
4 Spoon the filling into a 1.25 litre ovenproof dish. Combine the gremolata ingredients and sprinkle half over the filling.
5 Cook the polenta according to the packet, then stir in the cream and Parmesan. Spread over the osso buco and rough up with a fork. Bake for 25–30 minutes, until bubbling. Leave for 5 minutes. Sprinkle with the remaining gremolata.

NUTRITION PER SERVE (6)
Protein 43 g; Fat 18 g; Carbohydrate 24 g; Dietary Fibre 3 g; Cholesterol 172 mg; 1835 kJ (440 cal)

When the meat is tender and falling off the bones, remove the bones with tongs.

Spread the polenta topping evenly over the osso buco filling.

ASPARAGUS PIE

Preparation time: 40 minutes +
    45 minutes chilling
Total cooking time: 30 minutes
Serves 6

350 g (11 oz) plain flour
250 g (8 oz) butter, chilled and cubed
2/3 cup (170 ml/5 1/2 fl oz) iced water

FILLING
800 g (1 lb 10 oz) asparagus
30 g (1 oz) butter
1/2 teaspoon chopped fresh thyme
1 French shallot, chopped
60 g (2 oz) sliced ham
1/3 cup (80 ml/2 3/4 fl oz) cream
2 tablespoons grated Parmesan
1 egg
pinch of ground nutmeg
1 egg, extra, lightly beaten

1 To make the pastry, mix the flour
and a pinch of salt in a food processor
for 3 seconds. Add the butter and mix
until it is cut finely, but not entirely
blended into the flour—a few lumps
are desirable. With the motor running,
gradually pour in the iced water until
the dough comes together. It should
still have some small pebbles of butter.
2 Transfer to a lightly floured work
surface and press into a rectangle
about 30 x 12 cm (12 x 5 inches).
Fold one end into the centre, then the
opposite end over to cover the first.
Roll into a rectangle again and repeat
the folding three or four times. Wrap in
plastic wrap and chill for 45 minutes.
3 Remove the woody ends from the
asparagus. Slice thick spears in half
lengthways. Heat the butter in a large
frying pan and cook the asparagus,
thyme and shallot with a tablespoon of
water for 3 minutes, stirring often until
the asparagus is tender. Season well.
4 Preheat the oven to 200°C (400°F/
Gas 6) and grease a 20 cm (8 inch)
fluted, loose-based flan tin. Roll the
pastry out to a circle about 30 cm
(12 inches) across and line the tin,
leaving the rest of the pastry
overhanging the edge. Place half the
asparagus in the dish, top with the
ham, then the remaining asparagus.
5 Combine the cream, Parmesan, egg
and nutmeg. Season well and pour
over the asparagus. Fold the
overhanging pastry over the filling,
forming loose pleats. Brush with egg
and bake in the centre of the oven for
25 minutes, or until golden.

NUTRITION PER SERVE
Protein 15 g; Fat 46 g; Carbohydrate 46 g;
Dietary Fibre 4 g; Cholesterol 200 mg;
2730 kJ (650 cal)

Fold the ends of the dough over and press into a
rectangle. Repeat several times.

Pour the combined cream, egg, Parmesan and
nutmeg over the asparagus.

CHARGRILLED VEGETABLE AND PARMESAN PIE

Preparation time: 45 minutes +
  1 hour standing
Total cooking time: 1 hour 30 minutes
Serves 6

1 clove garlic, crushed
300 ml (10 fl oz) olive oil
2 large eggplants
1 large orange sweet potato
3 large zucchini
3 red capsicums
3 yellow capsicums
2 tablespoons polenta
90 g (3 oz) Parmesan, grated
1 egg, lightly beaten

PASTRY
450 g (14 oz) plain flour
2 teaspoons cumin seeds
2 teaspoons paprika
100 g (3¹/₂ oz) butter, chopped

1 Mix the garlic and oil together. Cut the eggplants and sweet potato into 5 mm (¹/₄ inch) slices and the zucchini into 5 mm (¹/₄ inch) lengths, then brush with the garlic oil. Quarter the capsicums and place, skin-side-up, under a hot grill for 10 minutes, or until the skins blacken and blister. Cool in a plastic bag, then peel.

2 Cook the eggplant, sweet potato and zucchini in batches in a chargrill pan over high heat, turning often, for 5–6 minutes, or until brown and tender. Set aside to cool.

3 Preheat the oven to 180°C (350°F/ Gas 4). Grease a deep 20 cm (8 inch) springform tin. Sift the flour into a bowl and add the cumin, paprika and ¹/₂ teaspoon salt. Gently heat the butter in a saucepan with 225 ml (7 fl oz) water. Bring to the boil, pour into the flour and mix with a wooden spoon. When cool enough to handle, tip onto a floured surface and press gently together. Rest for 5 minutes.

4 Set aside one quarter of the dough and roll out the rest between two sheets of baking paper until large enough to line the base and side of the tin, leaving some pastry overhanging. Sprinkle polenta over the base, then layer the red capsicum, zucchini, eggplant, sweet potato and yellow capsicum in the pie, brushing each layer with a little garlic oil, sprinkling with Parmesan and seasoning with salt and pepper as you go.

5 Roll out the remaining pastry between the baking paper to fit the top of the tin. Brush the edges of the bottom layer of pastry with egg. Cover with the pastry lid. Brush the edges with egg and trim with a sharp knife, crimping the edges to seal. Cut a small steam hole in the centre of the pie. Roll out the trimmings and use to decorate. Cook for 1 hour, or until crisp and golden (cover with foil if it browns too quickly). Cool for 1 hour before serving at room temperature.

NUTRITION PER SERVE
Protein 18 g; Fat 54 g; Carbohydrate 68 g; Dietary Fibre 7 g; Cholesterol 86 mg; 3445 kJ (820 cal)

Layer the chargrilled vegetables and grated Parmesan in the pastry case.

FISHERMAN'S PIE

Preparation time: 40 minutes
Total cooking time: 1 hour
Serves 4

800 g (1 lb 10 oz) white fish fillets
1½ cups (375 ml/12 fl oz) milk
1 onion, roughly chopped
2 cloves
50 g (1¾ oz) butter
2 tablespoons plain flour
pinch of ground nutmeg
2 tablespoons chopped fresh parsley
1 cup (150 g/5 oz) peas
750 g (1½ lb) potatoes, quartered
2 tablespoons hot milk
3 tablespoons grated Cheddar

1 Place the fish in a pan and cover with the milk. Add the onion and cloves and bring to the boil. Reduce the heat and simmer for 5 minutes, or until the fish is cooked and flakes easily with a fork.
2 Preheat the oven to 180°C (350°F/ Gas 4). Remove the fish from the pan, reserving the milk and onion. Discard the cloves. Allow the fish to cool then remove any bones and flake into bite-sized pieces with a fork.
3 Heat half of the butter in a pan, stir in the flour and cook, stirring, for 1 minute. Slowly add the reserved milk, stirring constantly until smooth. Cook, stirring, until the sauce begins to bubble, then cook for another minute. Remove from the heat, cool slightly, then add the nutmeg, parsley and peas. Season and gently fold in the fish. Spoon into a 1.25 litre casserole.
4 Cook the potatoes in boiling water until tender. Drain and add the hot milk and remaining butter. Mash until very smooth. Add the cheese. If the

mash is very stiff you can add a little more milk, but it should be fairly firm.
5 Spoon the potato over the filling and rough up with a fork. For a neater topping, spoon the potato into a piping bag and pipe over the filling. Bake for 30 minutes to heat through.

NUTRITION PER SERVE
Protein 55 g; Fat 25 g; Carbohydrate 40 g; Dietary Fibre 6 g; Cholesterol 200 mg; 2565 kJ (610 cal)

Cover the fish fillets with the milk and add the onion and cloves.

Heat half the butter in a pan and stir in the flour to make a roux.

For a neat topping to the pie, put the mash in a piping bag and pipe over the filling.

17

TANDOORI LAMB PIE

Preparation time: 45 minutes +
 20 minutes chilling
Total cooking time: 1 hour 30 minutes
Serves 4–6

1 cup (125 g/4 oz) plain flour
60 g (2 oz) butter, chilled and cubed
2 teaspoons coriander seeds
2 teaspoons cumin seeds
2 teaspoons poppy seeds
1 egg yolk
2 tablespoons iced water

FILLING
850 g (1 lb 11 oz) boned lamb
 shoulder
2 tablespoons oil
2 onions, chopped
1 clove garlic, crushed
2 teaspoons grated fresh ginger
1 teaspoon chilli powder
2 teaspoons garam masala
1 teaspoon ground cumin
1/2 teaspoon ground turmeric
2 carrots, chopped
11/4 cups (315 ml/10 fl oz) beef stock
1 tablespoon plain flour
1 teaspoon sugar
2 tablespoons lemon juice
200 g (61/2 oz) yoghurt
1 egg yolk, lightly beaten, to glaze

1 To make the pastry, mix the flour and butter in a food processor until the mixture is crumbly. Season with a pinch of salt. Add the coriander, cumin and poppy seeds and process until combined. Then add the egg yolk and water. Process in short bursts until the mixture just comes together, adding a little extra water if necessary. Turn out onto a floured surface and quickly bring together into a ball. Cover with plastic wrap and refrigerate for at least 20 minutes.

2 To make the filling, trim any excess fat from the lamb and cut into large cubes. Heat the oil in a pan and brown the lamb in batches. Return all the lamb to the pan. Add the onion and cook until translucent. Add the garlic, ginger and spices and stir over the heat for about 1 minute, or until aromatic. Stir in the carrot and stock. Bring to the boil, reduce the heat and simmer, covered, for 50 minutes, or until the lamb is tender. Remove from the heat. Mix together the flour and 2 tablespoons of water, until smooth. Stir into the meat, return to the heat and then stir until the mixture boils and thickens. Add the sugar, lemon juice and yoghurt and stir well. Season with a good pinch of salt.

3 Spoon the mixture into a deep 20 cm (8 inch) square or round pie dish and allow to cool. Preheat the oven to 200°C (400°F/Gas 6).

4 Roll out the pastry on a sheet of baking paper until it is large enough to cover the pie dish. Place the pastry over the filling and pinch the edges decoratively with your fingers. Then brush with the lightly beaten egg yolk and bake for 25–30 minutes, or until the pastry is browned and crisp.

NUTRITION PER SERVE (6)
Protein 40 g; Fat 25 g; Carbohydrate 25 g;
Dietary Fibre 3 g; Cholesterol 185 mg;
1920 kJ (455 cal)

STORAGE: The pie can be stored, covered, in the fridge for up to a day before baking.

Add the coriander, cumin and poppy seeds to the food processor.

Brown the lamb in batches, returning all the meat to the pan.

Stir the chopped carrot and beef stock into the lamb mixture.

Add the sugar, lemon juice and yoghurt to the pan and stir well.

Roll out the pastry until it is large enough to cover the pie dish.

Cover the filling with the pastry and pinch the edges for a decorative finish.

MINI SPINACH PIES

Preparation time: 45 minutes +
 30 minutes cooling
Total cooking time: 35 minutes
Makes 24

1/3 cup (80 ml/2¾ fl oz) olive oil
2 onions, finely chopped
2 cloves garlic, chopped
150 g (5 oz) small button mushrooms,
 roughly chopped
200 g (6½ oz) English spinach,
 chopped
½ teaspoon chopped fresh thyme
100 g (3½ oz) feta, crumbled
750 g (1½ lb) shortcrust pastry
milk, to glaze

1 Heat 2 tablespoons of the oil in
a frying pan over medium heat and
cook the onion and garlic for
5 minutes, or until soft and lightly
coloured. Add the mushrooms and
cook for another 4 minutes, or until
softened. Transfer to a bowl.
2 Heat 1 tablespoon of the oil in the
same pan over medium heat, add half
the spinach and cook, stirring well, for
2–3 minutes, or until softened. Add to
the bowl. Repeat with the remaining
oil and spinach. Add the thyme and
feta to the bowl and mix. Season well
and leave to cool.
3 Preheat the oven to 200°C (400°F/
Gas 6) and grease two 12-hole round-
based patty tins. Roll out half the
pastry between two sheets of baking
paper and cut out 24 rounds with a
7.5 cm (3 inch) cutter. Use these to line
the patty tins, then add the spinach
filling. Roll out the remaining pastry
and cut rounds of 7 cm (2¾ inches) to
fit the tops of the pies. Press the edges
with a fork to seal.

4 Prick the pie tops once with a fork,
brush with milk and bake for
15–20 minutes, or until golden. Serve
immediately or leave to cool on a
wire rack.

NUTRITION PER PIE
Protein 3 g; Fat 12 g; Carbohydrate 14 g;
Dietary Fibre 1 g; Cholesterol 12 mg;
725 kJ (175 cal)

Cook the spinach in a little oil in two batches until
it is just softened.

Spoon the spinach filling into the pastry-lined
patty tins.

Seal the edges of the pies with a fork, then prick
the tops once.

LAMB SHANK PIE

Preparation time: 30 minutes + 2 hours chilling
Total cooking time: 3 hours 10 minutes
Serves 6

8 lamb shanks
1/2 cup (60 g/2 oz) plain flour
2 tablespoons olive oil
4 red onions, quartered
8 cloves garlic, peeled
1 cup (250 ml/8 fl oz) red wine
1 litre beef stock
2 tablespoons finely chopped fresh rosemary
6 whole black peppercorns
1/4 cup (30 g/1 oz) cornflour
375 g (12 oz) puff pastry
1 egg, lightly beaten

1 Preheat the oven to 220°C (425°F/Gas 7). Lightly dust the shanks with flour, shaking off the excess. Heat the oil in a large frying pan and cook the shanks for 2 minutes each side, or until well browned. Transfer to a deep roasting tin and add the onion, garlic, wine, stock, rosemary and peppercorns. Cover and bake for 1 hour.
2 Stir the mixture, uncover and return to the oven for 1 hour 10 minutes, stirring occasionally, until the meat falls off the bones.
3 Remove the lamb bones with tongs. Mix the cornflour with 2 tablespoons water, then stir into the tin. Return to the oven for 10 minutes, or until thickened. Transfer to a large bowl, cool, then refrigerate for at least 2 hours, or overnight.
4 Preheat the oven to moderate 180°C (350°F/Gas 4). Grease a 23 cm (9 inch) pie plate with a rim. Spoon in the filling. Roll the pastry out between two sheets of baking paper until a little wider than the plate. Cut a 2 cm (3/4 inch) strip around the edge of the pastry, brush with water and place damp-side-down on the rim. Cover with the pastry circle, pressing down on the edges. Use the back of a knife to make small slashes around the edge. Trim, then re-roll the scraps to decorate. Brush with egg and bake for 45 minutes, or until the pastry is golden and has risen.

NUTRITION PER SERVE
Protein 50 g; Fat 24 g; Carbohydrate 47 g; Dietary Fibre 3 g; Cholesterol 157 mg; 2625 kJ (630 cal)

Cook the lamb shanks until the meat is so tender it is falling off the bones.

Stir the cornflour mixture into the tin and continue cooking until the sauce thickens.

SHEPHERD'S PIE

Preparation time: 30 minutes + cooling
Total cooking time: 1 hour 35 minutes
Serves 6

3 tablespoons olive oil
1 large onion, finely chopped
2 cloves garlic, crushed
2 celery sticks, finely chopped
3 carrots, diced
2 bay leaves
1 tablespoon fresh thyme, chopped
1 kg (2 lb) lamb mince
1¹/₂ tablespoons plain flour
¹/₂ cup (125 ml/4 fl oz) dry red wine
2 tablespoons tomato paste
400 g (13 oz) can crushed tomatoes
1.5 kg (3 lb) potatoes, chopped
¹/₄ cup (60 ml/2 fl oz) milk
100 g (3¹/₂ oz) butter
¹/₂ teaspoon ground nutmeg

1 Heat 2 tablespoons of the oil in a large, heavy-based saucepan and cook the onion for 3–4 minutes, or until softened. Add the garlic, celery, carrot, bay leaves and thyme and cook for 2–3 minutes. Transfer to a bowl and remove the bay leaves.

2 Add the remaining oil to the same pan and cook the mince over high heat for 5–6 minutes, or until it changes colour. Mix in the flour, cook for 1 minute, then pour in the red wine and cook for 2–3 minutes. Return the vegetables to the pan with the tomato paste and crushed tomato. Reduce the heat, cover and simmer for 45 minutes, stirring occasionally. Season and transfer to a shallow 3 litre casserole and leave to cool. Preheat the oven to 180°C (350°F/Gas 4).

3 Boil the potatoes in salted water for 20–25 minutes, or until tender. Drain, then mash with the milk and butter until smooth. Season with nutmeg and black pepper. Spoon over the mince and fluff with a fork. Bake for 30 minutes, until golden and crusty.

NUTRITION PER SERVE
Protein 42 g; Fat 35 g; Carbohydrate 37 g; Dietary Fibre 7 g; Cholesterol 159 mg; 2700 kJ (645 cal)

Return the softened vegetables to the pan with the mince.

Spoon the mashed potato over the cooked mince and then fluff with a fork.

CHICKEN AND CORN PIES

Preparation time: 25 minutes +
  2 hours refrigeration
Total cooking time: 50 minutes
Makes 6

1 tablespoon olive oil
650 g (1 lb 5 oz) chicken thigh fillets,
  cut into small pieces
1 tablespoon grated fresh ginger
400 g (13 oz) oyster mushrooms,
  halved
3 corn cobs, kernels removed
1/2 cup (125 ml/4 fl oz) chicken stock
2 tablespoons kecap manis
2 tablespoons cornflour
90 g (3 oz) coriander leaves, chopped
6 sheets shortcrust pastry
milk, to glaze

1 Grease six 10 cm (4 inch) metal pie tins. Heat the oil in a large frying pan over high heat and add the chicken. Cook for 5 minutes, or until golden. Add the ginger, mushrooms and corn and cook for 5–6 minutes, or until the chicken is just cooked through. Add the stock and kecap manis. Mix the cornflour with 2 tablespoons water, then stir into the pan. Boil for 2 minutes before adding the coriander. Cool then chill for 2 hours.
2 Preheat the oven to 180°C (350°F/ Gas 4). Using a saucer as a guide, cut a 15 cm (6 inch) round from each sheet of shortcrust pastry and line the pie tins. Fill the shells with the cooled filling, then cut out another six rounds large enough to make the lids. Trim away any extra pastry and seal the edges with a fork. Decorate with pastry scraps. Prick a few holes in the top of each pie, brush with a little milk and bake for 35 minutes until golden.

NUTRITION PER PIE
Protein 36 g; Fat 58 g; Carbohydrate 85 g; Dietary Fibre 8 g; Cholesterol 145 mg; 4145 kJ (990 cal)

Add the cornflour and then boil for 2 minutes to let it thicken the filling.

Cut out six rounds of pastry to fit the tops of the tins, then cover the filling.

TOURTIERE

Preparation time: 40 minutes +
   20 minutes chilling + cooling
Total cooking time: 1 hour
Serves 6

2¼ cups (280 g/9 oz) plain flour
½ teaspoon baking powder
120 g (4 oz) butter, chilled and cubed
½ teaspoon finely chopped fresh
   thyme
1 teaspoon lemon juice
1 egg, lightly beaten
1–2 tablespoons iced water

FILLING
1 small carrot
1 baby fennel bulb, thick outer
   leaves removed
4 French shallots
30 g (1 oz) butter
200 g (6½ oz) bacon, chopped
3 cloves garlic, crushed
500 g (1 lb) pork mince
1 teaspoon finely chopped fresh
   thyme
1 teaspoon finely chopped fresh sage
¼ teaspoon ground nutmeg
¾ cup (185 ml/6 fl oz) chicken stock
250 g (8 oz) potatoes, cut into small
   cubes
1 egg, lightly beaten

1 To make the pastry, sift the flour, baking powder and ¼ teaspoon salt into a large bowl and rub in the chilled butter with your fingertips until the mixture resembles fine breadcrumbs. Stir in the thyme, then make a well in the centre and add the lemon juice, egg and a little of the water. Mix with a flat-bladed knife, using a cutting action, until the mixture comes together in beads, adding more water if necessary.
2 Gently gather the dough together and lift out onto a lightly floured work surface. Press into a ball and flatten slightly into a disc, wrap in plastic wrap and chill for at least 20 minutes.
3 Finely chop the carrot, fennel and shallots in a food processor. Heat the butter in a large frying pan over medium heat and add the chopped vegetables, bacon, garlic and mince. Cook, stirring often, for 10 minutes, or

until the pork changes colour, then stir in the thyme, sage and nutmeg. Season well with salt and cracked black pepper. Add ¼ cup (60 ml/2 fl oz) of stock and simmer for 10 minutes, or until it is absorbed. Set aside to cool.
4 Preheat the oven to 200°C (400°F/Gas 6) and heat a baking tray. Grease an 18 cm (7 inch) pie dish. Place the remaining stock in a small saucepan with the potato and simmer for about 10 minutes, or until tender. Do not drain. Mash coarsely, then stir into the pork mixture.
5 Divide the dough into two portions, one slightly larger than the other. Roll out the larger portion between two sheets of baking paper until large enough to line the base and side of the dish. Spoon in the filling, levelling the surface. Brush the exposed pastry with beaten egg.
6 Roll out the remaining dough between the sheets of baking paper until large enough to cover the pie. Trim the edges and crimp to seal. Brush the surface with egg and make 6–8 small slits over the surface. Bake on the hot baking tray in the centre of the oven for 30 minutes until golden.

NUTRITION PER SERVE
Protein 33 g; Fat 30 g; Carbohydrate 42 g; Dietary Fibre 3.5 g; Cholesterol 189 mg; 2350 kJ (560 cal)

NOTE: The flavour of a tourtière improves over 24 hours and it is excellent served cold.

Remove the thick outer leaves from the baby fennel before chopping.

Cook the pork mixture, stirring often, until the meat changes colour.

Mash the potato and stock together, then stir into the pork mixture.

Trim the edges of the pastry to fit and then crimp them to seal.

SWEET POTATO, PUMPKIN AND COCONUT LATTICE PIES

Preparation time: 45 minutes +
 20 minutes refrigeration
Total cooking time: 55 minutes
Makes 8

2 tablespoons oil
1 onion, finely chopped
2 cloves garlic, crushed
1 teaspoon grated fresh ginger
1 small red chilli, chopped
250 g (8 oz) orange sweet potato,
 peeled and cubed
250 g (8 oz) pumpkin, peeled and
 cubed
1/2 teaspoon fennel seeds
1/2 teaspoon yellow mustard seeds
1/2 teaspoon ground turmeric
1/2 teaspoon ground cumin
150 ml (5 fl oz) can coconut milk
1/4 cup (15 g/1/2 oz) chopped fresh
 coriander
4 sheets puff pastry
1 egg yolk, to glaze

1 Heat the oil in a pan and cook the onion, garlic, ginger and chilli for 5 minutes, stirring continuously, until the onion is cooked. Add the sweet potato, pumpkin, fennel and mustard seeds, turmeric and cumin. Stir for 2 minutes, then add the coconut milk and 2 tablespoons of water. Cook over low heat, stirring frequently, for 20 minutes, or until the vegetables are tender. Stir through the coriander and set aside to cool.
2 Grease a large baking tray. Cut eight 9 cm (3 1/2 inch) circles from two sheets of the pastry and place them on the tray. Divide the filling between the circles and spread to within 1 cm

(1/2 inch) of the edge. Mound the filling slightly in the centre. Brush the edges of the pastry with a little water.
3 Using a lattice cutter or a sharp knife, cut out eight 10 cm (4 inch) circles from the remaining pastry. Carefully open out the lattices and fit them over the mixture. Press the edges together firmly to seal. Using the back of a knife, press the outside edge lightly at 1 cm (1/2 inch) intervals. Refrigerate for at least 20 minutes.

4 Preheat the oven to 190°C (375°F/ Gas 5). Mix the egg yolk with a teaspoon of water and brush the pastry. Bake for 20–25 minutes, or until golden.

NUTRITION PER PIE
Protein 7 g; Fat 30 g; Carbohydrate 40 g;
Dietary Fibre 3 g; Cholesterol 45 mg;
1800 kJ (430 cal)

Cut the orange sweet potato and pumpkin into even-sized cubes.

Mark the remaining two sheets of puff pastry with a lattice cutter.

Open out the lattices, fit them over the filling and press the edges to seal.

BEEF, STOUT AND POTATO PIE

Preparation time: 30 minutes
Total cooking time: 3 hours 10 minutes
Serves 6

2 tablespoons olive oil
1.25 kg (2 lb 8 oz) chuck steak, cut into small cubes
2 onions, sliced
2 rashers bacon, roughly chopped
4 cloves garlic, crushed
2 tablespoons plain flour
440 ml (14 fl oz) can stout
1½ cups (375 ml/12 fl oz) beef stock
1½ tablespoons chopped fresh thyme
2 large potatoes, thinly sliced

1 Heat 1 tablespoon of the oil over high heat in a large flameproof casserole. Add the beef in batches and cook, stirring, for 5 minutes, or until the meat is browned. Remove from the dish. Reduce the heat to low, add the remaining oil, then cook the onion and bacon for 10 minutes, stirring occasionally. Add the garlic and cook for another minute. Return the beef to the casserole.
2 Sprinkle the flour over the beef, cook for a minute, stirring, and then gradually add the stout, stirring constantly. Add the stock, increase the heat to medium–high and bring to the boil. Stir in the thyme, season well, then reduce the heat and simmer for 2 hours, or until the beef is tender and the mixture has thickened.
3 Preheat the oven to 200°C (400°F/ Gas 6). Lightly grease a 1.25 litre ovenproof dish and pour in the beef filling. Arrange potato slices in a single overlapping layer over the top to cover the meat. Brush lightly with olive oil and sprinkle with salt. Bake for 30–40 minutes, or until golden.

NUTRITION PER SERVE
Protein 49 g; Fat 13 g; Carbohydrate 14 g;
Dietary Fibre 2 g; Cholesterol 146 mg;
1665 kJ (400 cal)

Gradually add the stout to the beef mixture, stirring constantly.

Arrange the potato slices in a single overlapping layer to cover the meat.

BRIK A L'OEUF

Preparation time: 30 minutes
Total cooking time: 15 minutes
Makes 2

6 sheets filo pastry
30 g (1 oz) butter, melted
1 small onion, finely chopped
200 g (6½ oz) can tuna in oil, drained
6 pitted black olives, chopped
1 tablespoon chopped fresh
    parsley
2 eggs

1 Preheat the oven to 200°C (400°F/ Gas 6). Cut the pastry sheets in half widthways. Brush four sheets with melted butter and lay them on top of each other. Place half of the combined onion, tuna, olives and parsley at one end and make a well in the centre. Break an egg into the well, being careful to leave it whole. Season well.
2 Brush two more sheets with melted butter, place them together and lay them on top of the tuna and egg. Fold in the sides and roll up into a neat firm package, still keeping the egg whole.
3 Place on a baking tray and brush with melted butter. Repeat with the remaining pastry and filling. Bake for 15 minutes, or until golden.

NUTRITION PER PIE
Protein 35 g; Fat 35 g; Carbohydrate 25 g; Dietary Fibre 1 g; Cholesterol 260 mg; 2295 kJ (545 cal)

NOTE: The yolk is still soft after 15 minutes cooking. If you prefer a firmer egg, bake for longer. Tuna in oil is preferable to brine as it will keep the filling moist when cooked.

Carefully break an egg into the centre of the tuna mixture, without breaking the yolk.

Lay an extra two sheets of filo over the tuna and egg and fold in the sides.

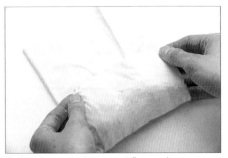
Roll up the pastry into a neat firm package, keeping the egg intact.

FILO VEGETABLE STRUDEL

Preparation time: 30 minutes +
  30 minutes standing
Total cooking time: 1 hour
Serves 6–8

1 large eggplant, sliced
1 red capsicum
3 zucchini, sliced lengthways
2 tablespoons olive oil
6 sheets filo pastry
50 g (1¾ oz) baby English spinach
  leaves
60 g (2 oz) feta cheese, sliced

1 Preheat the oven to 190°C (375°F/ Gas 5). Sprinkle the eggplant slices with a little salt and leave to drain in a colander for 30 minutes. Pat dry with paper towels.
2 Cut the capsicum into quarters and place, skin-side-up, under a hot grill for 10 minutes, or until the skin blackens. Peel away the skin. Brush the eggplant and zucchini with olive oil and grill for 5–10 minutes, or until golden brown. Set aside to cool.
3 Brush one sheet of filo pastry at a time with olive oil, then lay them on top of each other. Place half the eggplant slices lengthways down the centre of the filo and top with a layer

of zucchini, capsicum, spinach and feta cheese. Repeat the layers until the vegetables and cheese are used up. Tuck in the ends of the pastry, then roll up like a parcel; brush lightly with oil and place on a baking tray. Bake for 35 minutes, or until golden brown.

NUTRITION PER SERVE (8)
Protein 4 g; Fat 7 g; Carbohydrate 9 g;
Dietary Fibre 3 g; Cholesterol 5 mg;
485 kJ (115 cal)

NOTE: Unopened packets of filo can be stored in the fridge for up to a month. Once opened, use within 2–3 days.

Cut a large eggplant into thin slices with a sharp knife, then sprinkle with salt.

Build up layers of eggplant, zucchini, capsicum, spinach and feta cheese.

Tuck in the ends of the pastry, then roll up like a parcel to make a strudel.

RABBIT AND MUSHROOM PIE WITH POLENTA TOP

Preparation time: 30 minutes
Total cooking time: 1 hour 20 minutes
Serves 4–6

10 g (1/4 oz) dried porcini mushrooms
90 g (3 oz) butter
1 kg (2 lb) trimmed rabbit meat, cubed
    (buy fillets or boned saddles)
200 g (61/2 oz) pancetta or bacon,
    diced
1 large onion, finely chopped
200 g (61/2 oz) button mushrooms,
    quartered
150 g (5 oz) shimeji mushrooms
1 tablespoon plain flour
200 g (61/2 oz) crème fraîche
150 ml (5 fl oz) cream
2 teaspoons chopped fresh thyme
2 tablespoons chopped fresh parsley

TOPPING
2 cups (500 ml/16 fl oz) milk
30 g (1 oz) butter
1/2 cup (75 g/21/2 oz) instant polenta
1/2 cup (60 g/2 oz) grated Parmesan
pinch of ground nutmeg
1 egg, lightly beaten

1 Soak the porcini mushrooms in
1/2 cup (125 ml) warm water for
15 minutes. Meanwhile, heat half the
butter in a large, deep frying pan over
medium heat and cook the rabbit in
batches for 5 minutes each batch, or
until brown all over. Remove from the
pan. Add the pancetta to the pan and
cook for 4–5 minutes, or until golden.
Add the remaining butter and the
onion, reduce the heat and cook for
5 minutes, or until softened.
2 Add the button and shimeji
mushrooms to the pan and stir well.
Squeeze dry the porcini mushrooms
and chop. Add to the pan, along with
the liquid. Simmer for 10 minutes,
or until all the liquid evaporates. Add
the flour and stir for 1 minute. Stir in
the crème fraîche and cream and
season with pepper. Return the rabbit
to the pan and simmer for 20 minutes,
or until the sauce has reduced and
thickened. Add the fresh herbs.
3 Preheat the oven to 200°C (400°F/
Gas 6). Grease a 1.25 litre ovenproof
dish. Spoon in the rabbit and
mushroom filling.
4 To make the topping, put the milk,
butter and 1/2 teaspoon salt in a
saucepan and heat until almost

boiling. Add the polenta and stir
constantly for 5 minutes, or until thick
and smooth and the polenta comes
away from the side of the pan.
Remove from the heat and stir in the
Parmesan. Add the nutmeg, beat in the
egg and season. Spread over the filling
and bake for 20 minutes until golden.

NUTRITION PER SERVE (6)
Protein 57 g; Fat 53 g; Carbohydrate 10 g;
Dietary Fibre 2.5 g; Cholesterol 282 mg;
3260 kJ (780 cal)

VARIATION: You can use 1 kg (2 lb)
chicken thigh meat, bones removed,
instead of the rabbit.

Use a wooden spoon to spread the polenta
topping over the rabbit filling.

CHICKEN AND MUSHROOM PITHIVIER

Preparation time: 45 minutes +
   30 minutes refrigeration
Total cooking time: 40 minutes
Serves 4

50 g (1³/₄ oz) butter
2 rashers bacon, sliced
4 spring onions, chopped
100 g (3¹/₂ oz) button mushrooms,
   sliced
1 tablespoon plain flour
³/₄ cup (185 ml/6 fl oz) milk
1 tablespoon cream
1 cup (180 g/6 oz) chopped cooked
   chicken breast
¹/₃ cup (20 g/³/₄ oz) chopped fresh
   parsley
2 sheets puff pastry
1 egg yolk, lightly beaten, to glaze

1 Melt the butter in a pan and cook the bacon and spring onions, stirring, for 2–3 minutes. Add the mushrooms and cook, stirring, for 3 minutes. Stir in the flour and cook for 1 minute. Add the milk all at once and stir for 2–3 minutes, or until thickened. Simmer for 1 minute then remove from the heat. Stir in the cream, chicken and parsley. Set aside to cool.
2 Cut two 23 cm (9 inch) circles from the pastry sheets. Place one circle on a greased baking tray. Pile the chicken filling into the centre, mounding slightly in the centre and leaving a small border. Combine the egg yolk with 1 teaspoon of water, and brush the pastry edge.
3 Using a small pointed knife, and starting from the centre of the second circle, mark curved lines at regular intervals. Take care not to cut through the pastry. Place this sheet over the other and stretch a little to fit evenly. Press the edges together to seal. Using the back of a knife, push up the outside edge at 1 cm (¹/₂ inch) intervals. Cover and refrigerate for at least 30 minutes. Preheat the oven to 190°C (375°F/Gas 5). Brush the pie with egg and make a hole in the centre for steam to escape. Bake for 25 minutes until golden.

NUTRITION PER SERVE
Protein 25 g; Fat 40 g; Carbohydrate 35 g;
Dietary Fibre 2 g; Cholesterol 160 mg;
2395 kJ (570 cal)

Stir the cream, chicken and chopped parsley into the filling mixture.

Draw curved lines from the centre to the edge of the pastry.

Use the back of a knife to push up the edge of the pastry.

MOROCCAN LAMB PIE

Preparation time: 30 minutes + cooling
Total cooking time: 2 hours 40 minutes
Serves 6–8

3 tablespoons olive oil
2 onions, finely chopped
4 cloves garlic, crushed
1¹⁄₄ teaspoons ground cinnamon
1¹⁄₄ teaspoons ground cumin
1¹⁄₄ teaspoons ground coriander
¹⁄₂ teaspoon ground ginger
large pinch of cayenne pepper
1.2 kg (2 lb 7 oz) boned lamb leg, cut
    into small cubes
1¹⁄₂ cups (375 ml/12 fl oz) chicken
    stock
2 teaspoons grated lemon rind
1 tablespoon lemon juice
2 carrots, cut into small cubes
¹⁄₃ cup (60 g/2 oz) ground almonds
¹⁄₂ cup (30 g/1 oz) chopped fresh
    coriander
500 g (1 lb) puff pastry
1 egg, lightly beaten

1 Heat the oil in a large saucepan.
Add the onion, garlic, cinnamon,
cumin, ground coriander, ginger and
cayenne pepper and cook, stirring,
over medium heat for 30–40 seconds.
Add the lamb and stir until coated in
the spices. Add the stock, lemon rind
and lemon juice and cook, covered,
over low heat for 45 minutes.
2 Add the carrot, cover and simmer
for another 45 minutes, or until the
lamb is tender. Stir in the almonds,
increase the heat and boil for
30 minutes, or until the sauce becomes
very thick. Stir in the fresh coriander,
season and leave to cool.
3 Preheat the oven to 200°C (400°F/
Gas 6) and heat a baking tray. Grease
a 20 cm (8 inch) pie dish. Roll out the
pastry to a 40 cm (16 inch) round and
neaten the edge with a sharp knife.
Line the dish with the pastry, leaving
the rest overhanging the edge.
4 Spoon the filling into the dish,
levelling the surface. Fold the
overhanging pastry over the filling,
forming loose pleats. Using kitchen
scissors, cut out Vs of pastry where it
falls into deep folds towards the
middle. This reduces the thickness so

that the pastry can bake evenly.
5 Brush with egg and bake on the hot
tray in the centre of the oven for
20 minutes. Reduce the oven to
moderate 180°C (350°F/Gas 4), cover
the pie with foil and bake for another
20 minutes.

NUTRITION PER SERVE (8)
Protein 39 g; Fat 31 g; Carbohydrate 26 g;
Dietary Fibre 3 g; Cholesterol 115 mg;
2230 kJ (535 cal)

Boil the lamb mixture for 30 minutes, or until the
sauce becomes very thick.

Fold the overhanging pastry up and over the
filling, in loose pleats.

SALMON FILO PIE
WITH DILL BUTTER

Preparation time: 25 minutes + cooling
Total cooking time: 50 minutes
Serves 6

3/4 cup (150 g/5 oz) medium-grain
    white rice
90 g (3 oz) butter, melted
8 sheets filo pastry
500 g (1 lb) fresh salmon fillet, cut into
    small cubes
2 French shallots, finely chopped
1 1/2 tablespoons baby capers
150 g (5 oz) Greek-style yoghurt
1 egg
1 tablespoon grated lemon rind
3 tablespoons chopped fresh dill
1/4 cup (30 g/1 oz) dry breadcrumbs
1 tablespoon sesame seeds
2 teaspoons lemon juice

1 Put the rice in a large saucepan and add enough water to cover it by 2 cm (1 inch). Bring to the boil over medium heat, then reduce the heat to low, cover and cook for 20 minutes, or until all the water has been absorbed and tunnels appear on the surface of the rice. Set aside to cool.

2 Preheat the oven to 180°C (350°F/ Gas 4). Grease a 20 x 30 cm (8 x 12 inch) baking tin with melted butter. Cover the filo pastry with a damp tea towel. Mix the salmon with the shallots, capers, rice, yoghurt and egg. Add the lemon rind, 1 tablespoon of the dill and season well.

3 Layer four sheets of pastry in the base of the tin, brushing each one with melted butter and leaving the sides of the pastry overhanging the edge of the tin. Spoon in the salmon filling and pat down well. Fold the overhanging pastry over the filling.

4 Top with four more sheets of filo, brushing each one with melted butter and sprinkling all but the top layer with a tablespoon of breadcrumbs. Sprinkle the top with sesame seeds.

5 Score the top of the pie into diamonds without cutting right through the pastry. Bake for 25–30 minutes on the lowest shelf until golden brown. Reheat the remaining butter, add the lemon juice and remaining dill and pour some over each portion of pie.

NUTRITION PER SERVE
Protein 23 g; Fat 20 g; Carbohydrate 35 g;
Dietary Fibre 1 g; Cholesterol 110 mg;
1705 kJ (410 cal)

Combine the salmon, shallots, capers, rice, yoghurt, egg, lemon rind and dill.

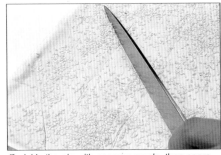
Sprinkle the pie with sesame seeds, then score the top into diamonds.

GAME PIE

Preparation time: 50 minutes
 + overnight setting
Total cooking time: 5 hours
Serves 4–6

JELLY
any bones reserved from the game
    meat
2 pig's trotters
1 onion, quartered
1 carrot, roughly chopped
1 celery stick, chopped
2 bay leaves
6 black peppercorns

FILLING
250 g (8 oz) pork belly, finely diced
4 rashers streaky bacon, chopped
400 g (13 oz) game meat (e.g. rabbit,
    pheasant), removed from carcass
    and finely diced (bones reserved)
$1/2$ small onion, finely chopped
$1/2$ teaspoon ground nutmeg
$1/2$ teaspoon ground cinnamon
2 dried juniper berries, crushed
1 teaspoon chopped fresh thyme

PASTRY
4 cups (500 g/1 lb) plain flour
90 g (3 oz) lard
1 egg, lightly beaten, to glaze

1 To make the stock for the jelly, place all the ingredients and 1.75 litres water in a large saucepan and bring to the boil over high heat. Remove any froth that forms on the surface. Reduce the heat and simmer for 3 hours, skimming off any froth occasionally. Strain, return to the pan and cook uncovered until the liquid has reduced to about 2 cups (500 ml/ 16 fl oz). Cool, then refrigerate.

2 To make the filling, combine all the ingredients in a bowl. Season well.

3 To make the pastry, sift the flour and $1/2$ teaspoon salt into a large bowl and make a well in the centre. Bring 200 ml ($6^{1/2}$ fl oz) water and the lard to the boil in a saucepan. Pour the boiling liquid into the flour and mix with a wooden spoon to form a dough. Gather together and lift onto a lightly floured work surface. Press together until smooth. Keep the dough warm by covering with foil and putting it in a warm place.

4 Preheat the oven to 190°C (375°F/ Gas 5). Grease an 18 cm (7 inch) springform tin. While the pastry is still warm, roll out two-thirds of the dough between two sheets of baking paper and line the base and side of the tin, leaving some overhanging. Spoon the filling into the tin, pressing down well. Roll out the remaining dough to about 4 mm ($1/4$ inch) thick and 20 cm (8 inches) across. Place on top of the tin and pinch the edges together to seal. Trim the edges and cut a small hole in the top of the pie.

5 Roll out the pastry trimmings to make decorations, securing to the pie top with a little beaten egg. Glaze the top of the pie with egg and bake for 1 hour 20 minutes. Cover the top with foil after about 45 minutes to prevent it colouring too much.

6 Remove the pie from the oven and allow to cool for about 25 minutes. Gently remove from the tin, brush the top and sides with beaten egg and place on a baking tray. Return to the oven and cook for another 20 minutes until golden brown and firm to touch. Remove from the oven and cool.

7 Warm the jelly to a pouring consistency. Place a small piping nozzle into the hole in the pie and pour in a little of the jelly. Leave to settle, then pour in more jelly until the pie is full (see HINT). Fill the pie completely so there are no gaps when the jelly sets. Refrigerate overnight but serve at room temperature.

NUTRITION PER SERVE (6)
Protein 40 g; Fat 20 g; Carbohydrate 63 g; Dietary Fibre 3.5 g; Cholesterol 113 mg; 2455 kJ (585 cal)

HINT: If there is some jelly left, you can freeze it and use it to add flavour to soups, casseroles or sauces.

Line the tin with the warm pastry, leaving some overhanging the edge.

Place the dough on top of the filling and pinch the edges together to seal.

Use a small, sharp knife to cut a hole in the top of the pie.

Insert a nozzle into the hole and pour in a little of the liquid jelly.

35

CHILLI CON CARNE PIE

Preparation time: 25 minutes +
    20 minutes chilling
Total cooking time: 2 hours 15 minutes
Serves 6–8

1¹/2 cups (185 g/6 oz) plain flour
100 g (3¹/2 oz) butter, chilled and
    cubed
3/4 cup (90 g/3 oz) grated Cheddar
1–2 tablespoons iced water

FILLING
2 tablespoons olive oil
1 onion, chopped
2 cloves garlic, chopped
¹/4 teaspoon chilli powder
2 teaspoons ground cumin
1 teaspoon ground coriander
¹/4 teaspoon cayenne pepper
1 teaspoon paprika
1 teaspoon dried oregano
750 g (1¹/2 lb) beef mince
2 tablespoons tomato paste
¹/2 cup (125 ml/4 fl oz) dry red wine
425 g (14 oz) can crushed tomatoes
1 tablespoon wholegrain mustard
300 g (10 oz) can red kidney beans,
    drained and rinsed
2 tablespoons chopped fresh
    flat-leaf parsley
1 tablespoon chopped fresh oregano
2/3 cup (170 g/5¹/2 oz) sour cream

1 Sift the flour into a bowl and rub in the butter with your fingertips until the mixture resembles fine breadcrumbs. Stir in the cheese. Make a well and add almost all the water. Mix with a flat-bladed knife, using a cutting action, until the dough comes together, adding more water if necessary.
2 Gather the dough together and lift out onto a lightly floured surface. Press it into a ball and flatten slightly into a disc. Cover in plastic wrap and refrigerate for at least 20 minutes.
3 Heat the oil in a large saucepan over medium heat and cook the onion for 5 minutes, or until softened. Add the garlic, spices and dried oregano and cook for 2 minutes. Add the mince and cook over high heat for 5 minutes, or until brown. Stir in the tomato paste and cook for 1 minute. Pour in the wine and simmer for 3 minutes. Add the tomato and mustard, bring to the boil, then reduce the heat and simmer for 30 minutes.
4 Add the kidney beans to the beef and cook for 30 minutes, or until any excess moisture has evaporated. Stir in the fresh herbs. Season well.
5 Preheat the oven to 200°C (400°F/ Gas 6). Lightly grease a 23 cm (9 inch) pie dish and spoon in the beef filling. Roll out the pastry to fit the top of the dish, then trim away the excess pastry and crimp the edges. Make two or three cuts in the top to let the steam escape. Bake for 10 minutes, then reduce the oven to 180°C (350°F/ Gas 4) and cook for 40–45 minutes, or until the top is golden. Cover the top with foil if it is browning too much. Serve with sour cream.

NUTRITION PER SERVE (8)
Protein 27 g; Fat 32 g; Carbohydrate 24 g;
Dietary Fibre 4 g; Cholesterol 111 mg;
2085 kJ (500 cal)

Simmer the chilli con carne filling until the excess liquid has evaporated.

Use a rolling pin to help you lift the pastry top over the filling.

SPINACH PIE

Preparation time: 30 minutes +
    30 minutes chilling
Total cooking time: 1 hour
Serves 8–10

2 cups (250 g/8 oz) plain flour
1/3 cup (80 ml/2³/4 fl oz) olive oil
1 egg, beaten
4–5 tablespoons iced water

FILLING
1 kg (2 lb) spinach, stalks removed,
    roughly chopped
1 tablespoon olive oil
1 large leek, sliced
4 cloves garlic, crushed
2 cups (500 g/1 lb) ricotta
1 cup (90 g/3 oz) grated pecorino
    cheese
300 g (10 oz) feta, crumbled
3 eggs, lightly beaten
3 tablespoons chopped fresh dill
1/2 cup (15 g/1/2 oz) chopped fresh
    flat-leaf parsley

1 Sift the flour and 1/2 teaspoon salt into a large bowl and make a well in the centre. Mix the oil, egg and most of the water, add to the flour and mix with a flat-bladed knife until the mixture comes together in beads, adding a little more water if necessary. Gather the dough and press into a ball. Wrap in plastic wrap and chill for at least 30 minutes.
2 Put the spinach in a large pan, sprinkle lightly with water, then cover and steam for 5 minutes until wilted. Drain, squeeze out the excess moisture, then finely chop.
3 Preheat the oven to 200°C (400°F/ Gas 6) and heat a baking tray. Grease a 25 cm (12 inch) loose-based fluted tart tin. Heat the oil in a frying pan and cook the leek and garlic over low heat for 5 minutes, or until soft. Mix with the ricotta, pecorino, feta, spinach, egg, dill and parsley and season with salt and pepper.
4 Roll out two-thirds of the pastry between two sheets of baking paper until large enough to line the tin. Fill

with the spinach mixture. Roll out the remaining pastry between the baking paper and top the pie. Trim the edges and make two or three steam holes.
5 Bake the pie on the hot tray for 15 minutes, then reduce the oven to 180°C (350°F/Gas 4) and cook for another 30 minutes. Cover with foil if the pie is overbrowning. Leave for 5–10 minutes before slicing.

NUTRITION PER SERVE (10)
Protein 20 g; Fat 26 g; Carbohydrate 20 g;
Dietary Fibre 4 g; Cholesterol 123 mg;
1660 kJ (395 cal)

Drain the wilted spinach well, then finely chop with a large, sharp knife.

HAM AND CHICKEN PIE

Preparation time: 40 minutes
Total cooking time: 1 hour
Serves 6–8

3 cups (375 g /12 oz) plain flour
180 g (6 oz) butter, chilled and cubed
2–3 tablespoons iced water
1 egg, lightly beaten, to glaze

FILLING
1 kg (2 lb) chicken mince
1 teaspoon dried mixed herbs
2 eggs, lightly beaten
3 spring onions, finely chopped
2 tablespoons chopped fresh parsley
2 teaspoons French mustard
1/3 cup (80 ml/2³/4 fl oz) cream
200 g (6¹/2 oz) sliced leg ham

1 Preheat the oven to 180°C (350°F/ Gas 4). Mix the flour and butter in a food processor for 20 seconds or until fine and crumbly. Add the water and process for 20 seconds or until the mixture comes together. Turn onto a lightly floured surface and press together until smooth. Roll out two-thirds of the pastry to line a 20 cm (8 inch) springform tin, leaving some pastry overhanging the side. Cover with plastic wrap and refrigerate until required. Wrap the remaining pastry in plastic wrap and refrigerate.
2 To make the filling, mix together the chicken, herbs, eggs, onions, parsley, mustard and cream and season well.
3 Spoon a third of the filling into the pastry-lined tin and smooth the surface. Top with half the ham and then another chicken layer followed by the remaining ham and then a final layer of chicken filling.
4 Brush around the inside edge of pastry with egg. Roll out the remaining pastry to make a pie top, pressing the pastry edges together. Trim the edge. Decorate the top with pastry trimmings. Brush the pie top with beaten egg and bake for 1 hour or until golden brown.

NUTRITION PER SERVE (8)
Protein 40 g; Fat 29 g; Carbohydrate 39 g; Dietary Fibre 2 g; Cholesterol 215 mg; 2445 kJ (583 cal)

Process the flour and butter in a food processor until fine and crumbly.

Combine the chicken, herbs, eggs, onion, parsley, mustard, cream, salt and pepper.

Layer the chicken filling and the ham in the pastry-lined tin.

Use a sharp knife to trim away the excess pastry from the edge of the pie.

VEAL PIE WITH JERUSALEM ARTICHOKE AND POTATO TOPPING

Preparation time: 40 minutes
Total cooking time: 1 hour 15 minutes
Serves 4–6

1 tablespoon olive oil
500 g (1 lb) lean veal mince
2 onions, finely chopped
3 cloves garlic, crushed
150 g (5 oz) bacon, diced
1/2 teaspoon dried rosemary
2 tablespoons plain flour
pinch of cayenne pepper
1/2 cup (125 ml/4 fl oz) dry white wine
150 ml (5 fl oz) cream
1 egg, lightly beaten
2 hard-boiled eggs, roughly chopped

TOPPING
500 g (1 lb) Jerusalem artichokes
400 g (13 oz) potatoes
100 g (3 1/2 oz) butter

1 To make the filling, heat the oil in a large frying pan and cook the mince, onion, garlic, bacon and rosemary, stirring often, for 10 minutes, or until the veal changes colour. Stir in the flour and cayenne pepper and cook for 1 minute. Pour in the wine and 1/2 cup (125 ml/4 fl oz) water. Season well. Simmer for 5 minutes, or until the sauce is very thick, then stir in the cream, beaten egg and chopped egg.
2 Preheat the oven to 210°C (415°F/ Gas 6–7). Lightly grease a 21 cm (8 inch) springform tin. Peel and chop

the artichokes and potatoes and boil together for 12–15 minutes until tender. Drain, add the butter, then mash until smooth.
3 Spoon the filling into the tin then spread with the topping. Bake for 15 minutes, then reduce the heat to 180°C (350°F/Gas 4) and bake for 30 minutes, or until golden on top.

NUTRITION PER SERVE (6)
Protein 31 g; Fat 38 g; Carbohydrate 17 g; Dietary Fibre 4 g; Cholesterol 258 mg; 2265 kJ (540 cal)

When the sauce has thickened, stir in the cream, beaten egg and chopped egg.

Mash the cooked potato and artichoke with butter until smooth.

LITTLE CHICKEN AND VEGETABLE POT PIES

Preparation time: 45 minutes +
  20 minutes chilling
Total cooking time: 1 hour 20 minutes
Makes 6

1¼ cups (150 g/5 oz) plain flour
90 g (3 oz) butter, chilled and
  cubed
1 tablespoon finely chopped fresh
  thyme
1 tablespoon finely chopped fresh
  flat-leaf parsley
3–4 tablespoons iced water

FILLING
750 g (1½ lb) chicken breast fillets
1 lemon, quartered
5 spring onions
2 bay leaves
1½ cups (375 ml/12 fl oz) chicken
  stock
¼ cup (60 ml/2 fl oz) dry white
  wine
60 g (2 oz) butter
1 large onion, thinly sliced
1 tablespoon finely chopped fresh
  tarragon
100 g (3½ oz) button mushrooms,
  thinly sliced
¾ cup (90 g/3 oz) plain flour
2 large carrots, cut into small
  cubes
1 celery stick, cut into small
  cubes
½ cup (90 g/3 oz) peas
1 egg, lightly beaten, to glaze

1 To make the pastry, sift the flour
and ¼ teaspoon salt into a large bowl.
Add the butter and rub it into the flour
with your fingertips until the mixture
resembles fine breadcrumbs. Stir in the
chopped herbs. Make a well in the
centre of the mixture, add almost all
the water and mix with a flat-bladed
knife, using a cutting action, until the
mixture comes together in beads,
adding a little more water if necessary.
2 Gently gather the dough together
and lift it out onto a lightly floured
work surface. Press together into a
ball. Flatten slightly into a disc, wrap
in plastic wrap and refrigerate for at

least 20 minutes to let the dough relax.
3 Preheat the oven to 180°C (350°F/
Gas 4). Place the chicken, lemon, 4 of
the spring onions, the bay leaves,
chicken stock, wine, 1½ cups
(375 ml/12 fl oz) water and
½ teaspoon salt in a large saucepan.
Bring to the boil over high heat.
Reduce the heat and simmer for
20 minutes, or until the chicken is
cooked through. Remove the chicken
from the liquid with a slotted spoon
and set aside. Return the liquid to the
heat and boil for 10 minutes, or until it
has reduced to 2 cups (500 ml/
16 fl oz), then strain into a bowl and
set aside. Roughly cut the chicken into
small pieces.
4 Melt the butter in a large saucepan
over medium heat. When it is
sizzling, add the onion and cook for
2–3 minutes, or until soft. Add the
tarragon and mushrooms and cook,
stirring occasionally, for 3–4 minutes,
or until the mushrooms are soft. Add
the flour and cook, stirring constantly,
for 3 minutes. Pour in the reserved
poaching liquid, bring to the boil and
cook, stirring often, for 2 minutes, or
until slightly thickened. Remove from
the heat, then stir in the carrot, celery,
peas and chicken. Divide the filling
evenly among six 1½ cup (375 ml/
12 fl oz) ramekins.

5 Divide the dough into six even
portions. Roll out each portion into
a flat disc, 12 cm (4½ inches) in
diameter (or use a cutter). Moisten the
ramekin rims and cover with pastry
rounds, pressing down firmly to seal
the edges. Re-roll any pastry trimmings
to make decorations. Prick the pie tops
with a fork, then brush with the egg.
Bake for about 30 minutes, or until the
pies are golden.

NUTRITION PER PIE
Protein 28 g; Fat 25 g; Carbohydrate 36 g;
Dietary Fibre 4 g; Cholesterol 154 mg;
1990 kJ (475 cal)

Roughly cut the poached chicken breasts into
small pieces.

Stir the carrot, celery, peas and chicken into the
thickened mixture.

Roll out each portion of dough to a 12 cm circle
or use a cutter for neat edges.

Cover the filling with the pastry tops, pressing
down firmly to seal the edges.

RABBIT PIE

Preparation time: 45 minutes +
  overnight soaking + chilling
Total cooking time: 2 hours 45 minutes
Serves 4

1 tablespoon vinegar
1/2 teaspoon salt
1 rabbit, cut into 12 portions
3 tablespoons plain flour, seasoned
    with salt and pepper
4 tablespoons olive oil
2 rashers bacon, chopped
2 onions, finely chopped
1 green apple, peeled, cored and
    chopped
12 pitted prunes
1 tablespoon plain flour
1 tablespoon soft brown sugar
375 ml (12 fl oz) beer or cider
1 teaspoon dried thyme
375 g (12 oz) puff pastry
1 egg yolk mixed with
    1 teaspoon water, to glaze

1 Add the vinegar and salt to a large bowl of water. Add the rabbit portions and leave to soak overnight in the fridge. Drain and rinse well. Dry with paper towels. Toss the rabbit in the seasoned flour.

2 Preheat the oven to 180°C (350°F/Gas 4). Heat 3 tablespoons of the olive oil in a large heavy-based frying pan. Cook the rabbit quickly, in batches, over medium heat until browned. Put in a 2 litre casserole.

3 Heat the remaining oil in the same frying pan and add the bacon, onion, apple and prunes. Cook over medium heat for 5 minutes or until lightly browned. Sprinkle with the flour and brown sugar and stir. Cook, stirring, for 5 minutes. Add the beer or cider and stir constantly for 3 minutes or until thickened. Stir in the thyme. Pour over the rabbit. Cover the dish with a tight-fitting lid. Bake for 2 hours or until the rabbit is tender.

4 Transfer to a deep 1.25 litre pie dish with a rim. Leave to cool and then refrigerate until cold. Place a pie funnel in the centre of the dish. Roll the pastry out to about 5 cm (2 inches) larger than the top of the pie dish. Cut small pieces of pastry to fit around the pie funnel. Mark the pastry to lid size and cut out a hole to fit over the pie funnel. Use the remaining scraps to cut small strips to fit on the rim of the pie plate. Press the joins together. Brush the pie plate rim and strips with egg and water glaze, position the pastry lid and press to seal. Use the back of a knife to push up the pastry edge at intervals. Refrigerate for at least 30 minutes. Brush the pastry top with egg glaze. Increase the oven to 210°C (415°F/Gas 6–7). Bake for 30–40 minutes or until the pastry is golden brown and cooked through. Reduce the oven temperature to 180°C (350°F/Gas 4) during the last 10 minutes of cooking and cover with foil to prevent the top browning too much.

NUTRITION PER SERVE
Protein 85 g; Fat 50 g; Carbohydrate 64 g; Dietary Fibre 5 g; Cholesterol 265 mg; 4450 kJ (1063 cal)

Add the beer or cider and stir constantly with a wooden spoon for 3 minutes.

When the rabbit filling is completely cold, place the pie funnel in the centre of the dish.

LAMB AND FILO PIE

Preparation time: 20 minutes
Total cooking time: 50 minutes
Serves 6

2 tablespoons oil
2 onions, chopped
1 clove garlic, chopped
1 teaspoon ground cumin
1 teaspoon ground coriander
1/2 teaspoon ground cinnamon
1 kg (2 lb) lamb mince
3 tablespoons chopped fresh parsley
2 tablespoons chopped fresh mint
1 tablespoon tomato paste
10 sheets filo pastry
250 g (8 oz) unsalted butter, melted

1 Heat the oil in a large frying pan. Add the onion and garlic and cook for 3 minutes or until just soft. Add the ground cumin, coriander and cinnamon, and cook, stirring, for another minute.

2 Add the mince to the pan and cook over medium–high heat for 10 minutes or until the meat is brown and all the liquid has evaporated. Use a fork to break up any lumps. Add the herbs, tomato paste and a little salt and mix well. Set aside to cool.

3 Preheat the oven to 180°C (350°F/ Gas 4). Lightly grease a 33 x 23 cm (13 x 9 inch) ovenproof dish with butter or oil. Remove 3 sheets of filo and cover the rest with a damp tea towel to prevent them drying out. Brush one sheet of pastry with melted butter. Place another 2 sheets of filo on top and brush the top one with butter. Line the dish with these sheets, letting the excess overhang.

4 Spread the lamb filling over the pastry and then fold the overhanging pastry back over the filling. Butter 2 sheets of filo, place one on top of the other and fold in half. Place over the top of the filling and tuck in the edges. Butter the remaining 4 sheets and cut roughly into squares. Scrunch these over the top of the pie. Bake for 40 minutes or until crisp and golden.

NUTRITION PER SERVE
Protein 47 g; Fat 46 g; Carbohydrate 17 g; Dietary Fibre 5 g; Cholesterol 105 mg; 2784 kJ (665 cal)

As the mince cooks, press down on any lumps, using a fork to break them up.

Gently brush each top sheet of filo pastry with melted butter.

Spread the lamb over the pastry and then fold the overhanging pastry over the filling.

Scrunch the squares of pastry roughly and arrange them over the top of the pie.

CREAMY MUSHROOM PIE

Preparation time: 45 minutes +
   35 minutes soaking and chilling
Total cooking time: 1 hour
Serves 4–6

2 cups (250 g/8 oz) plain flour
1/2 cup (75 g/21/2 oz) fine polenta
125 g (4 oz) butter, chilled and cubed
1/4 cup (60 ml/2 fl oz) cream
2–3 tablespoons iced water

FILLING
10 g (1/4 oz) dried porcini mushrooms
150 g (5 oz) oyster mushrooms
1 large leek
150 g (5 oz) butter
2 large cloves garlic, crushed
200 g (61/2 oz) shiitake mushrooms,
   thickly sliced
200 g (61/2 oz) Swiss brown
   mushrooms, thickly sliced
350 g (11 oz) field mushrooms, sliced
100 g (31/2 oz) enoki mushrooms
2 tablespoons plain flour
1/2 cup (125 ml/4 fl oz) dry white wine
1/2 cup (125 ml/4 fl oz) vegetable or
   chicken stock
1/4 cup (60 ml/2 fl oz) thick cream
2 tablespoons chopped fresh thyme
1 egg, lightly beaten, to glaze

1 To make the pastry, sift the flour into a large bowl, then stir in the polenta and 1/2 teaspoon of salt. Add the butter and rub into the dry ingredients with your fingertips until the mixture resembles fine breadcrumbs. Make a well in the centre, pour in the cream and mix with a flat-bladed knife, using a cutting action, until the mixture comes together in beads. Add a little water if the mixture is too dry.
2 Gently gather the dough together and lift out onto a lightly floured work surface. Press together into a ball and then flatten slightly into a disc. Wrap in plastic wrap and refrigerate for 20 minutes.
3 Soak the porcini mushrooms in 3 tablespoons boiling water for about 15 minutes. Cut any large oyster mushrooms into halves. Thoroughly wash the leek and thinly slice it.
4 Preheat the oven to hot 210°C

(415°F/Gas 6–7). Heat a baking tray in the oven. Lightly grease an 18 cm (7 inch) pie dish.
5 Drain the porcini mushrooms, reserving the soaking liquid, then coarsely chop them. Heat the butter in a large, deep frying pan over medium heat and cook the leek and garlic for 7–8 minutes, or until the leek is soft and golden. Add all the mushrooms to the pan and cook, stirring, for 5–6 minutes, or until soft.
6 Add the flour to the pan and stir for 1 minute. Pour in the wine and reserved mushroom soaking liquid and bring to the boil for 1 minute, then pour in the stock and cook for 4–5 minutes, or until the liquid has reduced. Stir in the cream and cook for 1–2 minutes, or until thickened. Stir in the thyme and season. Cool.
7 Divide the pastry into two portions. Roll out one portion between two sheets of baking paper to 2 mm (1/8 inch) thick to line the base and side of the pie dish. Line the pie dish, then spoon in the cooled mushroom filling. Lightly brush the edge of the pastry with egg.
8 Roll out the remaining pastry between the baking paper until about 2 mm (1/8 inch) thick and cover the pie. Pinch the edges together and pierce the top three times with a fork. Trim the edges. Roll the trimmings and cut into mushroom shapes. Arrange over the pie and lightly brush the top with more egg. Place on the hot tray and bake for 35–40 minutes, or until the pastry is golden brown. Set aside for 5 minutes before slicing.

NUTRITION PER SERVE (6)
Protein 14 g; Fat 48 g; Carbohydrate 51 g;
Dietary Fibre 8 g; Cholesterol 173 mg;
2900 kJ (695 cal)

Mix in the cream, using a cutting action, until the mixture comes together in beads.

Add all of the mushrooms to the pan and cook them until they are soft.

Spoon the cooled mushroom filling into the pastry-lined dish.

Cut the pastry trimmings into mushroom shapes to decorate the pie.

STEAK AND KIDNEY PIE

Preparation time: 20 minutes
Total cooking time: 2 hours
Serves 6

750 g (1 lb 8 oz) round steak
4 lamb kidneys
2 tablespoons plain flour
1 tablespoon oil
1 onion, chopped
30 g (1 oz) butter
1 tablespoon Worcestershire sauce
1 tablespoon tomato paste
1/2 cup (125 ml/4 fl oz) red wine
1 cup (250 ml/8 fl oz) beef stock
125 g (4 oz) button mushrooms, sliced
1/2 teaspoon dried thyme
1/3 cup (20 g/3/4 oz) chopped fresh
    parsley
375 g (12 oz) puff pastry
1 egg, lightly beaten, to glaze

1 Cut the meat into small cubes. Trim the skin from the kidneys. Quarter the kidneys and trim away any fat or sinew. Coat the meat and kidneys with the flour and shake off the excess.
2 Heat the oil in a pan. Add the onion and cook for 5 minutes, or until soft. Remove with a slotted spoon. Add the butter to the pan. Brown the meat and kidneys in batches and then return all the meat and onion to the pan.
3 Add the Worcestershire sauce, tomato paste, wine, beef stock, sliced mushrooms, thyme and parsley to the pan. Bring to the boil, then simmer, covered, for 1 hour or until the meat is tender. Season and leave to cool. Spoon into a 1.5 litre pie dish.
4 Preheat the oven to 210°C (415°F/ Gas 6–7). Roll the puff pastry out on a lightly floured surface so that it is 5 cm (2 inches) larger than the dish. Cut thin strips from the pastry and press onto the rim, sealing the joins. Place the pastry on top of the pie. Trim the edges and cut steam holes in the top. Decorate with pastry trimmings and brush the top with egg. Bake for 35–40 minutes or until golden brown.

NUTRITION PER SERVE
Protein 38 g; Fat 28 g; Carbohydrate 27 g;
Dietary Fibre 2 g; Cholesterol 244 mg;
2195 kJ (524 cal)

Cook the meat and kidneys in batches and then return it all to the pan.

Roll the puff pastry out on a lightly floured surface until it is a little larger than the dish.

BACON AND EGG PIE

Preparation time: 20 minutes + chilling
Total cooking time: 1 hour
Serves 4–6

1 sheet shortcrust pastry
2 teaspoons oil
4 rashers bacon, chopped
5 eggs, lightly beaten
1/4 cup (60 ml/2 fl oz) cream
1 sheet puff pastry
1 egg, extra, lightly beaten, to glaze

1 Preheat the oven to 210°C (415°F/ Gas 6–7). Lightly oil a 20 cm (8 inch) loose-bottomed flan tin. Place the shortcrust pastry in the tin and trim the pastry edges. Cut a sheet of greaseproof paper to cover the pastry-lined tin. Spread a layer of baking beads, dried beans or rice over the paper. Bake for 10 minutes and then discard the paper and rice. Bake the pastry for another 5–10 minutes or until golden. Allow to cool.
2 Heat the oil in a frying pan. Add the bacon and cook over medium heat for a few minutes or until lightly browned. Drain on paper towels and allow to cool slightly. Arrange the bacon over the pastry base and pour the mixed eggs and cream over the top.
3 Brush the edges of the pastry with the egg glaze, cover with puff pastry and press on firmly to seal. Trim the pastry edges and decorate the top with trimmings. Brush with egg glaze and bake for 30–35 minutes, or until puffed and golden.

NUTRITION PER SERVE (6)
Protein 14 g; Fat 26 g; Carbohydrate 23 g; Dietary Fibre 1 g; Cholesterol 215 mg; 1569 kJ (375 cal)

Spread a layer of dried beans or rice over the paper before blind baking.

Carefully pour the combined eggs and cream over the top of the bacon.

CHICKEN AND WATERCRESS STRUDEL

Preparation time: 30 minutes
Total cooking time: 50 minutes
Serves 6

3/4 cup (60 g/2 oz) fresh white
    breadcrumbs
1–2 teaspoons sesame seeds
1 bunch (60 g/2 oz) watercress
4 chicken breast fillets
25 g (3/4 oz) butter
3 tablespoons Dijon mustard
1 cup (250 ml/8 fl oz) thick cream
15 sheets filo pastry
100 g (3 1/2 oz) butter, melted

1 Preheat the oven to 190°C (375°F/ Gas 5) and bake the breadcrumbs and sesame seeds, on separate trays, until golden. Steam the watercress for 3–5 minutes, until just wilted, and squeeze out any water.
2 Slice the chicken into thin strips. Heat the butter in a pan and stir-fry the chicken until just cooked. Remove from the pan. Stir the mustard and cream into the pan and simmer until reduced to 1/2 cup (125 ml/4 fl oz). Remove from the heat and stir in the chicken and watercress.
3 Brush a sheet of filo with melted butter and sprinkle with toasted breadcrumbs. Lay another filo sheet on top, brush with butter and sprinkle

with breadcrumbs. Repeat with the remaining filo and breadcrumbs and place on a baking tray.
4 Place the chicken filling along the centre of the pastry. Fold the sides over and roll into a parcel, with the join underneath. Brush with the remaining butter and add the sesame seeds. Bake for 30 minutes, or until golden. Cool slightly before serving.

NUTRITION PER SERVE
Protein 25 g; Fat 65 g; Carbohydrate 30 g; Dietary Fibre 2 g; Cholesterol 235 mg; 3350 kJ (795 cal)

Steam the watercress until lightly cooked, then drain and squeeze out the water.

Layer the buttered sheets of filo pastry and place on a baking tray.

Fold in the pastry sides to enclose the filling, then roll up into a parcel.

MEDITERRANEAN PIE

Preparation time: 25 minutes +
   20 minutes refrigeration
Total cooking time: 35 minutes
Serves 4

3 cups (375 g/12 oz) plain flour
1 egg, lightly beaten
1/2 cup (125 ml/4 fl oz) buttermilk
100 ml (31/2 fl oz) olive oil

FILLING
2 tablespoons olive oil
100 g (31/2 oz) button mushrooms,
   sliced
400 g (13 oz) can tomatoes, drained
   and roughly chopped
100 g (31/2 oz) sliced salami
180 g (6 oz) jar artichokes, drained
4 tablespoons fresh basil leaves, torn
100 g (31/2 oz) mozzarella, grated
1/4 cup (30 g/1 oz) grated Parmesan
milk, to brush

1 Preheat the oven to 210°C (415°F/
Gas 6–7). Grease a large baking tray
and place in the oven to heat up. Sift
the flour into a large bowl and add the
egg and buttermilk. Add the oil and
mix with a large metal spoon until the
mixture comes together and forms a
soft dough (add a little water if the
mixture is too dry). Turn onto a lightly
floured surface and gather together
into a smooth ball. Cover with plastic
wrap and refrigerate for 20 minutes.
2 Heat the oil in a large frying pan,
add the button mushrooms and cook
over medium heat for 5 minutes,
or until they have softened and
browned a little.
3 Divide the pastry in half and roll
each portion, between two sheets of
baking paper, into a 30 cm (12 inch)
round. Layer the chopped tomato,
salami, mushrooms, artichokes, basil
leaves, mozzarella and Parmesan on
one of the pastry rounds, leaving a
narrow border. Season well.
4 Brush the border with milk. Top
with the remaining pastry circle to
enclose the filling, then pinch and seal
the edges together. Make three slits in
the top. Brush the top with milk. Place
on the preheated tray and bake for
30 minutes, or until golden.

NUTRITION PER SERVE
Protein 30 g; Fat 52 g; Carbohydrate 75 g;
Dietary Fibre 7 g; Cholesterol 95 mg;
3675 kJ (880 cal)

Gently gather the dough together to form a
smooth ball.

Brush the pastry border with milk to help the top
layer of pastry stick.

RAISED PORK PIE

Preparation time: 20 minutes + chilling
  + overnight setting
Total cooking time: 1 hour
Serves 6

1.2 kg (2 lb 7 oz) minced pork
2/3 cup (90 g/3 oz) pistachio nuts,
    shelled and chopped
2 green apples, peeled and finely
    chopped
6 fresh sage leaves, finely chopped
4 cups (500 g/1 lb) plain flour
150 g (5 oz) butter
2 eggs, lightly beaten
1 egg yolk, to glaze
200 ml (6 1/2 fl oz) vegetable stock
200 ml (6 1/2 fl oz) unsweetened apple
    juice
2 teaspoons gelatine

1 Preheat the oven to 200°C (400°F/ Gas 6). Mix together the pork, pistachio nuts, apple and sage leaves and season. Fry a piece of the mixture to taste and adjust the seasoning. Cover and refrigerate. Wrap a piece of plastic wrap around a 6 cm (2 1/2 inch) high, 20 cm (8 inch) straight-sided tin, then turn the tin over and grease the outside base and side.
2 Put the flour and 1 teaspoon salt in a bowl and make a well in the centre. Put the butter in a pan with 210 ml (7 fl oz) water, bring to the boil and add to the flour with the eggs. Mix with a wooden spoon until combined, then turn out onto a work surface and bring together to form a smooth dough. Wrap in plastic and refrigerate for 10 minutes.
3 Cut off a third of the pastry and wrap in plastic wrap—do not refrigerate. Roll the remainder into a circle large enough to just cover the outside of the tin. Lift onto a rolling pin and place over the tin, working fast before the pastry sets. Refrigerate until the pastry hardens. Carefully pull out the tin and remove the plastic wrap. Attach a paper collar made of two layers of greased baking paper around the outside of the pastry so it fits snugly and secure with a paper clip at the top and bottom. Fill the pie, then roll out the remaining pastry to form a lid. Attach it to the base with some water, pressing or crimping it to make it look neat. Cut a small hole in the top of the pie.
4 Put the pie on a baking tray, bake for 40 minutes and check the pastry top. If it is still pale, bake for another 10 minutes, then remove the paper. Brush with egg yolk mixed with 1 tablespoon water and bake for another 15 minutes, or until the sides are brown. Cool completely.
5 Bring the stock and half the apple juice to the boil. Sprinkle the gelatine over the surface of the remaining apple juice in a jug and leave to go spongy, then pour into the stock and mix until the gelatine dissolves. Place a small funnel (a piping nozzle works well) in the hole of the pie and pour in a little of the gelatine, leave to settle and then pour in some more until the pie is full. Fill the pie completely so there are no gaps when the gelatine sets. Leave in the fridge overnight.

NUTRITION PER SERVE
Protein 60 g; Fat 35 g; Carbohydrate 72 g; Dietary Fibre 5.5 g; Cholesterol 257 mg; 3545 kJ (845 cal)

STORAGE: If wrapped tightly with plastic wrap, pork pies will last in the fridge for 4–5 days.

Mix together the ingredients for the filling and then fry a little to test the seasoning.

Turn out the dough onto a work surface and then bring together with your hands.

Cover the outside of the tin with the pastry, working fast so that it does not set.

The greased paper collar should fit snugly around the outside of the pastry.

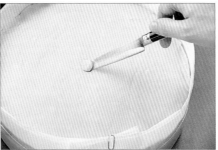

Cut a small hole in the top of the pie to allow the gelatine to be poured in.

Gradually pour the gelatine into the cooked and cooled pie until it is full.

SAUSAGE AND ONION PIE

Preparation time: 30 minutes
Total cooking time: 55 minutes
Serves 6–8

1 tablespoon olive oil
2 onions, chopped
1 clove garlic, chopped
1 kg (2 lb) pork sausages (see NOTE)
1 tablespoon chopped chives
1 teaspoon chopped fresh
    flat-leaf parsley
1 1/2 teaspoons English mustard
1 egg, lightly beaten
600 g (1 1/4 lb) shortcrust pastry
1 egg, lightly beaten, to glaze

1 Preheat the oven to 200°C (400°F/ Gas 6) and grease an 18 cm (7 inch) metal pie dish. Heat the oil in a frying pan and cook the onion and garlic for 5 minutes, or until soft and lightly golden. Transfer to a large bowl.
2 Remove the sausage meat from the casings, crumble slightly and add to the onion. Add the chives, parsley and mustard. Season well. Mix well, then stir in the beaten egg.
3 Roll out two-thirds of the pastry between two sheets of baking paper to make a round large enough to fit the base and side of the pie tin. Line the tin with the pastry and trim the edges. Fill with the sausage mixture.
4 Roll out the remaining dough between two pieces of baking paper to a round large enough to cover the pie. Brush the rim of the first piece of pastry with the egg glaze, then cover the top with the pastry and press the edges to seal. Make a small hole in the centre. Use the trimmings to decorate.

Brush the pie with beaten egg and bake for 10 minutes. Reduce the oven to 180°C (350°F/Gas 4) and bake for 40 minutes. Serve hot.

NUTRITION PER SERVE (8)
Protein 22 g; Fat 51 g; Carbohydrate 37 g; Dietary Fibre 3.5 g; Cholesterol 148 mg; 2835 kJ (680 cal)

NOTE: It's important to use lean, English-style pork sausages as they contain grains which soak up any excess liquid. Other sausages will make the pie too wet.

Using your fingers, remove the sausage meat from the casings.

Fill the pastry-lined pie dish with the sausage meat filling.

COTTAGE PIE

Preparation time: 30 minutes
Total cooking time: 1 hour 30 minutes
Serves 6–8

2 tablespoons olive oil
2 onions, chopped
2 carrots, diced
1 celery stick, diced
1 kg (2 lb) beef mince
2 tablespoons plain flour
1¹/₂ cups (375 ml/12 fl oz) beef stock
1 tablespoon soy sauce
1 tablespoon Worcestershire sauce
2 tablespoons tomato sauce
1 tablespoon tomato paste
2 bay leaves
2 teaspoons chopped fresh flat-leaf
    parsley

TOPPING
800 g (1 lb 10 oz) potatoes, diced
400 g (13 oz) parsnips, diced
30 g (1 oz) butter
¹/₂ cup (125 ml/4 fl oz) milk

1 Heat the oil in a large frying pan over medium heat and cook the onion, carrot and celery, stirring occasionally, for 5 minutes, or until softened and lightly coloured. Add the mince and cook for 7 minutes, then stir in the flour and cook for 2 minutes. Add the stock, soy sauce, Worcestershire sauce, tomato sauce, tomato paste and bay leaves and simmer over low heat for 30 minutes, stirring occasionally. Leave to cool. Remove the bay leaves and stir in the parsley.
2 To make the topping, boil the potato and parsnip in salted water for 15–20 minutes, or until cooked through. Drain, return to the pan and mash with the butter and enough of the milk to make a firm mash.
3 Preheat the oven to 180°C (350°F/ Gas 4) and lightly grease a 2.5 litre ovenproof dish. Spoon the filling into the dish and spread the topping over it. Fluff with a fork. Bake for 25 minutes, or until golden.

NUTRITION PER SERVE (8)
Protein 31 g; Fat 18 g; Carbohydrate 27 g;
Dietary Fibre 4 g; Cholesterol 78 mg;
1640 kJ (390 cal)

Mash the potato and parsnip together with a potato masher.

Spoon the cooled meat filling into the a lightly greased dish.

FAMILY-STYLE MEAT PIE

Preparation time: 30 minutes + cooling
+ 20 minutes refrigeration
Total cooking time: 1 hour 45 minutes
Serves 6

1 tablespoon oil
1 onion, chopped
1 clove garlic, crushed
750 g (1¹/₂ lb) beef mince
1 cup (250 ml/8 fl oz) beef stock
1 cup (250 ml/8 fl oz) beer
1 tablespoon tomato paste
1 tablespoon vegetable yeast extract
1 tablespoon Worcestershire sauce
2 teaspoons cornflour
375 g (12 oz) shortcrust pastry
375 g (12 oz) puff pastry
1 egg, lightly beaten, to glaze

1 Heat the oil in a large saucepan over medium heat and cook the onion for 5 minutes, or until golden. Increase the heat to high, add the garlic and mince and cook, breaking up any lumps, for about 5 minutes, or until the mince changes colour.
2 Add the stock, beer, tomato paste, yeast extract, Worcestershire sauce and ¹/₂ cup (125 ml/4 fl oz) water. Reduce the heat to medium and cook for 1 hour, or until there is little liquid left. Combine the cornflour with 1 tablespoon water, then stir into the mince and cook for 5 minutes, or until thick and glossy. Remove from the heat and cool completely.
3 Lightly grease an 18 cm (7 inch) pie tin. Roll the shortcrust pastry out between two sheets of baking paper until large enough to line the base and side of the tin. Use a small ball of pastry to help press the pastry into the tin, allowing any excess to hang over the side of the tin.
4 Roll out the puff pastry between two sheets of baking paper to make a 24 cm (9 inch) circle. Spoon the filling into the pastry shell and smooth it down. Brush the pastry edges with beaten egg, then place the puff pastry over the top. Cut off any excess with a sharp knife. Press the top and bottom pastries together, then scallop the edges with a fork or your fingers, and refrigerate for 20 minutes. Preheat the oven to 200°C (400°F/Gas 6) and heat a baking tray.
5 Brush the remaining egg over the top of the pie, place on the hot tray on the bottom shelf of the oven and bake for 25–30 minutes, or until golden and well puffed.

NUTRITION PER SERVE
Protein 38 g; Fat 44 g; Carbohydrate 52 g;
Dietary Fibre 3 g; Cholesterol 129.5 mg;
3120 kJ (745 cal)

Spoon the cooled mince meat filling into the pastry shell.

Trim the edges of the puff pastry pie top with a sharp knife.

PUMPKIN, LEEK AND CORN PIE

Preparation time: 30 minutes + cooling
Total cooking time: 1 hour 15 minutes
Serves 6

4 tablespoons olive oil
2 leeks, thinly sliced
2 large cloves garlic, chopped
1 butternut pumpkin, peeled, seeded
   and diced
3 corn cobs
1¹/₂ cups (185 g/6 oz) grated Cheddar
1 teaspoon chopped fresh rosemary
¹/₂ cup (15 g/¹/₂ oz) chopped fresh
   flat-leaf parsley
12 sheets filo pastry
5 eggs, lightly beaten

1 Preheat the oven to moderate 180°C (350°F/Gas 4). Grease a 32 x 24 cm (13 x 10 inch) ovenproof dish.
2 Heat 1 tablespoon of the oil in a small saucepan and cook the leek and garlic for 10 minutes, stirring occasionally, until soft and golden. Transfer to a large bowl and cool.
3 Meanwhile, cook the pumpkin in boiling water for 5 minutes, or until just tender. Drain and cool. Cook the corn in boiling water for 7–8 minutes, or until tender. Drain, leave until cool enough to handle, then cut away the kernels. Add these to the bowl with the pumpkin, cheese, rosemary and parsley, season and mix gently.
4 Cover the filo pastry with a damp tea towel to prevent drying out. Lightly brush one sheet of filo with oil and place in the dish. Layer five more sheets in the dish, brushing all but the last sheet with oil.
5 Gently stir the eggs into the pumpkin mixture, then spoon into the dish. Cover with the remaining filo pastry, again brushing each layer with oil, and tuck in the edges. Bake for 1 hour, or until the pastry is golden brown and the filling has set.

NUTRITION PER SERVE
Protein 22 g; Fat 29 g; Carbohydrate 38 g; Dietary Fibre 6 g; Cholesterol 180.5 mg; 2080 kJ (495 cal)

Spoon the pumpkin and corn mixture into the ovenproof dish.

Tuck the edges of the filo pastry into the side of the dish.

ROSEMARY LAMB COBBLER

Preparation time: 30 minutes
Total cooking time: 2 hours
Serves 4–6

600 g (1¼ lb) boned lamb leg, cut
    into small chunks
¼ cup (30 g/1 oz) plain flour,
    seasoned
30 g (1 oz) butter
2 tablespoons olive oil
8 spring onions, chopped
3 cloves garlic, crushed
2 cups (500 ml/16 fl oz) beef stock
1 cup (250 ml/8 fl oz) dry white wine
2 teaspoons wholegrain mustard
2 teaspoons finely chopped
    fresh rosemary
2 celery sticks, sliced
1 teaspoon grated lemon rind
1 teaspoon lemon juice
½ cup (125 g/4 oz) sour cream

COBBLER TOPPING
¾ cup (185 ml/6 fl oz) milk
1 egg
2 tablespoons melted butter
1½ cups (185 g/6 oz) plain flour
2 teaspoons baking powder
1 teaspoon finely chopped
    fresh rosemary
2 tablespoons finely chopped
    fresh flat-leaf parsley

1 Put the lamb pieces and flour in a plastic bag and shake well to evenly coat the lamb. Shake off any excess.
2 Heat the butter and 1 tablespoon of the olive oil in a large saucepan over high heat, then cook half the lamb for 5 minutes, or until well browned. Add the remaining oil if needed and cook the remaining lamb.

3 Add half the spring onion to the pan with the garlic and cook for 30 seconds, or until the spring onion is softened. Return all the lamb to the pan with the stock, wine, mustard, rosemary, celery, lemon rind and juice and bring to the boil. Reduce the heat and simmer, stirring occasionally, for 1¼ hours, or until the lamb is tender and the sauce has thickened.
4 Remove from the heat and stir a little of the sauce into the sour cream, then stir it all back into the lamb mixture with the remaining spring onion. Leave to cool while you make the topping.
5 Preheat the oven to 190°C (375°F/Gas 5). To make the topping, combine the milk, egg and melted butter in a large bowl. Add the combined sifted flour and baking powder with the herbs, 1 teaspoon salt and some cracked black pepper and stir until you have a thick, sticky batter—you may need to add a little more flour if it is too wet, or milk if it is too dry.
6 Spoon the lamb into a deep 18 cm (7 inch) pie dish and, using two spoons, cover the top with small dollops of the batter, leaving a little space for spreading. Cook for 30 minutes, or until the topping is risen and golden.

NUTRITION PER SERVE (6)
Protein 31 g; Fat 28 g; Carbohydrate 31 g;
Dietary Fibre 2.5 g; Cholesterol 153 mg;
2180 kJ (520 cal)

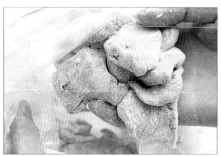

Put the lamb and flour in a plastic bag and shake until the meat is lightly covered.

Cook the lamb in two batches in a large saucepan until it is nicely browned.

Simmer the mixture until the meat is tender and the sauce has thickened.

Stir a little of the meaty sauce into the sour cream.

Stir the batter for the cobbler topping until it is thick and sticky.

Add spoonfuls of the batter to the top of the pie, leaving a little room for spreading.

VEGETABLE LATTICE PIE

Preparation time: 40 minutes + chilling
Total cooking time: 1 hour
Serves 6

185 g (6 oz) butter
2 cups (250 g/8 oz) plain flour
3 tablespoons iced water

FILLING
1 tablespoon oil
1 onion, finely chopped
1 small red capsicum, chopped
1 small green capsicum, chopped
150 g (5 oz) pumpkin, chopped
1 small potato, chopped
100 g (3½ oz) broccoli, cut into small
    florets
1 carrot, chopped
3 tablespoons plain flour
1 cup (250 ml/8 fl oz) milk
2 egg yolks
½ cup (60 g/2 oz) grated Cheddar
1 egg, lightly beaten, to glaze

1 Chop 125 g (4 oz) of the butter. Sift the flour into a large bowl and add the chopped butter. Using your fingertips, rub the butter into the flour until the mixture is fine and crumbly. Add almost all the water and use a knife to mix to a firm dough, adding more water if necessary. Turn onto a lightly floured surface and press together until smooth. Divide the dough in half, roll out one portion and line a deep 20 cm (8 inch) fluted flan tin. Refrigerate for 20 minutes. Roll the remaining pastry out to a 25 cm (10 inch) diameter circle. Cut into strips and lay half of them on a sheet of baking paper, leaving a 2 cm (¾ inch) gap between each strip. Interweave the remaining strips to form a lattice pattern. Cover with plastic wrap and refrigerate, keeping flat, until firm.

2 Preheat the oven to 180°C (350°F/ Gas 4). Cut a sheet of greaseproof paper to cover the pastry-lined tin. Spread a layer of baking beads or dried beans or rice over the paper. Bake for 10 minutes, remove from the oven and discard the paper and beans. Bake for another 10 minutes or until golden. Remove and allow to cool.

3 Heat the oil in a frying pan. Add the onion and cook for 2 minutes or until soft. Add the caspicum and cook, stirring, for another 3 minutes. Steam or boil the remaining vegetables until just tender; drain and cool. Combine the onion, capsicum and the other vegetables in a large bowl.

4 Heat the remaining butter in a small pan. Add the flour and cook, stirring, for 2 minutes. Add the milk gradually, stirring until smooth after each addition. Stir until the sauce boils and thickens. Boil for 1 minute and then remove from the heat. Add the egg yolks and cheese and stir until smooth.

Pour over the vegetables and stir together. Pour into the pastry case and brush the edges with egg. Using the baking paper to help, invert the lattice over the vegetables, trim the edges and brush with a little egg. Press the edges lightly to seal to the cooked pastry. Brush the top with egg and bake for 30 minutes or until the pastry is golden.

NUTRITION PER SERVE
Protein 17 g; Fat 39 g; Carbohydrate 48 g; Dietary Fibre 4 g; Cholesterol 190 mg; 2535 kJ (605 cal)

Add almost all the water to the bowl, mixing with a knife until a firm dough is formed.

Invert the lattice over the pie and slowly pull away the baking paper.

SPINACH AND FETA FILO ROLL

Preparation time: 30 minutes
Total cooking time: 50 minutes
Serves 4–6

1 bunch (500 g/1 lb) English spinach
2 tablespoons olive oil
8 spring onions, finely chopped
375 g (12 oz) feta cheese, crumbled
    (see NOTE)
1/4 cup (25 g/3/4 oz) grated Parmesan
1/4 cup (15 g/1/2 oz) chopped fresh dill
2 eggs, lightly beaten
1/2 teaspoon ground nutmeg
12 sheets filo pastry

1 Wash the spinach and put in a pan with just the water clinging to the leaves. Cover the pan and heat for 2 minutes, or until wilted. Drain, cool and squeeze out as much moisture as possible. Chop roughly and put in a large bowl.
2 Heat the olive oil in a pan and cook the spring onion for 2–3 minutes. Add the spinach, feta, Parmesan, dill, eggs and nutmeg. Season and stir well.
3 Grease a 30 cm (12 inch) round pizza tray. Preheat the oven to 190°C (375°F/Gas 5). Cover the filo with a damp tea towel and, working with one sheet at a time, lightly brush a sheet with oil, fold in half lengthways and brush again. Place 3 tablespoons of the filling along one long edge, fold in the sides and roll up firmly. Form the roll into a coil, brush again with some oil and place on the tray. Repeat with the remaining sheets and filling. Arrange the coils in a single layer. Sprinkle the top with a little more nutmeg. Bake for 40 minutes.

NUTRITION PER SERVE (6)
Protein 20 g; Fat 30 g; Carbohydrate 45 g;
Dietary Fibre 6 g; Cholesterol 175 mg;
2230 kJ (530 cal)

NOTE: Substitute dry cottage cheese for half the feta if you prefer a less salty flavour.

Wash the spinach thoroughly and heat with just the water clinging to the leaves.

Add the spring onion, feta, Parmesan, dill, eggs and nutmeg to the spinach.

Place some filling along one long edge of the pastry, fold in the sides and roll up.

Once the pastry has been rolled up to seal the filling, roll it into a firm coil.

MINI OYSTER PIES

Preparation time: 30 minutes +
 20 minutes cooling
Total cooking time: 45 minutes
Makes 30

2 cups (500 ml/16 fl oz) fish stock
1 tablespoon olive oil
2 leeks, chopped
30 g (1 oz) butter
1 tablespoon plain flour
1 teaspoon lemon juice
1 teaspoon chopped fresh chives
8 sheets puff pastry
30 fresh oysters
1 egg, lightly beaten, to glaze

1 Pour the stock into a saucepan and simmer over medium heat for 15 minutes, or until reduced by half—you will need 1 cup (250 ml/8 fl oz).
2 Heat the oil in a saucepan over medium heat. Add the leek and cook, stirring well, for 5 minutes, or until soft and lightly coloured. Transfer to a small bowl to cool slightly.

3 Melt the butter in a small saucepan over low heat. Add the flour and cook, stirring well, for 2 minutes, or until the flour is golden. Remove from the heat and gradually add the fish stock, stirring well. Return to the heat and bring to the boil, stirring constantly for 2 minutes, or until thickened. Add the lemon juice, chives and leek and season well. Set aside to cool for 20 minutes. Preheat the oven to 200°C (400°F/Gas 6) and grease two baking trays.
4 Using a 6 cm (2½ inch) round cutter, cut out 30 circles of pastry and put one oyster and a heaped teaspoon

of the filling on top of each, leaving a narrow border. Lightly brush the edges with beaten egg.
5 Cut thirty 8 cm (3 inch) circles from the remaining pastry. Cover the filling with these rounds and press the edges with a fork to seal. Brush the tops with the remaining beaten egg, put on the trays and bake for 15–20 minutes, or until golden and well puffed.

NUTRITION PER PIE
Protein 3.5 g; Fat 12 g; Carbohydrate 17 g;
Dietary Fibre 1 g; Cholesterol 24 mg;
785 kJ (190 cal)

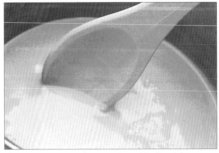

Gradually add the fish stock and boil, stirring constantly, until thickened.

Place an oyster and a heaped teaspoon of filling on each pastry round.

CHICKEN AND PRESERVED LEMON PIE

Preparation time: 40 minutes +
  20 minutes refrigeration + cooling
Total cooking time: 1 hour 15 minutes
Serves 4–6

2 tablespoons olive oil
2 leeks, thinly sliced
3/4 preserved lemon, pulp removed,
  rind washed and cut into thin strips
1 kg (2 lb) chicken thigh fillets, cut into
  bite-size pieces
2 tablespoons plain flour
1 cup (250 ml/8 fl oz) chicken stock
250 g (8 oz) kipfler potatoes, thinly
  sliced
2 tablespoons chopped fresh
  flat-leaf parsley
1 egg, lightly beaten, to glaze

PASTRY
100 g (3¹/2 oz) self-raising flour
150 g (5 oz) plain flour
60 g (2 oz) butter, chilled and cubed
60 g (2 oz) lard, chilled and cubed
3–4 tablespoons iced water
1 egg, lightly beaten

1 Heat the oil in a large frying pan, and cook the leek for 2–3 minutes, or until golden. Add the preserved lemon and cook for 3 minutes, or until fragrant. Remove from the pan.
2 Add a little extra oil to the pan if necessary and brown the chicken in batches, stirring, for 5 minutes. Return all the chicken to the pan with the leek and lemon. Sprinkle with flour and cook, stirring, for 2 minutes.
3 Gradually stir in the chicken stock, then add the potato. Bring to the boil, then reduce the heat and simmer for 7 minutes, or until thickened slightly. Stir in the parsley. Transfer to a bowl and allow to cool completely.
4 To make the pastry, sift the flours and a pinch of salt into a large bowl and rub in the chopped butter and lard with your fingertips until the mixture resembles fine breadcrumbs. Make a well, add almost all the water and mix with a flat-bladed knife, using a cutting action, until the mixture forms beads, adding more water if necessary.
5 Turn out the dough onto a lightly floured surface, gather into a ball, cover in plastic wrap and refrigerate for 20 minutes. Preheat the oven to 200°C (400°F/Gas 6). Heat a baking tray in the oven.
6 Spoon the filling into a 16 cm (6¹/2 inch) pie plate. Roll out the dough between two sheets of baking paper until large enough to cover the pie. Trim any excess pastry, then press to seal on the rim. Cut a few steam holes in the top and decorate with pastry trimmings. Brush with the egg glaze, place on the hot tray and bake for 35–40 minutes, or until the crust is crisp and golden.

NUTRITION PER SERVE (6)
Protein 40 g; Fat 39 g; Carbohydrate 40 g;
Dietary Fibre 4 g; Cholesterol 240 mg;
2795 kJ (665 cal)

When the chicken mixture has thickened slightly, stir in the parsley.

SPICED CHINESE ROAST DUCK PIES

Preparation time: 50 minutes +
    30 minutes refrigeration + cooling
Total cooking time: 1 hour
Makes 4

2 cups (250 g/8 oz) plain flour
2 teaspoons baking powder
50 g (1³/₄ oz) lard, chilled and grated

FILLING
¹/₃ cup (80 ml/2³/₄ fl oz) vegetable oil
1 tablespoon plus 1 teaspoon
    sesame oil
1 clove garlic, finely chopped
2 teaspoons finely chopped
    fresh ginger
150 g (5 oz) oyster mushrooms, sliced
1 Chinese roast duck (from Chinese
    barbecue shops), meat shredded
3 spring onions, cut into short lengths
    plus 4 spring onions, finely sliced
1 teaspoon sugar
1 teaspoon finely ground Sichuan
    pepper
¹/₄ cup (30 g/1 oz) plain flour
¹/₄ cup (60 ml/2 fl oz) Chinese rice
    wine
1¹/₂ cups (375 ml/12 fl oz) chicken
    stock
1 tablespoon light soy sauce

1 Sift the flour, baking powder and 1 teaspoon salt into a bowl. Mix the lard into the flour with your fingertips until the mixture resembles fine breadcrumbs. Make a well and gradually pour in ³/₄ cup (185 ml/ 6 fl oz) boiling water. Gradually stir the flour into the centre of the bowl until the dough comes together. Turn out, gather into a ball, wrap in plastic wrap and refrigerate for 30 minutes.
2 Heat 2 tablespoons vegetable oil and 1 teaspoon sesame oil in a frying pan over medium heat. Add the garlic and ginger and cook for 2 minutes, then add the mushrooms, duck meat, lengths of spring onion, sugar, Sichuan pepper and a pinch of salt and cook for 3–4 minutes. Add the flour and cook for 2 minutes, stirring well. Pour in the rice wine, stir again, then add the stock and soy sauce. Bring to the boil and cook, stirring for 2–3 minutes,

or until the mixture thickens. Remove from the heat and set aside to cool.
3 Preheat the oven to 180°C (350°F/ Gas 4). Grease four 6 cm (2¹/₂ inch) pie tins. Roll the pastry into a log, then roughly divide into eight pieces. Combine the remaining vegetable and sesame oils in a small bowl. Roll each piece of dough into a flat 10 cm (4 inch) round, brush with the oil mixture and sprinkle with the sliced spring onion. Roll into small logs, then coil each log into a cake.
4 Roll out four of the dough cakes into flat 16 cm (6¹/₂ inch) discs. Use to line the pie tins, then fill the pastry cases with the duck filling. Roll the remaining pastry into 15 cm (6 inch) circles and use as lids. Press with a fork to seal. Brush with the oil mixture and bake for 40–45 minutes, until the tops are golden.

NUTRITION PER PIE
Protein 30 g; Fat 46 g; Carbohydrate 56 g; Dietary Fibre 5 g; Cholesterol 120 mg; 3175 kJ (760 cal)

NOTE: Sichuan pepper, otherwise known as anise pepper or Chinese pepper, is a Chinese spice made from dried red berries.

Let the barbecued duck filling cool completely before spooning into the pastry cases.

HAM, CHEESE AND POTATO PIE

Preparation time: 25 minutes +
    cooling + 10 minutes standing
Total cooking time: 1 hour 45 minutes
Serves 6–8

1/4 cup (60 ml/2 fl oz) olive oil
3 onions, finely chopped
1 clove garlic, finely chopped
300 g (10 oz) ham, chopped
430 g (14 oz) desiree potatoes, diced
2 cups (250 g/8 oz) grated Cheddar
2 eggs
1/3 cup (80 ml/2³/4 fl oz) cream
2 teaspoons chopped chives
4 sheets puff pastry
1 egg, lightly beaten, to glaze

1 Heat the oil in a large frying pan over medium heat. Add the onion and garlic and cook, stirring occasionally, for 5 minutes, or until the onion softens. Add the ham and potato and cook, stirring occasionally, for 5–7 minutes, or until the potato softens slightly. Transfer to a large bowl and stir in the Cheddar.

2 Mix together the eggs and cream and pour into the bowl. Add the chives and mix thoroughly. Season and leave to cool.

3 Preheat the oven to 200°C (400°F/ Gas 6). Grease an 18 cm (7 inch) pie dish. Line the pie dish with two sheets of puff pastry, and brush the edge with beaten egg. Spoon the filling into the pie dish.

4 Cut the remaining sheets of pastry into quarters, and each quarter into three equal lengths. Place the strips, overlapping, around the top of the pie, leaving the centre open. Press down the edges so that the top and bottom layers stick together, then trim the edges with a sharp knife.

5 Brush the top of the pie with the beaten egg, and bake in the oven for 30 minutes. Reduce the temperature to 180°C (350°F/Gas 4) and cook the pie for another hour, covering the top with foil if it is browning too much. Leave for 10 minutes before serving.

NUTRITION PER SERVE (8)
Protein 24 g; Fat 44 g; Carbohydrate 39 g;
Dietary Fibre 3 g; Cholesterol 153 mg;
2700 kJ (645 cal)

Pour the creamy egg mixture into the bowl with the ham and cheese.

Overlap the pastry strips around the pie, leaving a gap in the middle.

ITALIAN EASTER PIE

Preparation time: 40 minutes +
 20 minutes cooling
Total cooking time: 1 hour 5 minutes
Serves 6–8

450 g (14 oz) spinach or silverbeet,
 stalks removed
1 cup (90 g/3 oz) fresh white
 breadcrumbs
1 cup (250 ml/8 fl oz) milk
500 g (1 lb) ricotta (see NOTE)
2 cups (200 g/6$^{1}/_{2}$ oz) grated
 Parmesan
8 eggs
pinch of ground nutmeg
pinch of cayenne pepper
10 small fresh marjoram leaves
150 g (5 oz) butter
20 sheets filo pastry

1 Bring 2 cups (500 ml/16 fl oz) salted
water to the boil in a large saucepan.
Add the spinach or silverbeet, cover
and cook, stirring occasionally, for
5 minutes, or until wilted. Drain well.
When cool enough to handle, wring
out all the liquid in a clean tea towel.
Chop well.
2 Preheat the oven to moderate 180°C
(350°F/Gas 4). Put the breadcrumbs
and milk in a large bowl, leave for
5 minutes, then add the ricotta, half
the Parmesan, 4 eggs, the nutmeg,
cayenne, marjoram and the chopped
spinach. Season well and mix.
3 Melt the butter, then lightly brush a
23 cm (9 inch) springform tin with it.
Line the base and the side with a sheet
of filo pastry. Brush with melted butter
and place another filo sheet on top,
positioned so that any exposed wall of
the tin is covered. Continue in this
way, using a total of 10 sheets of filo.
Don't worry about the filo forming
folds on the tin walls, just push them
flat as you brush with butter.
4 Spoon the filling into the tin. Make
four deep indentations in the surface
around the edge of the pie, then break
an egg into each. Season and sprinkle
with the remaining Parmesan. Fold
over any overhanging pastry. Cover
with the remaining filo, buttering
each layer.
5 Bake for 40 minutes, cover the top
with foil, then bake for another
20 minutes. Cool in the tin for
20 minutes before serving.

NUTRITION PER SERVE (8)
Protein 29 g; Fat 38 g; Carbohydrate 29 g;
Dietary Fibre 3 g; Cholesterol 286 mg;
2360 kJ (565 cal)

NOTE: Use ricotta from a wheel—pre-
packaged ricotta tends to be too moist.

Gently break an egg into each of the four
indentations you have made.

CHUNKY VEAL AND CAPSICUM PIE

Preparation time: 40 minutes +
  10 minutes resting + cooling
Total cooking time: 2 hours
Serves 6

1/3 cup (80 ml/2³/4 fl oz) olive oil
3 capsicums, seeded and cut into
    2.5 cm (1 inch) pieces
2 cloves garlic, crushed
1 kg (2 lb) neck, shoulder or breast of
    veal, cut into small pieces
1/4 cup (30 g/1 oz) plain flour,
    seasoned
40 g (1¹/2 oz) butter
2 onions, finely chopped
8 French shallots, peeled
1/4 teaspoon cayenne pepper
2 teaspoons red wine vinegar
3/4 cup (185 ml/6 fl oz) chicken
    stock
2 tablespoons chopped fresh flat-leaf
    parsley
375 g (12 oz) shortcrust pastry
1 egg, lightly beaten, to glaze

1 Heat half the oil in a large saucepan and cook the capsicum over medium heat for 2–3 minutes. Add the garlic, cover the pan and reduce the heat to low. Cook gently for 5 minutes, then remove from the pan.
2 Put the veal and flour in a plastic bag and shake until the veal is evenly coated, shaking off any excess. Heat the butter and the remaining oil over high heat in the same saucepan and cook the veal in batches until evenly browned. Return all the veal to the pan, add the onion, shallots and cayenne and reduce the heat to low. Cook, covered, for 10 minutes. Stir in the vinegar, cover and turn off the heat. Leave for 10 minutes.
3 Add the capsicum, stock and parsley to the meat, bring to the boil, then reduce the heat to low. Cover and simmer for 20 minutes, or until the meat is tender.
4 Uncover and cook for another 30–40 minutes to reduce the liquid until it thickens and darkens. Season to taste and cool slightly. Preheat the oven to 200°C (400°F/Gas 6) and preheat a baking tray. Lightly grease an 18 cm (7 inch) pie dish.
5 Spoon the filling into the pie dish, levelling the surface. Roll the dough out between two sheets of baking paper to a size slightly larger than the top of the pie dish. Carefully cover the filling and press the pastry over the edge to seal. Trim the edges. Decorate with pastry trimmings and brush the top with egg. Place on the hot tray and bake for 30 minutes, or until golden.

NUTRITION PER SERVE
Protein 44 g; Fat 37 g; Carbohydrate 33 g;
Dietary Fibre 2.5 g; Cholesterol 201 mg;
2660 kJ (635 cal)

Spoon the filling into the lightly greased pie dish, then level the surface.

VENISON AND JUNIPER BERRY PIES

Preparation time: 30 minutes + cooling
  + 30 minutes refrigeration
Total cooking time: 3 hours
Makes 6

1/4 cup (60 ml/2 fl oz) olive oil
2 cloves garlic, crushed
150 g (5 oz) streaky bacon, diced
800 g (1 lb 10 oz) venison or beef
   rump, diced (see VARIATION)
1/4 cup (30 g/1 oz) plain flour,
   seasoned
1/2 cup (125 ml/4 fl oz) dry red wine
1 teaspoon dried juniper berries,
   ground
3 bay leaves
1 tablespoon fresh thyme, chopped
2 teaspoons grated orange rind
2 cups (500 ml/16 fl oz) beef stock
200 g (6 1/2 oz) small pickling onions,
   trimmed
1 egg, lightly beaten
sour cream, to serve

PASTRY
450 g (14 oz) plain flour
300 g (10 oz) frozen lard (see NOTE)
150 ml (5 fl oz) iced water

1 Heat 1 tablespoon of the oil in a large flameproof casserole dish and cook the garlic and bacon over low heat for 4–5 minutes, or until softened but not browned. Remove from the dish with a slotted spoon.
2 Add the remaining oil to the pan and increase the heat to high. Cook the meat in batches for 3 minutes, or until lightly browned. Return all the meat to the pan and sprinkle with the flour, stirring well.
3 Pour the wine into the pan and cook, stirring constantly, for 2–3 minutes, or until nearly all of the wine has evaporated. Return the garlic and bacon to the pan with the ground juniper berries, bay leaves, thyme, orange rind and beef stock. Add enough water to cover the meat and bring to the boil, then reduce the heat and simmer, covered, for 1 hour.
4 Add the onions and cook for another 45–60 minutes, or until the meat is tender, stirring occasionally

and adding a little water if the mixture begins to catch on the base of the pan. Season, remove from the heat and allow to cool. Remove the bay leaves.
5 Preheat the oven to 200°C (400°F/ Gas 6). While the meat is cooling, make the pastry. Sift the flour and 1/4 teaspoon salt into a large bowl and roughly grate the frozen lard onto the flour. Rub the lard into the flour with your fingertips until the mixture resembles coarse breadcrumbs. Add the water 1 tablespoon at a time until the dough just comes together, being careful not to overwork the dough. Shape into a ball and flatten slightly. Cover with plastic wrap and refrigerate for at least 30 minutes.
6 On a lightly floured surface, roll out two-thirds of the pastry and cut out six circles large enough to line the base and sides of six 9.5 cm (4 inch) pie tins. Divide the filling among the tins and roll out the remaining pastry to make six lids. Brush the rims of the pastry lining with beaten egg, then place the lids on top, pinching to seal. Trim the edges and brush the tops with beaten egg. Make small steam holes on the tops of the pies.
7 Bake for 20 minutes, then reduce the temperature to 180°C (350°F/Gas 4) and cook for another 25–30 minutes, or until the pastry is crisp and golden. Serve with sour cream on the side.

NUTRITION PER PIE
Protein 43 g; Fat 64 g; Carbohydrate 52 g; Dietary Fibre 4 g; Cholesterol 159 mg; 4025 kJ (960 cal)

VARIATION: Any other red meat can be used instead of venison or beef.
NOTE: Freeze the lard before use to make it is easy to grate into the flour.

Pour the wine into the pan and cook, stirring, until it has nearly evaporated.

Remove the casserole dish from the heat and discard the bay leaves.

Roll out the remaining pastry to make six lids for the pies.

Brush the edge of the pastry with egg, then place the lids on top, pinching to seal.

BEEF AND CARAMELISED ONION PIE

Preparation time: 40 minutes +
    20 minutes cooling
Total cooking time: 2 hours 20 minutes
Serves 6–8

1/3 cup (80 ml/2³/₄ fl oz) oil
2 large red onions, thinly sliced
1 teaspoon dark brown sugar
1 kg (2 lb) lean rump steak, diced
1/4 cup (30 g/1 oz) plain flour,
    seasoned
2 cloves garlic, crushed
225 g (7 oz) button mushrooms, sliced
1 cup (250 ml/8 fl oz) beef stock
150 ml (5 fl oz) stout
1 tablespoon tomato paste
1 tablespoon Worcestershire sauce
1 tablespoon chopped fresh thyme
350 g (11 oz) potatoes, diced
2 carrots, diced
600 g (1¹/₄ lb) quick flaky pastry
1 egg, lightly beaten

1 Heat 2 tablespoons of the oil in a frying pan over medium heat and cook the onion for 5 minutes, or until light brown, then add the sugar and cook for 7–8 minutes, or until the onion caramelises. Remove from the pan. Wipe the pan clean.

2 Toss the beef in flour and shake off the excess. Heat the remaining oil in the same pan and cook the meat in batches over high heat until browned. Return all the meat to the pan, add the garlic and mushrooms and cook for 2 minutes. Add the stock, stout, tomato paste, Worcestershire sauce and thyme. Bring to the boil, then reduce the heat and simmer, covered, for 1 hour. Add the potato and carrot and simmer for 30 minutes. Remove from the heat and allow to cool.

3 Preheat the oven to 190°C (375°F/ Gas 5). Grease a 1.25 litre pie dish. Pour in the filling, then top with the onion. Roll the pastry out between two sheets of baking paper until it is 2.5 cm (1 inch) wider than the pie dish. Cut a 2 cm (³/₄ inch) strip around the edge of the pastry circle, brush with water and place damp-side-down on the rim of the dish.

4 Cover with the remaining pastry, pressing the edges together. Knock up the rim by making small slashes in the edges of the pastry with the back of a knife. Re-roll the trimmings and use them to decorate the pie. Brush with egg and bake for 25 minutes, or until golden.

NUTRITION PER SERVE (8)
Protein 36 g; Fat 32 g; Carbohydrate 47 g;
Dietary Fibre 4 g; Cholesterol 113 mg;
2615 kJ (625 cal)

Spoon the caramelised onion over the filling in the pie dish.

Place the strip of pastry damp-side-down on the rim of the dish.

ITALIAN ZUCCHINI PIE

Preparation time: 30 minutes +
  30 minutes refrigeration +
  30 minutes draining
Total cooking time: 1 hour
Serves 6

2^1/$_2$ cups (310 g/10 oz) plain flour
^{1}/$_3$ cup (80 ml/2^3/$_4$ fl oz) olive oil
1 egg, beaten
3–4 tablespoons iced water

FILLING
600 g (1^1/$_4$ lb) zucchini
150 g (5 oz) provolone cheese, grated
120 g (4 oz) ricotta
3 eggs
2 cloves garlic, crushed
2 teaspoons finely chopped fresh basil
pinch of ground nutmeg
1 egg, lightly beaten, to glaze

1 To make the pastry, sift the flour and ^{1}/$_2$ teaspoon salt into a large bowl and make a well. Combine the oil, egg and almost all the water and add to the flour. Mix with a flat-bladed knife, using a cutting action, until the mixture comes together in beads, adding a little more water if necessary. Gather into a ball, wrap in plastic wrap and refrigerate for 30 minutes.

2 Preheat the oven to moderately hot 200°C (400°F/Gas 6) and heat a baking tray. Grease an 18 cm (7 inch) pie dish. To make the filling, grate the zucchini and toss with ^{1}/$_4$ teaspoon salt. Place in a colander for 30 minutes to drain. Squeeze out any excess liquid with your hands. Place in a large bowl and add the provolone, ricotta, eggs, garlic, basil and nutmeg. Season well and mix thoroughly.

3 Roll out two-thirds of the pastry between two sheets of baking paper until large enough to line the base and side of the dish. Remove the top sheet and invert into the dish.

4 Spoon the filling into the pastry shell and level the surface. Brush the exposed rim of the dough with egg. Roll out two-thirds of the remaining dough between the baking paper to make a lid. Cover the filling with it, pressing the edges together firmly. Trim the edges. Crimp the rim. Prick the top all over with a skewer and brush with egg.

5 Roll the remaining dough into a strip about 30 x 10 cm (12 x 4 inches). Using a long sharp knife, cut this into nine lengths 1 cm (^{1}/$_2$ inch) wide. Press three ropes together at one end and press these onto the workbench to secure them. Plait the ropes. Make two more plaits with the remaining lengths. Trim the ends and space the plaits parallel across the centre of the pie. Brush with egg. Bake on the hot tray for 50 minutes, or until golden.

NUTRITION PER SERVE
Protein 21 g; Fat 27 g; Carbohydrate 40 g;
Dietary Fibre 4 g; Cholesterol 184.5 mg;
2010 kJ (480 cal)

Spoon the zucchini filling into the pastry shell and level the surface.

SALMON PIE

Preparation time: 25 minutes +
  refrigeration
Total cooking time: 50 minutes
Serves 4–6

60 g (2 oz) butter
1 onion, finely chopped
200 g (6½ oz) button mushrooms,
  sliced
2 tablespoons lemon juice
220 g (7 oz) salmon fillet, boned,
  skinned, cubed
2 hard-boiled eggs, chopped
2 tablespoons chopped fresh dill
2 tablespoons chopped fresh parsley
1 cup (185 g/6 oz) cooked rice
¼ cup (60 ml/2 fl oz) cream
375 g (12 fl oz) puff pastry
1 egg, lightly beaten, to glaze

1 Lightly oil an oven tray. Melt half
the butter in a frying pan and cook the
onion for 5 minutes, or until soft but
not browned. Add the mushrooms and
cook for 5 minutes. Stir in the lemon
juice and transfer to a bowl.
2 Melt the remaining butter in the
pan, add the salmon and cook for
2 minutes. Remove from the heat, cool
slightly and add the egg, dill, parsley,
salt and pepper. Stir gently and set
aside. Stir together the rice and cream.
3 Roll out half the pastry to a
rectangle measuring 18 x 30 cm
(7 x 12 inches) and place on the tray.
Spread with half the rice mixture,
leaving a small border all the way
around. Top with the salmon mixture,
then the mushroom mixture, and finish
with the remaining rice.
4 Roll out the remaining pastry to
20 x 32 cm (8 x 13 inches) to cover the
filling. Crimp the edges to seal.
Refrigerate for 30 minutes. Preheat the
oven to 210°C (415°F/Gas 6–7). Brush
with beaten egg and bake for
15 minutes. Reduce the heat to
180°C (350°F/Gas 4) and bake for
15–20 minutes until golden.

NUTRITION PER SERVE (6)
Protein 30 g; Fat 60 g; Carbohydrate 70 g;
Dietary Fibre 4 g; Cholesterol 180 mg;
3700 kJ (885 cal)

Add the sliced mushrooms to the softened
onions and stir for about 5 minutes.

When the salmon has cooled slightly, stir in the
egg, dill, parsley, salt and pepper.

Spread the salmon mixture evenly over the layer
of creamy rice.

Hang the pastry top over a rolling pin to make it
easy to place over the filling.

LOW-FAT SPINACH PIE

Preparation time: 25 minutes
Total cooking time: 45 minutes
Serves 6

1.5 kg (3 lb) English spinach
2 teaspoons olive oil
1 onion, chopped
4 spring onions, chopped
750 g (1¹/₂ lb) reduced-fat cottage
    cheese
2 eggs, lightly beaten
2 cloves garlic, crushed
pinch of ground nutmeg
¹/₄ cup (15 g/¹/₂ oz) chopped fresh
    mint
8 sheets filo pastry
30 g (1 oz) butter, melted
¹/₂ cup (40 g/1¹/₄ oz) fresh
    breadcrumbs

1 Preheat the oven to 180°C (350°F/ Gas 4). Lightly spray a square 1.5 litre capacity ovenproof dish with oil. Trim and wash the spinach, then place in a large pan with the water clinging to the leaves. Cover and cook for 2–3 minutes, until just wilted. Drain, cool then squeeze dry and chop.

2 Heat the oil in a small pan. Add the onion and spring onion and cook for 2–3 minutes, until softened. Combine in a bowl with the chopped spinach. Stir in the cottage cheese, egg, garlic, nutmeg and mint. Season and mix thoroughly.

3 Brush a sheet of filo pastry with a little butter. Fold in half widthways and line the base and sides of the dish. Repeat with 3 more sheets. Keep the unused sheets moist by covering with a damp tea towel.

4 Sprinkle the breadcrumbs over the pastry. Spread the filling into the dish.

Fold over any overlapping pastry. Brush and fold another sheet and place on top. Repeat with 3 more sheets. Tuck the pastry in at the sides. Brush the top with any remaining butter. Score squares or diamonds on top using a sharp knife. Bake for 40 minutes, or until golden. Cut into squares to serve.

NUTRITION PER SERVE
Protein 35 g; Fat 10 g; Carbohydrate 30 g; Dietary Fibre 8 g; Cholesterol 75 mg; 1500 kJ (360 cal)

Squeeze any excess moisture out of the cooled spinach with your hands.

Line the base and sides of the dish with the greased and folded filo.

When you have lined the top with pastry, tuck it in at the sides.

PUMPKIN AND FETA PIE

Preparation time: 30 minutes +
  cooling + 20 minutes refrigeration
Total cooking time: 1 hour 25 minutes
Serves 6

700 g (1 lb 7 oz) butternut pumpkin,
  cubed
4 cloves garlic, unpeeled
5 tablespoons olive oil
2 small red onions, halved and sliced
1 tablespoon balsamic vinegar
1 tablespoon soft brown sugar
100 g (3½ oz) feta, broken into
  small pieces
1 tablespoon chopped fresh rosemary

PASTRY
2 cups (250 g/8 oz) plain flour
125 g (4 oz) butter, chilled and cubed
½ cup (60 g/2 oz) grated Parmesan
3–4 tablespoons iced water

1 Preheat the oven to 200°C (400°F/
Gas 6). Place the pumpkin and garlic
cloves on a baking tray, drizzle with
2 tablespoons oil and bake for
25–30 minutes, or until the pumpkin is
tender. Transfer the pumpkin to a large
bowl and the garlic to a plate. Leave
the pumpkin to cool.
2 Meanwhile, heat 2 tablespoons oil
in a pan, add the onion and cook over
medium heat, stirring occasionally, for
10 minutes. Add the vinegar and sugar
and cook for 15 minutes, or until the
onion is caramelised. Remove from the
heat and add to the pumpkin. Leave to
cool completely.
3 While the vegetables are cooling,
make the pastry. Sift the flour and
1 teaspoon salt into a large bowl and
rub in the butter with your fingertips
until the mixture resembles fine
breadcrumbs. Stir in the Parmesan.
Make a well, add almost all the water
and mix with a flat-bladed knife, using
a cutting action, until the mixture
comes together in beads. Add a little
more water if necessary to bring the
dough together.
4 Gather the dough together and lift
onto a lightly floured work surface.
Press together into a ball and flatten
slightly into a disc. Cover in plastic
wrap and refrigerate for 20 minutes.
5 Add the feta and rosemary to the
pumpkin. Squeeze out the garlic flesh
and mix it through the vegetables.
Season, to taste.
6 Roll out the dough between two
sheets of baking paper to a 35 cm
(14 inch) circle. Remove the top sheet
of paper and place the bottom paper
with the pastry on a tray. Arrange the
pumpkin and feta mixture on top,
leaving a 6 cm (2½ inch) border. Fold
over the edges, pleating as you fold,
and bake for 30 minutes, or until crisp
and golden.

NUTRITION PER SERVE
Protein 14 g; Fat 39 g; Carbohydrate 42 g;
Dietary Fibre 4 g; Cholesterol 73 mg;
2360 kJ (565 cal)

Fold the edges of the pastry over the pumpkin
and feta filling.

CREAMY SNAPPER PIES

Preparation time: 25 minutes
Total cooking time: 1 hour 20 minutes
Makes 6

2 tablespoons olive oil
4 onions, thinly sliced
1¹/₂ cups (375 ml/12 fl oz) fish stock
3¹/₂ cups (875 ml/28 fl oz) cream
1 kg (2 lb) skinless snapper fillets, cut
   into large bite-size pieces
2 sheets puff pastry
1 egg, lightly beaten

1 Preheat the oven to 220°C (425°F/
Gas 7). Heat the oil in a large deep-
sided frying pan, add the onion and
stir over medium heat for 20 minutes,
or until it is golden brown and
slightly caramelised.
2 Add the stock to the pan, bring to
the boil and cook for 10 minutes, or
until the liquid has nearly evaporated.
Stir in the cream, bring to the boil, then
reduce the heat and simmer for
20 minutes, or until the liquid reduces
by half or coats the back of a spoon.
3 Divide half the sauce among
six 1¹/₄ cup (315 ml/10 fl oz) deep
ovenproof dishes. Put some fish in
each dish, then top with the sauce.
4 Cut the pastry sheets into rounds
slightly larger than the tops of the
dishes. Brush the edges of the pastry
with a little of the egg. Press onto the
dishes. Brush lightly with the
remaining beaten egg. Bake for
30 minutes, or until the pastry is crisp,
golden and puffed.

NUTRITION PER PIE
Protein 43 g; Fat 85 g; Carbohydrate 27 g;
Dietary Fibre 1.6 g; Cholesterol 345 mg;
4347 kJ (1033 cal)

Stir the sliced onion with a wooden spoon until
slightly caramelised.

Reduce the heat and simmer until the liquid coats
the back of a spoon.

Put some fish in each dish, dividing the pieces
equally among the six dishes.

Put a round of pastry on top of each dish and
gently press the edges.

73

CHEESE AND ONION PIE

Preparation time: 25 minutes +
    10 minutes cooling
Total cooking time: 45 minutes
Serves 4

2 tablespoons olive oil
2 onions, chopped
1¹/₂ cups (185 g/6 oz) grated Cheddar
1 tablespoon chopped fresh flat-leaf
    parsley
1 teaspoon English mustard
2 teaspoons Worcestershire sauce
2 eggs, beaten
2 sheets puff pastry

1 Preheat the oven to 190°C (375°F/ Gas 5). Heat the oil in a large frying pan over medium heat, add the onion and cook for 5–7 minutes, or until soft and golden. Transfer to a bowl and allow to cool for 10 minutes.
2 Add the cheese, parsley, mustard and Worcestershire sauce to the onion and mix well. Add half the egg to the bowl and season well.
3 Cut each sheet of pastry into a 23 cm (9 inch) circle. Lay one sheet of pastry on a lined baking tray. Spread the filling over the pastry base, piling it higher in the middle and leaving a narrow border. Lightly brush the border with some of the beaten egg

and place the second sheet on top, stretching it slightly to neatly fit the bottom. Press and seal the edges well and brush the top with the remaining beaten egg. Cut two slits in the top for steam to escape.
4 Bake for 10 minutes, then reduce the heat to 180°C (350°F/ Gas 4) and cook for another 20–25 minutes, or until the pastry is crisp and golden.

NUTRITION PER SERVE
Protein 21 g; Fat 47 g; Carbohydrate 34 g;
Dietary Fibre 2 g; Cholesterol 158 mg;
2625 kJ (630 cal)

Mix the cheese, parsley, mustard and Worcestershire sauce through the onion.

Brush the border of the pastry with some of the beaten egg.

Lift the second pastry circle over the cheese and onion filling.

WELSH LAMB PIE

Preparation time: 20 minutes + cooling
Total cooking time: 2 hours 35 minutes
Serves 6

750 g (1½ lb) boned lamb shoulder, cubed
3/4 cup (90 g/3 oz) plain flour, seasoned
2 tablespoons olive oil
200 g (6½ oz) bacon, finely chopped
2 cloves garlic, chopped
4 large leeks, sliced
1 large carrot, chopped
2 large potatoes, diced
1¼ cups (315 ml/10 fl oz) beef stock
1 bay leaf
2 teaspoons chopped fresh parsley
375 g (12 oz) quick flaky pastry
1 egg, lightly beaten, to glaze

1 Toss the meat in the flour. Heat the oil in a large frying pan over medium heat and brown the meat in batches for 4–5 minutes, then remove from the pan. Cook the bacon in the pan for 3 minutes. Add the garlic and leek and cook for 5 minutes, or until soft.
2 Put the meat in a large saucepan, add the leek and bacon, carrot, potato, stock and bay leaf and bring to the boil, then reduce the heat, cover and simmer for 30 minutes. Uncover and simmer for 1 hour, or until the meat is cooked and the liquid has thickened. Season to taste. Remove the bay leaf, stir in the parsley and set aside to cool.
3 Preheat the oven to 200°C (400°F/ Gas 6). Place the filling in an 18 cm (7 inch) pie dish. Roll out the pastry between two sheets of baking paper until large enough to cover the pie. Trim the edges and pinch to seal.
4 Decorate the pie with pastry trimmings. Cut two slits in the top for steam to escape. Brush with egg and bake for 45 minutes, or until the pastry is crisp and golden.

NUTRITION PER SERVE
Protein 42 g; Fat 28 g; Carbohydrate 43 g; Dietary Fibre 5 g; Cholesterol 147 mg; 2465 kJ (590 cal)

Cook the filling until the liquid has thickened and then remove the bay leaf.

Cut out shapes from the pastry trimmings to decorate the pie.

INDIAN-STYLE SPICY LAMB AND APRICOT PIE

Preparation time: 40 minutes +
    20 minutes refrigeration + cooling
Total cooking time: 2 hours 45 minutes
Serves 8–10

2¹/₂ cups (310 g/10 oz) plain flour
160 g (5¹/₂ oz) ghee, chilled and cut
    into small pieces
1 teaspoon cumin seeds
1 teaspoon sugar
3–6 tablespoons iced water

FILLING
1.4 kg (2 lb 13 oz) boned lamb
    shoulder, cubed (see NOTES)
1 cup (250 g/8 oz) natural yoghurt
2 teaspoons garam masala
1¹/₂ tablespoons grated fresh ginger
1 teaspoon chilli powder
2 teaspoons ghee
2 onions, sliced
3 cloves garlic, crushed
1 long fresh green chilli, finely
    chopped
6 cardamom pods, crushed
1 teaspoon ground coriander
2 teaspoons ground cumin
2 x 425 g (14 oz) cans crushed
    tomatoes
100 g (3¹/₂ oz) dried apricots, halved,
    soaked in 1 cup (250 ml/8 fl oz)
    warm water
¹/₂ cup (125 g/4 oz) thick natural
    yoghurt, to serve

1 To make the pastry, sift the flour
into a food processor and add the
ghee, cumin seeds, sugar and
1 teaspoon salt. Process until the
mixture resembles fine breadcrumbs,
then gradually add the water until the
pastry comes together in beads. Do
not over-process. Gently gather the
dough together into a ball, place on a
lightly floured surface and press into a
disc. Refrigerate for 20 minutes.
2 Combine the lamb, yoghurt, garam
masala, ginger, chilli powder and
¹/₂ teaspoon salt in a large bowl.
3 Heat the ghee in a large saucepan,
add the onion and cook over medium
heat for 10 minutes, or until soft and
golden. Add the garlic and fresh chilli
and cook for 1 minute, then add the

remaining spices and cook for
another minute.
4 Add the lamb and yoghurt mixture
to the pan and cook, stirring often,
until combined. Add the tomato, bring
to the boil, reduce the heat and
simmer for 1¹/₄ hours, then add the
apricots and simmer for another
15 minutes, or until the lamb is tender.
Set aside to cool.
5 Preheat the oven to 220°C (425°F/
Gas 7). Preheat a baking tray. Grease a
deep 23 cm (9 inch) fluted tart tin or
pie dish. Roll out two-thirds of the
pastry between two sheets of baking
paper until large enough to fit the tin.
Remove the top sheet of paper and
invert the pastry into the tin. Fill the
pastry shell with the lamb curry. Brush
the edges with a little water. Roll out
the remaining pastry between the
sheets of baking paper until large
enough to cover the top of the pie
dish. Position the lid on top of the
filling. Make two or three slits for the
steam to escape, then trim the pastry
edges with a sharp knife.
6 Place the pie on the heated baking
tray and bake on the lowest shelf for
30 minutes. Move to the centre shelf
and bake for another 30 minutes, or
until brown. Leave for 10 minutes
before slicing. Serve with a dollop of
thick yoghurt.

NUTRITION PER SERVE (10)
Protein 19 g; Fat 21 g; Carbohydrate 34 g;
Dietary Fibre 4 g; Cholesterol 94 mg;
1660 kJ (395 cal)

NOTES: Ask your butcher to bone the
lamb shoulder for you.
Because of the ghee content in the
pastry for this pie, it is very difficult to
make successfully by hand. It is better
to use a food processor as described in
the recipe. The filling mixture may
seem a little runny when ready to go
in the pie, but once it is cooked the
sauce thickens.

Gently gather the dough together into a ball and
place on a lightly floured surface.

Add the spices to the onion mixture and cook for another minute.

Spoon the lamb curry mixture into the pastry shell. The filling will thicken when baked.

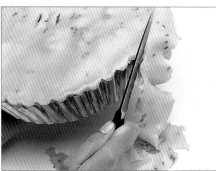

Make steam holes on top of the pie and trim the pastry edges with a sharp knife.

LOW-FAT CHICKEN PIES

Preparation time: 50 minutes
+ 30 minutes refrigeration
Total cooking time: 1 hour
Makes 4

300 g (10 oz) chicken breast fillet
1 bay leaf
2 cups (500 ml/16 oz) chicken stock
2 large potatoes, chopped
250 g (8 oz) orange sweet potato,
    chopped
2 celery sticks, chopped
2 carrots, chopped
1 onion, chopped
1 parsnip, chopped
1 clove garlic, crushed
1 tablespoon cornflour
1 cup (250 ml/8 fl oz) skim milk
1 cup (150 g/5 oz) frozen peas,
    thawed
1 tablespoon chopped chives
1 tablespoon chopped fresh parsley
1 1/2 cups (185 g/6 oz) self-raising flour
20 g (3/4 oz) butter
1/3 cup (80 ml/2 3/4 fl oz) milk
1 egg, lightly beaten
1/2 teaspoon sesame seeds

1 Put the chicken, bay leaf and stock in a large, deep frying pan and simmer over low heat for 10 minutes, until the chicken is cooked through. Lift out the chicken and cut into small pieces. Add the chopped potato, sweet potato, celery and carrot to the pan and simmer, covered, for 10 minutes, until just tender. Remove the vegetables from the pan with a slotted spoon.
2 Add the onion, parsnip and garlic to the pan and simmer, uncovered, for 10 minutes, or until very soft. Discard the bay leaf. Purée in a food processor until smooth.

3 Stir the cornflour into 2 tablespoons of the skim milk to make a smooth paste. Stir into the puréed mixture with the remaining milk and then return to the pan. Stir over low heat until the mixture boils and thickens. Preheat the oven to 200°C (400°F/Gas 6).
4 Combine the puréed mixture with the vegetables, chicken and herbs. Season and spoon into four 1 3/4 cup (440 ml/14 fl oz) ovenproof dishes.
5 To make the pastry, sift the flour into a large bowl, rub in the butter with your fingertips, then make a well in the centre. Combine the milk with 1/3 cup (80 ml/2 3/4 fl oz) water and add enough to the dry ingredients to make a soft dough. Turn out onto a

lightly floured surface and knead until just smooth. Cut the dough into four portions and roll out to 1 cm (1/2 inch) larger than the tops of the dishes. Brush the edge of the dough with egg and fit over the top of each dish, pressing the edge firmly to seal.
6 Brush the pastry tops lightly with beaten egg and sprinkle with the sesame seeds. Bake for 30 minutes, until the pastry tops are golden.

NUTRITION PER PIE
Protein 30 g; Fat 10 g; Carbohydrate 65 g;
Dietary Fibre 9.5 g; Cholesterol 100 mg;
2045 kJ (490 cal)

Purée the cooked onion, parsnip and garlic together until smooth.

Add enough liquid to the dry ingredients to make a soft dough.

Brush the edge of the pastry top with egg and then press over the pie dish.

BEEF AND RED WINE PIES

Preparation time: 50 minutes
Total cooking time: 2 hours 40 minutes
Makes 6

1/4 cup (60 ml/2 fl oz) oil
1.5 kg (3 lb) chuck steak, cubed
2 onions, chopped
1 clove garlic, crushed
1/4 cup (30 g/1 oz) plain flour
1 1/4 cups (315 ml/10 fl oz) dry red
   wine
2 cups (500 ml/16 fl oz) beef stock
2 bay leaves
2 sprigs fresh thyme
2 carrots, chopped
4 sheets ready-rolled shortcrust pastry
1 egg, lightly beaten
4 sheets ready-rolled puff pastry

1 Heat 2 tablespoons of the oil in a large pan, add the meat and fry in batches until browned all over. Remove all the meat from the pan. Heat the remaining oil in the same pan, add the onion and garlic and cook, stirring, until golden brown. Add the flour and stir over medium heat for 2 minutes, or until well browned.
2 Remove from the heat and gradually stir in the combined wine and stock. Return to the heat and stir until the mixture boils and thickens. Return the meat to the pan with the bay leaves and thyme, and simmer for 1 hour. Add the carrot and simmer for 45 minutes, or until the meat and carrot are tender and the sauce has thickened. Season to taste, and remove the bay leaves and thyme sprigs. Cool.
3 Preheat the oven to 200°C (400°F/ Gas 6). Lightly grease six 9 cm (3 1/2 inch) metal pie tins. Cut the shortcrust pastry sheets in half

diagonally. Line the base and side of each pie tin with the pastry and trim the edges. Line each pie with baking paper and fill with baking beads. Place on a baking tray and bake for 8 minutes. Remove the paper and beads and bake for a further 8 minutes, or until the pastry is lightly browned. Cool.
4 Spoon the filling into the pastry cases and brush the edge with some of the beaten egg. Cut the puff pastry

sheets in half diagonally and cover the tops of the pies. Trim the excess, pressing the edges with a fork to seal. Cut a slit in the top of each pie. Brush the tops with the remaining egg, and bake for 20–25 minutes, or until the pastry is golden brown.

NUTRITION PER PIE
Protein 60 g; Fat 47 g; Carbohydrate 51 g;
Dietary Fibre 3 g; Cholesterol 200 mg;
3648 kJ (873 cal)

Fry the steak in batches in a large pan until browned all over.

Line the base and side of each pie tin with the shortcrust pastry.

Cover the filling with puff pastry and trim off the excess with a sharp knife.

SPINACH AND FETA TRIANGLES

Preparation time: 30 minutes
Total cooking time: 40 minutes
Makes 8

1 kg (2 lb) English spinach (see
    VARIATION)
1/4 cup (60 ml/2 fl oz) olive oil
1 onion, chopped
10 spring onions, sliced
1/3 cup (20 g/3/4 oz) chopped fresh
    parsley
1 tablespoon chopped fresh dill
large pinch of ground nutmeg
1/3 cup (35 g/1 1/3 oz) grated
    Parmesan
150 g (5 oz) crumbled feta
90 g (3 oz) ricotta
4 eggs, lightly beaten
40 g (1 1/4 oz) butter, melted
1 tablespoon olive oil, extra
12 sheets filo pastry

1 Trim any coarse stems from the spinach. Wash the leaves thoroughly, roughly chop and place in a large pan with just a little water clinging to the leaves. Cover and cook gently over low heat for 5 minutes, or until the leaves have wilted. Drain well and allow to cool slightly before squeezing tightly to remove the excess water.
2 Heat the oil in a frying pan. Add the onion and cook over low heat for 10 minutes, or until soft and golden. Add the spring onion and cook for a further 3 minutes. Remove from the heat. Stir in the drained spinach, parsley, dill, nutmeg, Parmesan, feta, ricotta and egg. Season well.
3 Preheat the oven to 180°C (350°F/ Gas 4). Grease two baking trays. Combine the melted butter with the

extra oil. Work with three sheets of pastry at a time, keeping the rest covered with a damp tea towel. Brush each sheet with butter mixture and lay them on top of each other. Cut in half lengthways.
4 Place 4 tablespoons of the filling on an angle at the end of each strip. Fold the pastry over to enclose the filling and form a triangle. Continue folding over until you reach the end of the pastry. Put on the baking trays and brush with the remaining butter mixture. Bake for 20–25 minutes, or until the pastry is golden brown.

NUTRITION PER TRIANGLE
Protein 15 g; Fat 25 g; Carbohydrate 10 g;
Dietary Fibre 4.5 g; Cholesterol 125 mg;
1325 kJ (315 cal)

VARIATION: If you are unable to buy English spinach, silverbeet can be used instead. Use the same quantity and trim the coarse white stems from the leaves.
NOTE: Feta is a traditional Greek-style salty cheese. Any leftover should be stored immersed in lightly salted water and kept refrigerated. Rinse and pat dry before using.

Brush each sheet of filo pastry with the mixture of melted butter and oil.

Fold the pastry over the spinach filling to enclose it and form a triangle.

Continue folding the triangle over until you reach the end of the pastry sheet.

CORNISH PASTIES

Preparation time: 1 hour + chilling
Total cooking time: 45 minutes
Makes 6

2¹/₂ cups (310 g/10 oz) plain flour
125 g (4 oz) butter, chilled and cubed
4–5 tablespoons iced water
160 g (5¹/₂ oz) round steak, diced
1 small potato, finely chopped
1 small onion, finely chopped
1 small carrot, finely chopped
1–2 teaspoons Worcestershire sauce
2 tablespoons beef stock
1 egg, lightly beaten

1 Grease a baking tray. Mix the flour, butter and a pinch of salt in a food processor for 15 seconds, or until crumbly. Add the water and process in short bursts until it comes together. Turn out onto a floured surface and form into a ball. Wrap in plastic and chill for 30 minutes. Preheat the oven to 210°C (415°F/Gas 6–7).
2 Mix together the steak, potato, onion, carrot, Worcestershire sauce and stock. Season well.
3 Divide the dough into six portions and roll out to 3 mm (¹/₈ inch) thick. Cut into six 16 cm (6¹/₂ inch) rounds. Divide the filling evenly and put in the centre of each pastry circle.
4 Brush the pastry edges with egg and fold over. Pinch to form a frill and place on the tray. Brush with egg and bake for 15 minutes. Lower the heat to 180°C (350°F/Gas 4) and bake for 25–30 minutes, or until golden.

NUTRITION PER PASTY
Protein 15 g; Fat 20 g; Carbohydrate 40 g;
Dietary Fibre 3 g; Cholesterol 100 mg;
1665 kJ (395 cal)

Process the flour, butter and salt until the mixture resembles fine breadcrumbs.

Mix together the steak, potato, onion, carrot, Worcestershire sauce and stock.

Fold the pastry over the filling to form a semi-circle and pinch to close.

PORK AND VEAL PIE

Preparation time: 40 minutes +
 30 minutes refrigeration
Total cooking time: 1 hour 40 minutes
Serves 8

2 sheets shortcrust pastry
2 tablespoons oil
1 onion, finely chopped
1 clove garlic, crushed
1 kg (2 lb) lean pork and veal mince
2 tablespoons chopped fresh parsley
2 tablespoons chopped fresh thyme
2 eggs
4 cups (320 g/11 oz) fresh white
 breadcrumbs
4 gherkins, roughly chopped
125 g (4 oz) ham steak, diced
1 sheet puff pastry

1 Grease a shallow 22.5 cm (9 inch) flan tin. Cut one sheet of pastry in half and join to the other pastry sheet, pressing the join together. Line the base and side of the tin and trim the edge. Refrigerate for 30 minutes. Preheat the oven to 200°C (400°F/ Gas 6).
2 Put the flan tin on a baking tray. Cover the base of the pastry with baking paper and baking beads or rice. Bake blind for 10 minutes, then remove the paper and beads and bake for a further 10–15 minutes, or until lightly browned. Allow to cool.
3 Heat the oil in a frying pan and fry the onion and garlic over medium heat for 5 minutes, or until soft. Remove from the heat. Combine the mince, herbs, 1/4 cup (60 ml/2 fl oz) water, 1 egg and the breadcrumbs in a food processor until fine but not smooth. Place in a bowl and add the onion mixture, gherkins and ham. Season

well. Mix well and fry a small amount of mixture to taste for seasoning.
4 Press the mixture firmly into the cold pastry base, forming a dome shape. Lightly beat the remaining egg and brush the edges of the pastry. Place the puff pastry over the mince to make a lid, and press the edges firmly to seal. Trim any excess pastry.
5 Brush the pastry all over with the rest of the egg and make two small slashes in the top of the pie. Using the

back of a knife, score the top of the pie with a lattice pattern.
6 Bake for 20 minutes, then reduce the oven to 180°C (350°F/Gas 4) and bake for 50 minutes, or until the pastry is golden brown. Serve cold with pickles.

NUTRITION PER SERVE
Protein 40 g; Fat 25 g; Carbohydrate 55 g; Dietary Fibre 3.5 g; Cholesterol 170 mg; 2625 kJ (625 cal)

Cut one piece of shortcrust pastry in half and join to the other sheet of pastry.

Press the meat filling into the pastry base, forming a dome shape.

Cover with the puff pastry and press the edges of the two pastries firmly together.

PUMPKIN AND PESTO CHICKEN FILO PIES

Preparation time: 30 minutes
Total cooking time: 50 minutes
Makes 4

4 chicken breast fillets
1 tablespoon oil
250 g (8 oz) pumpkin
1 bunch English spinach
12 sheets filo pastry
100 g ($3^1/2$ oz) butter, melted
$1/4$ cup (25 g/$3/4$ oz) dry breadcrumbs
100 g ($3^1/2$ oz) ricotta
$1/3$ cup (90 g/3 oz) pesto (see NOTE)
1 tablespoon pine nuts, chopped

1 Preheat the oven to 200°C (400°F/ Gas 6). Season the chicken. Heat half the oil in a frying pan and brown the chicken on both sides, then remove from the pan.
2 Cut the peeled pumpkin into 5 mm ($1/4$ inch) slices. Heat the remaining oil in the same pan and lightly brown the pumpkin on both sides. Allow to cool.
3 Put the spinach leaves in a pan of boiling water and stir until just wilted. Drain well and pat dry with paper towels. Layer 3 sheets of filo pastry, brushing each with some of the melted butter, sprinkling between the layers with breadcrumbs.
4 Wrap each chicken breast in a quarter of the spinach and place on one short side of the filo, leaving a gap of about 2 cm ($3/4$ inch). Top the chicken with a quarter of the pumpkin slices, then spread a quarter of the ricotta down the centre of the pumpkin. Top with a tablespoon of the pesto.
5 Fold the sides of the pastry over the filling, then roll the parcel up until

it sits on the unsecured end. Repeat with the remaining ingredients. Place the parcels on a lightly greased baking tray, brush with any remaining butter and sprinkle with the pine nuts. Bake for 15 minutes, cover loosely with foil and bake for a further 20 minutes, or until the pastry is golden brown.

NUTRITION PER PIE
Protein 35 g; Fat 40 g; Carbohydrate 30 g; Dietary Fibre 2.5 g; Cholesterol 132 mg; 2635 kJ (630 cal)

NOTE: Bottled pesto will not do justice to this recipe—either make your own or use fresh pesto from a deli.

Remove the spinach from the boiling water and drain well.

Top the chicken with a quarter of the lightly browned pumpkin slices.

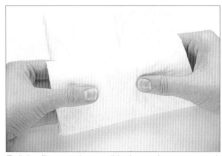

Roll the filo parcel up until it sits on the unsecured end of the pastry.

PICNIC PORK PIES

Preparation time: 20 minutes
Total cooking time: 1 hour 15 minutes
Makes 6

400 g (13 oz) pork mince
$^1/_4$ cup (35 g/1$^1/_4$ oz) shelled
    pistachios, chopped
$^1/_2$ apple, finely chopped
1 teaspoon finely chopped fresh sage
    leaves
2$^1/_4$ cups (280 g/9 oz) plain flour
80 g (2$^3/_4$ oz) butter
1 egg, lightly beaten
1 egg yolk
$^1/_2$ cup (125 ml/4 fl oz) vegetable
    stock
$^1/_2$ cup (125 ml/4 fl oz) unsweetened
    apple juice
1$^1/_2$ teaspoons gelatine

1 Preheat the oven to 200°C (400°F/ Gas 6). Combine the mince, pistachios, apple and sage in a large bowl and season very well. Fry a teaspoon of the filling and adjust the seasoning if necessary. Cover and refrigerate until needed.

2 Put the flour and $^1/_2$ teaspoon of salt in a large bowl and make a well in the centre. Put the butter in a small pan with $^1/_3$ cup (80 ml/2$^3/_4$ fl oz) of water and bring to the boil. Pour into the centre of the well, add the beaten egg and mix to form a smooth dough.

3 Grease six $^1/_3$ cup (80 ml/2$^3/_4$ fl oz) muffin holes. Set aside one third of the dough and divide the rest into six portions. Roll each portion into a small circle and line the muffin cups with the dough, leaving a little dough hanging over the side of each cup. Divide the filling among the pastry-filled cups, packing the filling down and making a small dome shape in the centre—the filling will shrink as it cooks. Divide the remaining dough into six portions and roll each into a small circle to make the lids. Brush the edges with water and lay one on top of each pie. Fold up the pastry hanging over the edge and roll or crimp it. Cut a small hole in the top of each pie. Brush with the egg yolk mixed with a tablespoon of water.

4 Put the muffin tin on a baking tray and bake for 30 minutes; then check the pastry top. If they are still pale, bake for another 5–10 minutes. Leave to rest for 5 minutes, then lift the pies out of the muffin tray, put them on the baking tray and bake for 15 minutes, or until the sides of the pies are golden brown (be careful not to break the pies when you move them).

5 Bring the stock and half the apple juice to the boil in a small pan. Sprinkle the gelatine over the surface of the remaining apple juice and leave to go spongy, then pour on the boiling stock and mix until the gelatine dissolves. Place a small funnel (a piping nozzle works well) in the hole of each pie and pour in a little of the gelatine mixture. Leave to settle, then pour in a little more until the pies are full. It is important to fill the pies completely to make sure there are no gaps when the gelatine mixture sets. You may need more or less liquid, depending on how much the meat shrinks. Allow to cool completely before serving.

NUTRITION PER PIE
Protein 25 g; Fat 17 g; Carbohydrate 32 g; Dietary Fibre 3 g; Cholesterol 25 mg; 1565 kJ (375 cal)

Mix together the mince, pistachios, apple and sage and season with salt and pepper.

Bring the melted butter and water to the boil and pour into the centre of the well.

Line the muffin holes, leaving a little pastry hanging over the sides.

Spoon the filling into the pastry shells and pack firmly into a dome shape.

Put the pastry lids on top, then fold up the pastry hanging over the side and roll it.

Put a funnel in the hole of the pie and pour in some of the gelatine mixture.

TUNA PANCAKE PIES

Preparation time: 15 minutes +
  20 minutes standing
Total cooking time: 50 minutes
Serves 6

PANCAKES
1¹/₄ cups (150 g/5 oz) plain flour
¹/₄ cup (45 g/1¹/₂ oz) rice flour
2 eggs, lightly beaten
melted butter or oil, for greasing

FILLING
1 tablespoon oil
1 onion, finely chopped
2 cloves garlic, crushed
¹/₂ cup (80 g/2³/₄ oz) capers
¹/₂ cup (80 g (2³/₄ oz) black olives,
  pitted, chopped
1 tomato, diced
250 g (8 oz) English spinach, roughly
  chopped
3 tablespoons chopped fresh
  flat-leaf parsley
1 tablespoon lemon juice
185 g (6 oz) can tuna in springwater,
  drained and flaked

2 eggs, lightly beaten
2 teaspoons cornflour
¹/₃ cup (80 ml/2³/₄ fl oz) olive oil,
  for shallow-frying

1 Sift the flours into a bowl, make a well and gradually whisk in the eggs and 2¹/₂ cups (625 ml/21 fl oz) water. Mix to a smooth lump-free batter. Cover and set aside for 20 minutes.
2 Heat a large frying pan and brush lightly with melted butter or oil. Pour ¹/₄ cup (60 ml/2 fl oz) batter into the pan and swirl into a 20 cm (8 inch) pancake. Cook over low heat for 1 minute, or until bubbles appear on the surface and the underside is golden. Turn over and cook for 20 seconds. Transfer to a plate and repeat to make 12 pancakes.
3 For the filling, heat the oil in a frying pan, add the onion and garlic and cook over medium heat for 2–3 minutes, or until the onion is soft. Add the capers, olives and tomato and cook, stirring occasionally, for 5–8 minutes, or until the liquid has evaporated. Reduce the heat to low,

add the spinach, cover and steam for 2 minutes, or until the leaves wilt. Remove from the heat and stir in the parsley, lemon juice and tuna. Cool and drain any excess liquid. Season.
4 For the coating, lightly stir the eggs, cornflour and ¹/₄ cup (60 ml/2 fl oz) water together in a shallow dish.
5 Lay the pancakes on a work surface. Place 1 tablespoon of filling in the centre of each. Fold into a parcel and secure with a toothpick.

6 Heat the oil in a frying pan over medium heat. Dip the filled pancakes into the egg coating, letting the excess drain off. Fry the pancakes in batches for 3 minutes each side, or until golden and heated through. Serve hot.

NUTRITION PER SERVE
Protein 18 g; Fat 23 g; Carbohydrate 29 g;
Dietary Fibre 4 g; Cholesterol 141 mg;
1610 kJ (385 cal)

Place a tablespoon of filling in the centre of each pancake, fold over and secure.

Turn the pancakes over and cook until golden and heated through.

MOROCCAN BEEF PIES

Preparation time: 45 minutes +
 30 minutes refrigeration
Total cooking time: 1 hour 20 minutes
Makes 4

1 tablespoon oil
2 cloves garlic, crushed
1 onion, cut into thin wedges
2 teaspoons ground cumin
2 teaspoons ground ginger
2 teaspoons paprika
pinch saffron threads
500 g (1 lb) round steak, cubed
1½ cups (375 ml/12 fl oz) beef stock
1 small cinnamon stick
100 g (3½ oz) pitted prunes, halved
2 carrots, sliced
1 teaspoon grated orange rind
2 cups (250 g/8 oz) plain flour
125 g (4 oz) butter, chilled and cubed
1 egg, lightly beaten
1–2 tablespoons iced water
¼ preserved lemon, rinsed, pith and
 flesh removed, finely chopped
200 g (6½ oz) thick natural yoghurt

1 Heat the oil in a large saucepan, add the garlic and onion and cook for 3 minutes, or until softened. Add the cumin, ginger, paprika and saffron and stir for 1 minute, or until fragrant. Add the meat and toss until coated. Add the stock, cinnamon stick, prunes and carrot. Bring to the boil, reduce the heat and simmer, covered, for 30 minutes. Increase the heat to medium, add the orange rind and cook, uncovered, for 20 minutes, or until the liquid has reduced and thickened slightly. Remove the cinnamon stick and cool completely.
2 To make the pastry, sift the flour into a large bowl. Rub the butter into the flour with your fingertips until it resembles fine breadcrumbs. Make a well in the centre and add the egg and water and mix with a flat-bladed knife, using a cutting action, until the mixture comes together in beads.
3 Gently gather the dough together and lift out onto a lightly floured work surface. Press into a ball, wrap in plastic and refrigerate for 30 minutes.
4 Preheat the oven to 200°C (400°F/ Gas 6). Grease four 9 cm (3½ inch) pie tins. Divide the dough into four pieces and roll out between two sheets of baking paper to make 20 cm (8 inch) circles. Press into the tins, leaving the excess overhanging.
5 Divide the filling among the tins. Fold over the excess pastry, pleating as you go. Place on a baking tray and bake for 20–25 minutes, or until golden. Combine the preserved lemon and yoghurt and serve with the pies.

NUTRITION PER PIE
Protein 40 g; Fat 40 g; Carbohydrate 64 g;
Dietary Fibre 6.5 g; Cholesterol 205 mg;
3183 kJ (760 cal)

Cook the beef mixture until the liquid has reduced and thickened slightly.

Gently gather the dough together and press into a ball before chilling.

Fold the overhanging pastry over the filling, pleating as you go.

VEGETABLE PIE WITH CHEESE TOPPING

Preparation time: 25 minutes +
  20 minutes refrigeration
Total cooking time: 1 hour 30 minutes
Serves 6

1 cup (125 g/4 oz) plain flour
60 g (2 oz) butter, chilled and cubed
1 egg yolk
2 teaspoons poppy seeds
1–2 tablespoons iced water

FILLING
30 g (1 oz) butter
2 tablespoons oil
1 onion, cut into thin wedges
1 leek, sliced
3 potatoes, cut into large chunks
300 g (10 oz) orange sweet potato,
  cut into large chunks
300 g (10 oz) pumpkin, cubed
200 g (6½ oz) swede, peeled and
  cubed
1 cup (250 ml/8 fl oz) vegetable stock
1 red capsicum, cubed
200 g (6½ oz) broccoli, cut into large
  florets
2 zucchini, cut into large pieces
1 cup (125 g/4 oz) grated Cheddar

1 Preheat the oven to 200°C (400°F/ Gas 6). To make the pastry, sift the flour into a large bowl and add the butter. Rub in the butter with your fingertips until it resembles fine breadcrumbs. Make a well in the centre and add the egg yolk, poppy seeds and water and mix with a flat-bladed knife, using a cutting action, until the mixture comes together in beads. Gently gather together and lift out onto a lightly floured work surface. Press into a disc, wrap in plastic and refrigerate for 20 minutes.
2 Roll out the dough between two sheets of baking paper, then fit into a 23 cm (9 inch) pie plate. Trim away any excess pastry. Prick the base with a fork and bake for 15–20 minutes, or until dry and golden.
3 Heat the butter and oil in a large saucepan and cook the onion and leek over medium heat for 5 minutes, or until soft and golden. Add the potato, sweet potato, pumpkin and swede and cook, stirring occasionally, until the vegetables start to soften. Add the stock and simmer for 30 minutes.
4 Add the remaining vegetables, reduce the heat and simmer for 20 minutes, or until the vegetables are soft—some may break up slightly. The mixture should be just mushy. Season and leave to cool a little.
5 Spoon the filling into the shell, sprinkle with cheese and cook under a medium grill for 5–10 minutes, or until the cheese is golden brown.

NUTRITION PER SERVE
Protein 14 g; Fat 27 g; Carbohydrate 32 g; Dietary Fibre 6.5 g; Cholesterol 90 mg; 1790 kJ (428 cal)

Prick the base of the pastry all over with a fork and bake until dry and golden.

Cook the vegetables until they are very soft when tested with a knife.

VEGETABLE AND POLENTA PIE

Preparation time: 20 minutes +
  15 minutes standing + refrigeration
Total cooking time: 50 minutes
Serves 6

2 eggplants, thickly sliced
1¹/₃ cups (350 ml/11 fl oz) vegetable
  stock
1 cup (150 g/5 oz) fine polenta
¹/₂ cup (50 g/1¹/₂ oz) finely grated
  Parmesan
1 tablespoon olive oil
1 large onion, chopped
2 cloves garlic, crushed
1 large red capsicum, diced
2 zucchini, thickly sliced
150 g (5 oz) button mushrooms, cut
  into quarters
400 g (13 oz) can chopped tomatoes
3 teaspoons balsamic vinegar
olive oil, for brushing

1 Spread the eggplant in a colander and sprinkle generously with salt. Leave for 15 minutes, then rinse, pat dry and cut into cubes.
2 Line a 22 cm (9 inch) round cake tin with foil. Pour the stock and 1¹/₃ cups (350 ml/11 fl oz) water into a saucepan and bring to the boil. Add the polenta in a thin stream and stir over low heat for 5 minutes, or until the liquid is absorbed and the mixture is thick and comes away from the side of the pan.
3 Remove from the heat and stir in the cheese until it melts all through the polenta. Spread into the tin, smoothing the surface as much as possible. Refrigerate until set.
4 Preheat the oven to 200°C (400°F/ Gas 6). Heat the oil in a large

saucepan and add the onion. Cook over medium heat, stirring occasionally, for 3 minutes, or until soft. Add the garlic and cook for a further 1 minute. Add the eggplant, capsicum, zucchini, mushrooms and tomato. Bring to the boil, then reduce the heat and simmer, covered, for 20 minutes, or until the vegetables are tender. Stir occasionally. Stir in the vinegar and season.
5 Transfer the vegetable mixture to a 22 cm (9 inch) pie dish, piling it up

slightly in the centre.
6 Turn out the polenta, peel off the foil and cut into 12 wedges. Arrange smooth-side-down in a single layer, over the vegetables—don't worry about any gaps. Brush lightly with a little olive oil and bake for 20 minutes, or until lightly brown and crisp.

NUTRITION PER SERVE
Protein 8 g; Fat 8.5 g; Carbohydrate 23 g;
Dietary Fibre 4.5 g; Cholesterol 8 mg;
855 kJ (205 cal)

Cook the polenta, stirring, until all the liquid is absorbed and it is very thick.

Reduce the heat and simmer until the vegetables are tender.

Arrange the polenta wedges, smooth-side-down, over the vegetable mixture.

POTATO AND GOATS CHEESE PIES

Preparation time: 25 minutes
Total cooking time: 1 hour
Makes 4

4 potatoes, peeled
4 slices prosciutto
150 g (5 oz) goats cheese
1 cup (250 g/8 oz) sour cream
2 eggs, lightly beaten
1/2 cup (125 ml/4 fl oz) cream

1 Brush four 1 cup (250 ml/8 fl oz) ramekins with melted butter. Preheat the oven to 180°C (350°F/Gas 4).
2 For each pie, thinly slice a potato and pat dry with paper towels. Line the base of a ramekin with half a slice of prosciutto. Layer half the potato slices neatly into the dishes. Put the other half slice of prosciutto on top and crumble a quarter of the goats cheese over it. Cover with the remaining potato slices and press down firmly. The potato should fill the dish to the top.

3 Mix together the sour cream, eggs and cream and season well. Pour into the ramekins, allowing it to seep through the layers. Place on a baking tray and bake for 50–60 minutes, or until the potato is soft when tested with a skewer. Leave for 5 minutes, then run a knife around the edge and turn out onto serving plates.

NUTRITION PER PIE
Protein 25 g; Fat 55 g; Carbohydrate 20 g;
Dietary Fibre 2 g; Cholesterol 255 mg;
2645 kJ (630 cal)

Cut the goats cheese into four slices, using a sharp knife.

Build up layers of potato, prosciutto and goats cheese in the ramekin.

Mix together the sour cream, eggs and cream and pour over the pies.

TOFU TRIANGLES

Preparation time: 30 minutes +
    4 hours refrigeration
Total cooking time: 20 minutes
Serves 4

150 g (5 oz) firm tofu
2 spring onions, chopped
3 teaspoons chopped fresh coriander
    leaves
1/2 teaspoon grated orange rind
2 teaspoons soy sauce
1 tablespoon sweet chilli sauce
2 teaspoons grated fresh ginger
1 teaspoon cornflour
1/2 cup (125 ml/4 fl oz) seasoned rice
    vinegar
1/4 cup (60 g/2 oz) sugar
1 small Lebanese cucumber, finely
    diced
1 small red chilli, thinly sliced
1 spring onion, extra, thinly sliced on
    the diagonal
2 sheets puff pastry
1 egg, lightly beaten

1 Drain the tofu, then pat dry and cut
into small cubes.
2 Put the spring onion, coriander,
rind, soy and chilli sauces, ginger,
cornflour and tofu in a bowl and
gently mix. Cover, then refrigerate for
3–4 hours.
3 To make a dipping sauce, put the
vinegar and sugar in a small saucepan
and stir over low heat until the sugar
dissolves. Remove from the heat and
add the cucumber, chilli and extra
spring onion. Cool completely.
4 Preheat the oven to 220°C (425°F/
Gas 7). Cut each pastry sheet into four
squares. Drain the filling and divide
into eight. Place one portion in the
centre of each square and brush the
edges with egg. Fold into a triangle
and seal the edges with a fork.
5 Put the triangles on two lined
baking trays, brush with egg and
bake for 15 minutes. Serve with the
dippping sauce.

NUTRITION PER SERVE
Protein 9 g; Fat 24 g; Carbohydrate 48 g;
Dietary Fibre 2 g; Cholesterol 66 mg;
1946 kJ (464 cal)

Gently mix the tofu and other ingredients together
in a bowl.

Remove the saucepan from the heat and add the
spring onion, cucumber and chilli.

Fold the pastry to enclose the filling, then seal the
edges with a fork.

POTATO AND SALMON PARCELS

Preparation time: 30 minutes
Total cooking time: 40 minutes
Makes 12

750 g (1¹/₂ lb) floury potatoes, peeled
40 g (1¹/₄ oz) butter
¹/₄ cup (60 ml/2 fl oz) cream
1 cup (125 g/4 oz) grated Cheddar
210 g (7 oz) can red salmon, skin and
    bones removed, flaked
1 tablespoon chopped fresh dill
4 spring onions, finely chopped
3 sheets puff pastry
1 egg, lightly beaten, to glaze

1 Cut the potatoes into small pieces and cook in a pan of boiling water until tender. Mash with the butter and the cream until there are no lumps. Lightly grease two oven trays.
2 Add the cheese, salmon, dill and spring onion to the potato and mix well. Preheat the oven to 200°C (400°F/Gas 6). Cut each pastry sheet into four squares. Divide the mixture among the squares (approximately ¹/₄ cup in each). Lightly brush the edges with beaten egg. Bring all four corners to the centre to form a point and press together to make a parcel.
3 Put the parcels on the greased trays and glaze with egg. Bake for 15–20 minutes, or until the pastry is golden brown.

NUTRITION PER PARCEL
Protein 30 g; Fat 55 g; Carbohydrate 70 g;
Dietary Fibre 5 g; Cholesterol 180 mg;
3700 kJ (885 cal)

NOTE: Before removing the pastries from the oven, lift them gently off the tray and check that the bottom of the parcels are cooked through. Take care not to overcook the parcels or they may burst open.
HINT: If you like your puff pastry to taste extra buttery, brush it with melted butter before baking.

Cook and drain the potato, then mash well with the butter and cream.

Mix the cheese, salmon, dill and spring onion into the mashed potato.

Cut each pastry sheet into four squares and then divide the filling among them.

Bring up the corners to the centre and press together to make a parcel.

POTATO FILO PIES

Preparation time: 1 hour
Total cooking time: 1 hour 20 minutes
Makes 6

6 Roma tomatoes, halved
    lengthways
3 tablespoons olive oil
50 g (1¾ oz) butter
3 cloves garlic, crushed
800 g (1 lb 10 oz) potatoes, unpeeled
    and sliced
500 g (1 lb) English spinach, trimmed
12 sheets filo pastry
100 g (3½ oz) butter, melted
2 tablespoons sesame seeds

1 Preheat the oven to 200°C (400°F/
Gas 6). Place the tomato halves, cut-
side-up, on a baking tray, drizzle with
1 tablespoon of the oil and sprinkle
with a little salt. Bake for 40 minutes.
2 Heat the butter and remaining oil in
a large non-stick pan and cook the
garlic and potato, tossing occasionally,
for 10 minutes, or until the potato is
tender. Set aside on paper towels.
Cook the spinach in the pan for
1–2 minutes, or until wilted. Cool and
then squeeze out any excess moisture.
3 Reduce the oven to 180°C (350°F/
Gas 4). Work with one sheet of pastry
at a time and cover the rest with a
damp tea towel. Brush the pastry with
melted butter and place another sheet

on top. Brush with butter and repeat
with another two layers. Cut in half
widthways. Place a few potato slices at
one end of each half, leaving a wide
border on each side. Top with two
tomato pieces and some spinach.
4 Fold in the sides of the pastry and
roll up. Place on a lightly greased
baking tray, brush with melted butter
and sprinkle with sesame seeds. Use
the remaining filo and filling to make
another five parcels. Bake for
25–30 minutes, or until lightly golden.

NUTRITION PER PIE
Protein 9 g; Fat 30 g; Carbohydrate 35 g;
Dietary Fibre 6 g; Cholesterol 60 mg;
1940 kJ (465 cal)

Build up the layers of filo pastry, brushing each
with melted butter.

Place a few slices of potato at one end and top
with tomato and spinach.

Fold in the sides of the pastry and then roll up
around the filling, into a parcel.

RICH BEEF PIE

Preparation time: 35 minutes + chilling
Total cooking time: 2 hours 45 minutes
Serves 6

FILLING
2 tablespoons oil
1 kg (2 lb) chuck steak, cubed
1 large onion, chopped
1 large carrot, finely chopped
2 cloves garlic, crushed
2 tablespoons plain flour
1 cup (250 ml/8 fl oz) beef stock
2 teaspoons fresh thyme leaves
1 tablespoon Worcestershire sauce

PASTRY
2 cups (250 g/8 oz) plain flour
150 g (5 oz) butter, chilled and cubed
1 egg yolk
3–4 tablespoons iced water
1 egg yolk and 1 tablespoon milk,
    to glaze

1 Heat 1 tablespoon of the oil in a large pan and brown the meat in batches. Remove all the meat from the pan and set aside. Heat the remaining oil, then add the onion, carrot and garlic and cook over medium heat until browned.

2 Return all the meat to the pan and stir in the flour. Cook for 1 minute, then remove from the heat and slowly stir in the beef stock, mixing the flour in well. Add the thyme leaves and Worcestershire sauce, and bring to the boil. Season to taste.

3 Reduce the heat to very low, cover and simmer for 1¹/₂–2 hours, or until the meat is tender. During the last 15 minutes of cooking remove the lid and allow the liquid to reduce until very thick. Cool completely.

4 To make the pastry, sift the flour into a large bowl and add the butter. Using your fingertips, rub the butter into the flour until it resembles fine breadcrumbs. Add the egg yolk and 2 tablespoons of iced water, and mix with a knife using a cutting action until the mixture comes together in beads, adding a little more water if necessary. Turn out onto a lightly floured surface and gather together to form a smooth dough. Wrap in plastic wrap and refrigerate for 30 minutes.

5 Preheat the oven to 200°C (400°F/ Gas 6). Divide the pastry into two pieces and roll out one of the pieces on a sheet of baking paper until large enough to line a 23 cm (9 inch) pie dish. Line the pie dish with the pastry. Fill with the cold filling and roll out the remaining piece of pastry until large enough to fully cover the dish. Dampen the edges of the pastry with your fingers dipped in water. Lay the top piece of pastry over the pie and gently press the bottom and top pieces of pastry together. Trim the overhanging edges with a sharp knife and re-roll the trimmings to make decorations for the pie top.

6 Cut a few slits in the top of the pastry to allow the steam to escape. Beat together the egg yolk and milk, and brush it over the top of the pie. Cook in the oven for 20–30 minutes, or until the pastry is golden.

NUTRITION PER SERVE
Protein 40 g; Fat 35 g; Carbohydrate 35 g;
Dietary Fibre 3 g; Cholesterol 235 mg;
2580 kJ (615 cal)

To make the pastry, rub the butter into the flour with your fingertips.

Mix the egg yolk and water into the flour mixture with a flat-bladed knife.

Gather the mixture together on a lightly floured surface to form a smooth dough.

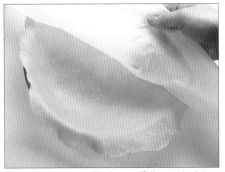

The baking paper will help you lift the pastry into the pie dish.

Spoon in the filling then top the pie with the second piece of pastry.

Press the pieces of pastry together and trim off the excess with a sharp knife.

BACON AND WHOLE EGG FILO PIES

Preparation time: 30 minutes
Total cooking time: 30 minutes
Makes 6

1 teaspoon oil
4 spring onions, chopped
6 lean bacon rashers, chopped
1/2 cup (125 ml/4 fl oz) milk
1/4 cup (60 ml/2 fl oz) cream
2 tablespoons chopped fresh parsley
pinch of ground nutmeg
7 eggs
10 sheets filo pastry
melted butter, for brushing

1 Heat the oil in a pan and cook the spring onion and bacon for 2–3 minutes, then set aside to cool. Mix together the milk, cream, parsley, ground nutmeg and 1 egg and season with salt and pepper.

2 Brush 1 sheet of filo pastry with the melted butter, then brush another sheet and lay it on top. Repeat until you have a stack of 5 sheets. Cut into 6 squares. Repeat with the remaining 5 sheets of pastry. Place 2 squares together at an angle to form a rough 8-pointed star and fit into a 1 cup (250 ml/8 fl oz) muffin tin. Repeat with the remaining squares.

3 Preheat the oven to 200°C (400°F/ Gas 6). Divide the spring onion and bacon mixture evenly between the filo pastry cups. Then pour over the egg and cream mixture and carefully break an egg on the top of the pie. Bake for 10 minutes, then reduce the oven to moderate 180°C (350°F/Gas 4) and bake for a further 10–15 minutes, or until the pastry is lightly crisp and golden and the egg is just set. Serve the pies immediately.

NUTRITION PER PIE

Protein 15 g; Fat 15 g; Carbohydrate 10 g; Dietary Fibre 1 g; Cholesterol 245 mg; 1130 kJ (270 cal)

Season the egg, milk, cream, parsley and nutmeg mixture.

Make an 8-pointed star from two pastry squares and place in the muffin tin.

Carefully break an egg over the filling inside the pastry shell.

96

CHICKEN CORIANDER PIE

Preparation time: 40 minutes
Total cooking time: 45 minutes
Serves 4

50 g (1³/4 oz) butter
2 onions, chopped
100 g (3¹/2 oz) button mushrooms,
    sliced
250 g (8 oz) cooked chicken, chopped
4 hard-boiled eggs
1 tablespoon plain flour
280 ml (9 fl oz) chicken stock
1 egg yolk
3 tablespoons chopped fresh
    coriander
250 g (8 oz) block or packet puff
    pastry
1 egg, lightly beaten, to glaze

1 Melt half of the butter in a large pan.
Add the onion and mushrooms and
cook for about 5 minutes, or until soft,
then stir in the chicken. Spoon half of
the mixture into a 20 cm (8 inch)
round, straight-sided pie dish. Slice the
eggs and lay over the chicken. Top
with the remaining mixture.
2 Preheat the oven to 200°C (400°F/
Gas 6). Melt the remaining butter in a
pan, add the flour and cook for
1 minute. Gradually add the stock and
cook for 4 minutes, stirring constantly,
then remove from the heat. Stir in the
egg yolk and coriander and season.
Leave to cool, then pour over the
chicken filling.
3 Roll out the pastry into a square
larger than the pie dish. Dampen the
dish rim with water and lay the pastry
over, pressing down firmly to seal.
Trim the edges and roll out the leftover
pastry into a long strip. Slice it into
three equal lengths and make a plait.
Brush the top of the pie with beaten
egg and place the plait around the
edge. Brush again with beaten egg.
Make a few slits in the centre and bake
for 35 minutes, or until golden.

NUTRITION PER SERVE
Protein 25 g; Fat 35 g; Carbohydrate 30 g;
Dietary Fibre 3 g; Cholesterol 385 mg;
2220 kJ (530 cal)

Add the chicken to the cooked onion and
mushrooms in the pan.

Slice the hard-boiled eggs and arrange them over
the chicken filling.

Stir the egg yolk and coriander into the heated
stock and flour.

Lay the decorative plait around the edge of the
pie, securing with beaten egg.

Decorative finishes

Traditionally, savoury pies were decorated to distinguish them at a glance from sweet pies. Today we are unlikely to bake more than one pie in a day, so confusion shouldn't be a problem.

Decorating seals pie edges, uses up pastry trimmings and helps identify the filling. Pies are usually double crusted (with a pastry base and top) or just crusted on the top, whereas tarts have no top. Pies or tarts made in pie dishes with a lip can all be decorated around the edge. These decorations can be very simple (pressing a fork or thumb around the edge), or quite intricate. Secure pastry shapes to the edge of the pie with glaze (often egg white, though for a rich colour, use a lightly beaten egg), then glaze them as well.

PIE & TART EDGES

Fork pressed—press a lightly floured fork around the edge.
Fluted—press the edge between your thumbs at a slight angle, to create a ripple effect.
Crimped—press the pastry between thumb and forefinger, while indenting with the other forefinger.
Scalloped—mark or cut out semi-circles with a spoon.
Chequerboard—make cuts in the edge; turn every other square inwards.

Leaves—cut out leaf shapes with a cutter or template and secure over the lip of the pie.
Plait—cut three long strips and plait them to the length of the circumference of the tart. Secure with a little water or egg glaze.
Rope—twist two long sausages of pastry together. Secure with egg glaze.
Feathering—lift the pastry off the lip so it stands upright and snip diagonally into the edge of the pie. Push one point inwards and then one point outwards.

PIE TOPS

When decorating with pastry trimmings, don't make the shapes too thick or they won't cook through. Re-roll pastry trimmings to an even thickness and cut out shapes with biscuit cutters. If you want to make a shape you don't have a cutter for, draw it on a piece of stiff card and cut out to make a template. The shapes can indicate the pie filling, such as fish or animals, or be purely whimsical like hearts or stars. The shapes are secured to the pastry top with a little glaze.

You can also place pastry shapes on or around the edge of an open tart. If the filling is quite liquid, cook the shapes separately and arrange on the middle of the tart after it is baked and the filling has set.

If your tart cooks for a long time, check that the edges are not over-browning and cover with pieces of foil if necessary.

LATTICE TOPS

A lattice makes a very impressive top for a pie and is actually quite easy to make. On a sheet of baking paper, roll the pastry out to a square or rectangle a little larger than the pie (just as you would to cover normally). Using a fluted pastry wheel, or a small, sharp knife, cut strips of pastry about 1.5 cm (5/8 inch) wide. Use a ruler to make perfect straight lines. Lay half the strips on another sheet of baking paper, all in the same direction, and about 1 cm (1/2 inch) apart. Fold alternate strips of pastry back away from you (all the way back to start with). Lay a strip of pastry horizontally across the unfolded strips, then fold them back into place. Fold the lower strips back this time, and lay another strip of pastry across. Repeat with all the strips, alternating the vertical strips. If the pastry is very soft, refrigerate it until firm.

Invert the lattice onto the pie and peel the paper away. Press the edges to seal, and trim off the excess pastry. Alternatively, if you bake often you can make life easy for yourself and buy a special lattice-cutter. Simply roll out your pastry and roll over it once with your cutter, gently open the lattice out and lift it onto your pie and then trim the edges.

CLOCKWISE, FROM TOP LEFT: Crimped; Chequerboard; Scalloped; Rope; Lattice; Fork pressed; Plait; Leaves; Fluted

Savoury Tarts

VEGETABLE TART WITH SALSA VERDE

Preparation time: 30 minutes +
    30 minutes refrigeration
Total cooking time: 50 minutes
Serves 6

1³/₄ cups (215 g/7 oz) plain flour
120 g (4 oz) chilled butter, cubed
¹/₄ cup (60 ml/2 fl oz) cream
1–2 tablespoons iced water

SALSA VERDE
1 clove garlic
2 cups (40 g/1¹/₄ oz) fresh flat-leaf
    parsley
¹/₃ cup (80 ml/2³/₄ fl oz) extra virgin
    olive oil
3 tablespoons chopped fresh dill
1¹/₂ tablespoons Dijon mustard
1 tablespoon red wine vinegar
1 tablespoon drained baby capers

FILLING
1 large (250 g/8 oz) Desiree potato,
    cut into 2 cm (1 inch) cubes
1 tablespoon olive oil
2 cloves garlic, crushed
1 red capsicum, cut into cubes
1 red onion, sliced
2 zucchini, sliced
2 tablespoons chopped fresh dill
1 tablespoon chopped fresh thyme
1 tablespoon drained baby capers
150 g (5 oz) marinated quartered
    artichoke hearts, drained
²/₃ cup (30 g/1 oz) baby English
    spinach leaves

1 Sift the flour and ¹/₂ teaspoon salt into a large bowl. Add the butter and rub in with your fingertips until it resembles fine breadcrumbs. Add the cream and water and mix with a knife until it comes together in beads. Gather together on a lightly floured work surface, press into a disc, wrap in plastic and chill for 30 minutes.
2 Preheat the oven to 200°C (400°F/ Gas 6). Grease a 27 cm (11 inch) loose-based flan tin. Roll the dough out between two sheets of baking paper large enough to line the tin, trimming off the excess. Cover with baking paper, then add baking beads and bake for 15–20 minutes. Remove the paper and beads, reduce the heat to 180°C (350°F/Gas 4) and bake for 20 minutes, or until golden.
3 Mix all the salsa verde ingredients in a food processor until almost smooth.
4 Boil the potato until just tender. Drain. Heat the oil in a large frying pan and cook the garlic, capsicum and onion for 3 minutes, stirring often. Add the zucchini, dill, thyme and capers and cook for 3 minutes. Reduce the heat, add the potato and artichokes, and heat through. Season to taste.
5 Spread 3 tablespoons of the salsa verde over the pastry. Spoon the filling into the case and drizzle with half the remaining salsa. Pile spinach in the centre and drizzle with salsa verde.

NUTRITION PER SERVE
Protein 5.5 g; Fat 30 g; Carbohydrate 27 g;
Dietary Fibre 3.5 g; Cholesterol 50 mg;
1590 kJ (380 cal)

Use a flat-bladed knife to mix the water into the dough until it comes together in beads.

Mix together the salsa verde ingredients in a food processor until almost smooth.

MEDITERRANEAN RICOTTA TARTS

Preparation time: 20 minutes +
   20 minutes cooling
Total cooking time: 30 minutes
Makes 4

1/3 cup (30 g/1 oz) dry breadcrumbs
2 tablespoons virgin olive oil
1 clove garlic, crushed
1/2 red capsicum, quartered and cut
   into thin strips
1 zucchini, cut into thin strips
2 slices prosciutto, chopped
375 g (12 oz) firm ricotta (see NOTE)
1/3 cup (40 g/1 1/2 oz) grated Cheddar
1/3 cup (30 g/1 oz) grated Parmesan
2 tablespoons shredded fresh basil
4 black olives, pitted and sliced

1 Preheat the oven to 180°C (350°F/ Gas 4). Lightly grease four 8 cm (3 inch) fluted tart tins. Lightly sprinkle 1 teaspoon breadcrumbs over the base and side of each tin.
2 To make the topping, heat half the oil in a frying pan, add the garlic, capsicum and zucchini and cook, stirring, over medium heat for 5 minutes, or until the vegetables are soft. Remove from the heat and add the prosciutto. Season to taste.
3 Place the ricotta in a large bowl and add the cheeses and remaining breadcrumbs. Season. Press the mixture into the tins and smooth the surface. Sprinkle with basil.
4 Scatter the topping over the ricotta mixture, top with the olives, then drizzle with the remaining oil.
5 Bake for 20 minutes, or until the tarts are slightly puffed and golden. Cool completely (the tarts will deflate on cooling) and remove from the tins. Do not refrigerate.

NUTRITION PER TART
Protein 20 g; Fat 27 g; Carbohydrate 8 g; Dietary Fibre 1 g; Cholesterol 66 mg; 1457 kJ (348 cal)

NOTE: Use firm ricotta or very well-drained ricotta, or the tarts will be difficult to remove from the tins.

Sprinkle breadcrumbs over the base and side of each tin.

Cook the vegetables in a frying pan over medium heat until soft.

Press the ricotta mixture into the tins, then smooth the surface.

Bake the tarts until they are puffed and golden around the edges.

CARAMELISED ONION, ROCKET AND BLUE CHEESE TARTS

Preparation time: 30 minutes +
  30 minutes refrigeration
Total cooking time: 1 hour 10 minutes
Makes 6

2 cups (250 g/8 oz) plain flour
125 g (4 oz) butter, chilled and
  cubed
1/4 cup (30 g/1 oz) grated Parmesan
1 egg, lightly beaten
1/4 cup (60 ml/2 fl oz) iced water

FILLING
2 tablespoons olive oil
3 onions, thinly sliced
100 g (3 1/2 oz) baby rocket leaves
100 g (3 1/2 oz) blue cheese, crumbled
3 eggs, lightly beaten
1/4 cup (60 ml/2 fl oz) cream
1/2 cup (60 g/2 oz) grated Parmesan
pinch of grated fresh nutmeg

1 To make the pastry, sift the flour into a large bowl and add the butter. Rub the butter into the flour with your fingertips until it resembles fine breadcrumbs. Stir in the Parmesan.
2 Make a well in the centre of the dry ingredients, add the egg and water and mix with a flat-bladed knife, until the mixture comes together in beads.
3 Lift the dough onto a lightly floured work surface, press into a disc, wrap in plastic and chill for 30 minutes.
4 Preheat the oven to 200°C (400°F/ Gas 6). Divide the pastry into six. Roll the dough out between two sheets of baking paper to fit six 8 cm (3 inch) fluted loose-based tart tins, trimming off the excess.
5 Line the pastry shells with a piece of crumpled baking paper that is large enough to cover the base and side of each tin and pour in some baking beads or rice. Bake for 10 minutes, then remove the paper and baking beads and return the pastry to the oven for 10 minutes, or until the base is dry and golden. Cool slightly. Reduce the oven to 180°C (350°F/ Gas 4).
6 Heat the oil in a large frying pan, add the onion and cook over medium heat for 20 minutes, or until the onion is caramelised.
7 Add the rocket and stir until wilted. Remove from the pan and cool.
8 Divide the onion mixture among the tart bases, then sprinkle with the blue cheese. Whisk together the eggs, cream, Parmesan and nutmeg and pour evenly over each of the tarts. Place on a baking tray and bake for 20–30 minutes. Serve hot or cold.

NUTRITION PER TART
Protein 18 g; Fat 40 g; Carbohydrate 33 g; Dietary Fibre 2.5 g; Cholesterol 215 mg; 2388 kJ (570 cal)

Rub the butter into the flour until the dough resembles fine breadcrumbs.

Use a small ball of pastry to help you press the pastry neatly into the tins.

SMOKED SALMON TARTLETS

Preparation time: 30 minutes +
  10 minutes refrigeration
Total cooking time: 30 minutes
Makes 24

250 g (8 oz) cream cheese, softened
1½ tablespoons wholegrain mustard
2 teaspoons Dijon mustard
2 tablespoons lemon juice
2 tablespoons chopped fresh dill
6 sheets puff pastry
300 g (10 oz) smoked salmon,
  cut into thin strips
65 g (2¼ oz) baby capers

1 Preheat the oven to 210°C (415°F/ Gas 6–7). Line a large baking tray with baking paper. Mix together the cream cheese, mustards, lemon juice and dill. Cover and refrigerate.

2 Cut four 9.5 cm (3¾ inch) rounds from each sheet of pastry with a fluted cutter and place on the baking tray. Prick the pastries all over. Cover and refrigerate for 10 minutes.

3 Bake in batches for 7 minutes, remove from the oven and use a spoon to flatten the centre of each pastry. Return to the oven and bake for a further 5 minutes, or until the pastry is golden. Allow to cool, then spread a rounded teaspoon of the cream cheese mixture over each pastry, leaving a 1 cm (½ inch) border. Arrange the salmon over the top. Decorate with a few capers.

NUTRITION PER TARTLET
Protein 6 g; Fat 15 g; Carbohydrate 15 g; Dietary Fibre 0.5 g; Cholesterol 25 mg; 869 kJ (210 cal)

Use a sharp knife to cut the smoked salmon into thin strips.

Put the cream cheese, mustards, lemon juice and dill in a bowl and mix well.

Using a spoon, flatten the centre of each pastry before returning to the oven.

Spread the cream cheese mixture onto the cooled pastries.

TOMATO, PARMESAN AND ANCHOVY TARTS

Preparation time: 10 minutes + cooling
Total cooking time: 1 hour 35 minutes
Serves 10

3 tablespoons olive oil
1 onion, finely chopped
2 tablespoons chopped fresh parsley
1 teaspoon dried basil
1 teaspoon sugar
2 x 800 g (1 lb 10 oz) cans tomatoes
2 sheets shortcrust pastry
2 teaspoons chopped anchovy fillets
2 tablespoons grated Parmesan
3 eggs, lightly beaten

1 Heat the oil in a frying pan and gently fry the onion for 15 minutes, or until golden. Add the parsley, basil and sugar and cook for 20–30 seconds, stirring constantly.
2 Drain the tomatoes and chop into a pulp. Add to the pan, then reduce the heat and simmer for 30 minutes, or until dark and quite dry. Cool.
3 Preheat the oven to 180°C (350°F/ Gas 4) and grease two 20 cm (8 inch) shallow fluted loose-based tart tins. Line each tin with a sheet of pastry and prick with a fork. Line with baking paper, fill with baking beads and bake for 10 minutes. Remove the baking paper and beads. Bake for a further 10 minutes, or until dry.
4 Stir the anchovies, Parmesan and eggs through the filling, then put into the pastry cases and level the surfaces. Bake for 30 minutes, or until set.

NUTRITION PER SERVE
Protein 6 g; Fat 17 g; Carbohydrate 18 g;
Dietary Fibre 2 g; Cholesterol 65 mg;
1045 kJ (250 cal)

Drain the canned tomatoes and roughly chop them into a pulp.

Line each tin with pastry and prick the bottom with a fork to reduce puffing.

Add the chopped anchovies, Parmesan and eggs to the filling mixture.

RATATOUILLE TARTS

Preparation time: 40 minutes +
  15 minutes refrigeration +
  20 minutes standing
Total cooking time: 1 hour 10 minutes
Makes 12

3 cups (375 g/12 oz) plain flour
170 g (5¹/₂ oz) butter, chilled and
  chopped
¹/₂ cup (125 ml/4 fl oz) iced water

RATATOUILLE FILLING
1 eggplant (about 500 g/1 lb)
¹/₄ cup (60 ml/2 fl oz) oil
1 onion, chopped
2 cloves garlic, crushed
2 zucchini, sliced
1 red capsicum, chopped
1 green capsicum, chopped
250 g (8 oz) cherry tomatoes, halved
1 tablespoon balsamic vinegar
1 cup (125 g/4 oz) grated Cheddar

1 Sift the flour into a bowl and add the butter. Using your fingertips, rub the butter into the flour until the mixture resembles fine breadcrumbs. Make a well in the centre and add the water. Mix together with a flat-bladed knife, adding a little more water if necessary, until the dough just comes together.
2 Gather the dough into a ball and divide into 12 portions. Grease 12 loose-based fluted 8 cm (3 inch) tart tins. Roll each portion of dough out on a sheet of non-stick baking paper to a circle a little larger than the tins. Lift the pastry into the tins and press well into the sides, then trim away any excess pastry. Refrigerate for 15 minutes. Preheat the oven to 200°C (400°F/Gas 6).

3 Put all the tins on baking trays, prick the pastry bases all over with a fork and bake for 20–25 minutes, or until the pastry is fully cooked and lightly golden. Cool completely.
4 Meanwhile, to make the ratatouille filling, cut the eggplant into 2 cm (³/₄ inch) cubes, put into a colander and sprinkle generously with salt. Leave for 20 minutes, then rinse, drain and pat dry with paper towels.
5 Heat 2 tablespoons of the oil in a large frying pan. Cook the eggplant for 8–10 minutes, or until browned. Drain on paper towels. Heat the remaining oil and add the onion. Cook over medium heat for 5 minutes, or until very soft. Add the garlic and cook for 1 minute, then add the zucchini and capsicum and cook, stirring frequently, for 10 minutes, or until softened. Add the eggplant and tomatoes. Cook, stirring, for 2 minutes. Transfer to a bowl, stir in the vinegar, then cover and cool completely.
6 Preheat the oven to 180°C (350°F/ Gas 4). Divide the filling among the shells with a slotted spoon, draining off any excess liquid. Sprinkle with Cheddar and cook for 10–15 minutes, or until the cheese has melted and the tarts are warmed through.

NUTRITION PER TART
Protein 7.5 g; Fat 20 g; Carbohydrate 25 g; Dietary Fibre 3.5 g; Cholesterol 45 mg; 1328 kJ (317 cal)

NOTE: The ratatouille filling can be made a day ahead and stored in an airtight container in the fridge.

Rub the butter into the sifted flour until the mixture resembles fine breadcrumbs.

Press the pastry well into the side of the tin and cut away any excess.

Prick the pastry bases with a fork to reduce the amount they will puff up.

Sprinkle a generous amount of salt on the eggplant cubes.

Add the eggplant and tomatoes, then cook, stirring, for 2 minutes.

Pour the balsamic vinegar over the vegetables and mix well.

THAI THREE MUSHROOM TART

Preparation time: 25 minutes
Total cooking time: 1 hour 10 minutes
Serves 8

375 g (12 oz) block puff pastry
1 teaspoon sesame oil
2 teaspoons oil
150 g (5 oz) shiitake mushrooms, trimmed
150 g (5 oz) button mushrooms, halved
150 g (5 oz) oyster mushrooms, halved
1/2 cup (125 ml/4 fl oz) coconut milk
1 stalk lemon grass, chopped

1 1/2 teaspoons grated fresh ginger
1 clove garlic, chopped
2 tablespoons chopped fresh coriander leaves and stems
1 egg
1 tablespoon plain flour
1 spring onion, sliced diagonally

1 Preheat the oven to 210°C (415°F/ Gas 6–7). Grease a shallow 19 x 28 cm (7 1/2 x 11 inch) or 25 cm (10 inch) round loose-based tart tin. Roll out the pastry to line the base and sides of the tin and trim off any excess. Prick all over with a fork. Bake for 20 minutes, or until crisp, then cool. While cooling, gently press down the pastry if it has puffed too high. Reduce the oven to 200°C (400°F/Gas 6).

2 Heat the oils in a pan, add the shiitake and button mushrooms and stir until lightly browned. Add the oyster mushrooms, then cool. Pour away any liquid.
3 Process the coconut milk, lemon grass, ginger, garlic and coriander until fairly smooth. Add the egg and flour and blend in short bursts until combined. Season to taste.
4 Pour the mixture into the pastry and add the mushrooms and spring onion. Bake for 30 minutes, or until set.

NUTRITION PER SERVE
Protein 5 g; Fat 15 g; Carbohydrate 20 g; Dietary Fibre 2 g; Cholesterol 35 mg; 1045 kJ (250 cal)

Trim the shiitake mushrooms and halve the oyster and button mushrooms.

Trim the excess pastry quickly and easily by running a rolling pin over the tin.

Add the egg and flour to the coconut milk mixture and blend in short bursts.

ROASTED TOMATO AND ZUCCHINI TARTLETS

Preparation time: 45 minutes
Total cooking time: 1 hour 20 minutes
Makes 6

3 Roma tomatoes, halved lengthways
1 teaspoon balsamic vinegar
1 teaspoon olive oil
3 small zucchini, sliced
375 g (12 oz) block puff pastry
1 egg yolk, beaten, to glaze
12 small black olives
24 capers, rinsed and drained

PISTACHIO MINT PESTO
$1/2$ cup (75 g/$2^1/2$ oz) unsalted shelled
    pistachio nuts
2 cups (40 g/$1^1/4$ oz) firmly packed
    fresh mint leaves
2 cloves garlic, crushed
$1/3$ cup (80 ml/$2^3/4$ fl oz) olive oil
$1/2$ cup (50 g/$1^3/4$ oz) grated
    Parmesan

1 Preheat the oven to 150°C (300°F/ Gas 2). Place the tomatoes, cut-side-up, on a baking tray. Roast for 30 minutes, brush with the combined vinegar and oil and roast for a further 30 minutes. Increase the oven to 210°C (415°F/Gas 6–7).
2 To make the pesto, place the pistachios, mint and garlic in a food processor and process for 15 seconds. With the motor running, slowly pour in the olive oil. Add the Parmesan and process briefly.
3 Preheat the grill and line with foil. Place the zucchini in a single layer on the foil and brush with the remaining balsamic vinegar and oil. Grill for about 5 minutes, turning once.
4 Roll the pastry out to 25 x 40 cm

(10 x 16 inches) and cut out six 12 cm (5 inch) circles. Put on a greased baking tray and brush with egg yolk. Spread a tablespoon of pesto on each, leaving a 2 cm ($3/4$ inch) border. Divide the zucchini among the pastries and top with tomato halves. Bake for

15 minutes, or until golden. Top with olives, capers and black pepper.

NUTRITION PER TARTLET
Protein 15 g; Fat 60 g; Carbohydrate 35 g;
Dietary Fibre 6 g; Cholesterol 80 mg;
3040 kJ (725 cal)

Roast the tomatoes for 30 minutes, then brush with the vinegar and oil.

Add the grated Parmesan to the pesto and process briefly until well mixed.

Arrange a few grilled zucchini slices over the pesto, leaving a clear border.

SPINACH AND RICOTTA LATTICE TART

Preparation time: 50 minutes +
  15 minutes refrigeration
Total cooking time: 50 minutes
Serves 6

2 cups (250 g/8 oz) plain flour
125 g (4 oz) butter, chilled and cubed
1 egg
2 tablespoons sesame seeds
2–3 tablespoons iced water

SPINACH AND RICOTTA FILLING
50 g (1³/₄ oz) butter
1 cup (125 g/4 oz) finely chopped
  spring onions
2 cloves garlic, crushed
500 g (1 lb) English spinach, trimmed,
  washed and roughly shredded
2 tablespoons chopped fresh mint
³/₄ cup (185 g/6 oz) ricotta cheese
¹/₂ cup (50 g/1³/₄ oz) grated
  Parmesan
3 eggs, beaten
1–2 tablespoons milk

1 Place the flour and butter in a food processor and process for 15 seconds, or until the mixture resembles fine breadcrumbs. Add the egg, sesame seeds and water. Process in short bursts until the mixture just comes together, adding a little extra water if necessary. Turn out onto a lightly floured surface and quickly gather into a ball. Cover the pastry with plastic wrap and refrigerate for at least 15 minutes. Place a baking tray in the oven and preheat the oven to 180°C (350°F/Gas 4).
2 To make the filling, melt the butter in a large pan, add the spring onions and garlic and cook until soft. Add the spinach a little at a time, then stir in the mint. Remove from the heat and allow to cool slightly before stirring in the ricotta, Parmesan and the beaten eggs. Season and mix well.
3 Grease a shallow 23 cm (9 inch) loose-based tart tin. Take two-thirds of the pastry and, on a sheet of baking paper, roll it out thinly to line the tin, pressing it well into the sides. Fill the pastry shell with the spinach and ricotta filling.
4 Roll out the remaining pastry and cut into 1.5 cm (⁵/₈ inch) strips. Interweave the pastry strips in a lattice pattern over the top of the tart. Dampen the edge of the pastry base and gently press the strips down. Trim the edges of the pastry by pressing down with your thumb or by rolling a rolling pin across the top of the tin. Brush with milk. Place on the baking tray and bake for about 40 minutes, or until the pastry is golden.

NUTRITION PER SERVE
Protein 20 g; Fat 35 g; Carbohydrate 35 g;
Dietary Fibre 5 g; Cholesterol 215 mg;
2220 kJ (530 cal)

NOTE: Depending on how thick you like to roll your pastry, there may be about 100 g (3¹/₂ oz) of pastry trimmings left over. It is easier to have this little bit extra when making the lattice strips as they will be long enough to cover the top of the pie. The extra pastry can be covered and frozen for future use as decorations, or made into small tart shells.

Wash spinach very thoroughly as it can be gritty, then trim and roughly shred.

Allow the filling mixture to cool a little before adding the cheeses and egg.

Lift pastry into a tin by draping it over the rolling pin and removing the paper.

Roll out the remaining pastry and cut into thin strips for the lattice.

Interweave the lattice strips over the top of the spinach and ricotta filling.

Dampen the edge of the pastry shell, press down the lattice and trim.

BEETROOT AND FETA TART

Preparation time: 40 minutes +
  15 minutes refrigeration
Total cooking time: 1 hour
Serves 6

³/₄ cup (110 g/3¹/₂ oz) plain
    wholemeal flour
³/₄ cup (90 g/3 oz) plain flour
125 g (4 oz) butter, chilled and cubed
1 egg yolk
1–2 tablespoons iced water

FILLING
300 g (10 oz) ricotta cheese
300 g (10 oz) feta cheese, crumbled
3 eggs, lightly beaten
300 g (10 oz) baby beetroots, with
    short stalks attached
1 tablespoon walnut or olive oil
1 tablespoon red wine vinegar
¹/₄ cup (30 g/1 oz) chopped pecans
2 tablespoons fresh coriander leaves

1 Place the flours, butter and a pinch of salt in a food processor and mix for 15 seconds, or until crumbly. Add the egg yolk and water. Process in short bursts until the mixture just comes together, adding more water if needed. Turn out onto a floured surface and gather into a ball. Wrap in plastic and chill for 15 minutes. Preheat the oven to 180°C (350°F/Gas 4).
2 Mix together the ricotta and feta with a fork. Add the eggs and mix well. Grease a 23 cm (9 inch) loose-based tart tin. Roll out the pastry on a floured surface to line the tin, pressing it well into the sides. Using a sharp knife, trim off any excess pastry. Cover with baking paper, fill with baking beads or rice and bake for 10 minutes.

Remove the paper and beads and bake for 10 minutes. Spoon the filling into the base and cook for 30 minutes, or until the filling is firm and puffed (the filling will flatten down when removed from the oven).
3 Boil or steam the beetroots until tender, peel, then cut in half. Drizzle

with the combined oil and vinegar, and season well. Arrange over the tart and scatter with pecans and coriander.

NUTRITION PER SERVE
Protein 25 g; Fat 45 g; Carbohydrate 25 g;
Dietary Fibre 4 g; Cholesterol 230 mg;
2455 kJ (585 cal)

The baby beetroots should be well scrubbed and trimmed, leaving just a short stem.

Process the flours and butter until the mixture resembles fine breadcrumbs.

Blind bake the pastry shell, then add the ricotta and feta filling.

TOMATO AND THYME TART

Preparation time: 35 minutes +
   15 minutes refrigeration
Total cooking time: 30 minutes
Serves 6

CREAM CHEESE PASTRY
2 cups (250 g/8 oz) plain flour
125 g (4 oz) butter, chilled and cubed
125 g (4 oz) cream cheese, chopped
1 tablespoon fresh thyme leaves

1/2 cup (40 g/1 1/4 oz) fresh
   breadcrumbs
1/3 cup (30 g/1 oz) grated Parmesan
2 tablespoons fresh lemon thyme
   leaves
6 Roma tomatoes, sliced
3 spring onions, sliced
1 egg yolk, beaten with
   1 teaspoon of water, to glaze

1 Mix the flour, butter, cream cheese and thyme in a food processor. Add 2 tablespoons of water and process in short bursts until the mixture just comes together, adding more water if needed. Turn out onto a floured surface and gather together into a ball. Press into a large triangle. Cover with plastic wrap and chill for 15 minutes. Place on a greased baking tray and prick all over with a fork.
2 Preheat the oven to 210°C (415°F/Gas 6–7). Place the breadcrumbs, most of the Parmesan and 1 tablespoon of lemon thyme on the pastry, leaving an 8 cm (3 inch) border. Overlap the tomatoes and some of the spring onions on top, keeping the border. Add black pepper, the remaining spring onions, Parmesan and lemon thyme. Fold the pastry border over,

pleating as you go, and press to seal. Brush with the egg and water glaze. Bake for 10 minutes, reduce the oven to 180°C (350°F/Gas 4) and cook for 15–20 minutes, or until golden.

NUTRITION PER SERVE
Protein 10 g; Fat 30 g; Carbohydrate 40 g; Dietary Fibre 3 g; Cholesterol 110 mg; 1840 kJ (440 cal)

Roma tomatoes are also known as plum or egg tomatoes. Cut them into slices.

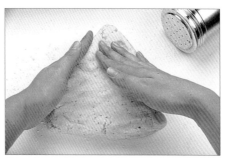
Press the pastry dough into a rough triangle shape before chilling.

Turn the pastry border up and over to make a traditional free-form tart.

113

CHEESE AND CHIVE SOUFFLE TART

Preparation time: 40 minutes
Total cooking time: 55 minutes
Serves 6–8

80 g (2³/₄ oz) butter
¹/₃ cup (40 g/1¹/₄ oz) plain flour
1 cup (250 ml/8 fl oz) cream
²/₃ cup (170 g/5¹/₂ oz) sour cream
4 eggs, separated
1 cup (130 g/4¹/₂ oz) grated Gruyère
     cheese
3 tablespoons chopped chives
¹/₄ teaspoon ground nutmeg
pinch of cayenne pepper
12 sheets filo pastry

1 Preheat the oven to 190°C (375°F/ Gas 5). Grease a deep 20 cm (8 inches) loose-based fluted tart tin. Melt half the butter in a pan. Sift in the flour and cook, stirring, for 1 minute. Remove from the heat and gradually whisk in the cream and sour cream.
2 Return to the heat and whisk constantly until the mixture boils and thickens. Remove from the heat and whisk in the egg yolks. Then cover the surface with plastic wrap and set aside to allow to cool slightly. Whisk in the cheese, chives, nutmeg and cayenne.
3 Melt the remaining butter and brush some over each sheet of pastry. Fold each one in half and use to line the tin, allowing the edges to overhang.
4 Beat the egg whites until stiff peaks

form, then stir a spoonful into the cheese mixture to loosen it up. Gently fold in the rest of the beaten egg white. Spoon the mixture into the pastry shell and then fold the pastry over the top. Brush the top with the remaining melted butter and bake for 40–45 minutes, or until puffed and golden. Serve immediately.

NUTRITION PER SERVE (8)
Protein 10 g; Fat 40 g; Carbohydrate 15 g;
Dietary Fibre 1 g; Cholesterol 200 mg;
1895 kJ (450 cal)

Fold each buttered sheet of filo in half, and use to line the tart tin.

Fold a spoonful of the beaten egg white into the cheese mixture.

Carefully fold the filo pastry over the top of the filling, then brush with melted butter.

ITALIAN SUMMER TART

Preparation time: 40 minutes +
  50 minutes refrigeration
Total cooking time: 1 hour
Serves 4–6

1¹/₂ cups (185 g/6 oz) plain flour
90 g (3 oz) butter, chilled and cubed
1 egg yolk
2–3 tablespoons iced water

FILLING
1 tablespoon olive oil
2 small red onions, sliced
1 tablespoon balsamic vinegar
1 teaspoon soft brown sugar
1 tablespoon fresh thyme leaves
170 g (5¹/₂ oz) jar marinated quartered
  artichokes, drained
2 slices prosciutto, cut into strips
12 black olives

1 Place the flour and butter in a food processor and process for 15 seconds, or until the mixture resembles fine breadcrumbs. Add the egg yolk and water. Process in short bursts until the mixture just comes together, adding a little extra water if necessary. Turn out onto a floured surface and gather into a ball. Cover with plastic wrap and refrigerate for at least 30 minutes.
2 Roll the pastry between two sheets of baking paper until large enough to fit a 35 x 10 cm (14 x 4 inch) loose-based tart tin. Press it well into the sides and trim off the excess. Cover and refrigerate for 20 minutes.
3 Preheat the oven to 190°C (375°F/ Gas 5). Cover the pastry shell with baking paper and fill evenly with baking beads, rice or beans. Bake for 15 minutes. Remove the paper and beads and bake for a further 15 minutes, or until the pastry is golden and dry. Cool on a wire rack.
4 Heat the oil in a pan, add the onion slices and cook, stirring occasionally, for 15 minutes. Add the balsamic vinegar and brown sugar and cook for a further 15 minutes. Remove from the heat, stir through the thyme leaves and set aside to cool.
5 Spread the onion evenly over the pastry shell. Arrange the quartered artichoke pieces on top, then fill the spaces between the artichokes with rolled-up pieces of prosciutto and the black olives. Serve the tart at room temperature.

NUTRITION PER SERVE (6)
Protein 6 g; Fat 15 g; Carbohydrate 25 g;
Dietary Fibre 2 g; Cholesterol 70 mg;
1155 kJ (275 cal)

Once the mixture resembles fine crumbs, add the egg yolk and a little water.

Fill the spaces with rolled-up pieces of prosciutto and black olives.

PISSALADIERE

Preparation time: 50 minutes +
    40 minutes standing
Total cooking time: 2 hours
Serves 8

7 g (¹/₄ oz) dried yeast
1 teaspoon caster sugar
2¹/₂ cups (310 g/10 oz) plain flour
2 tablespoons powdered milk
1 tablespoon oil

TOMATO AND ONION TOPPING
¹/₃ cup (80 ml/2³/₄ fl oz) olive oil
3–4 cloves garlic, finely chopped
6 onions, cut into thin rings
425 g (14 oz) can chopped tomatoes
1 tablespoon tomato paste
¹/₄ cup (15 g/¹/₂ oz) chopped fresh
    parsley
1 tablespoon chopped fresh thyme
olive oil, for brushing
3 x 45 g (1¹/₂ oz) cans anchovy fillets,
    drained and halved lengthways
36 small black olives

1 Lightly grease two 30 cm (12 inch) pizza trays. Place the yeast, sugar and 1 cup (250 ml/8 fl oz) of warm water in a small bowl. Set aside in a warm place for 5–10 minutes, or until frothy (if the yeast doesn't froth, you will need to start again with a fresh batch). Sift 2 cups (250 g/8 oz) of the plain flour, ¹/₂ teaspoon salt and the milk powder into a large bowl and make a well in the centre. Add the oil and yeast and mix thoroughly.
2 Turn out onto a lightly floured surface and knead for 10 minutes, gradually adding small amounts of the remaining flour, until the dough is smooth and elastic. Place in an oiled

bowl and brush the surface with a little oil, cover with plastic wrap and set aside in a warm place for 30 minutes, or until doubled in size.
3 To make the topping, heat the oil in a pan. Add the garlic and onion and cook, covered, over low heat for about 40 minutes, stirring frequently. The onion should be softened but not browned. Remove the lid and cook, stirring often, for a further 30 minutes, or until lightly golden. Take care not to burn. Set aside to cool.
4 Cook the chopped tomato in a pan, stirring frequently, for 20 minutes, or until thick and reduced to about 1 cup (250 ml/8 fl oz). Remove from the heat and stir in the tomato paste and herbs. Season with black pepper. Cool, then stir into the cooled onion mixture.
5 Preheat the oven to 220°C (425°F/ Gas 7). Punch down the dough, then turn out onto a lightly floured surface and knead for 2 minutes. Divide the dough in half. Return one portion to the bowl and cover. Roll the other portion out to a 30 cm (12 inch) circle and press evenly into the tin. Brush with some olive oil. Spread half the onion and tomato mixture evenly onto the dough, leaving a small border. Arrange half the anchovy fillets over the top in a lattice pattern and place an olive in each square. Repeat with the rest of the dough and topping. Bake for 15–20 minutes, or until the dough is cooked through and lightly browned (if you bake both tarts in the oven at the same time, they will take a little longer to cook).

NUTRITION PER SERVE
Protein 9 g; Fat 17 g; Carbohydrate 35 g;
Dietary Fibre 5 g; Cholesterol 8 mg;
1390 kJ (330 cal)

Pour the oil and frothy yeast into the flour mixture and mix thoroughly.

Cook the onion over low heat until it has softened but not browned.

Stir the tomato paste and herbs into the cooked tomatoes, then season with pepper.

Punch down the dough to expel any excess air before kneading.

Press one portion of dough evenly into the prepared tin and brush with olive oil.

Arrange half of the anchovy fillets in a lattice pattern over the top.

ROASTED VEGETABLE AND FETA TARTS

Preparation time: 1 hour
Total cooking time: 1 hour
Serves 6

1 small red capsicum, cubed
1 small yellow capsicum, cubed
300 g (10 oz) eggplant, cubed
2 zucchini, sliced
125 g (4 oz) cherry tomatoes
3 cloves garlic, crushed
2 tablespoons olive oil
1 teaspoon cumin seeds
3–4 sheets shortcrust pastry
300 g (10 oz) feta cheese
300 g (10 oz) ricotta cheese
2 teaspoons balsamic vinegar
1 tablespoon chopped fresh parsley

1 Preheat the oven to 200°C (400°F/ Gas 6). Place the capsicum, eggplant, zucchini and tomatoes in a baking dish lined with baking paper. Mix together the garlic, olive oil, cumin seeds and a pinch of salt. Drizzle over the vegetables. Roast for about 30 minutes, or until tender.

2 Line twelve 8 cm (3 inch) fluted loose-based tart tins with the pastry, pressing it well into the sides, and trim off any excess. Prick the bases with a fork and bake for 10 minutes, or until cooked and golden.

3 Mash together the feta and ricotta cheeses with a fork until smooth. Spoon into the tart shells and smooth with the back of a spoon dipped in hot water. Bake for 15–20 minutes, or until golden and warmed through.

4 Drizzle the balsamic vinegar over the roasted vegetables and mix well. Then spoon into each cooked tart and sprinkle with parsley.

NUTRITION PER SERVE
Protein 25 g; Fat 50 g; Carbohydrate 50 g;
Dietary Fibre 5 g; Cholesterol 90 mg;
3070 kJ (730 cal)

HINT: If you roll out all the trimmings from the pastry to line the tins you should only need to use 3 sheets, otherwise use 4 sheets and keep the trimmings for another recipe.

Cut the vegetables into small cubes before roasting.

Drizzle the flavoured oil over the chopped vegetables and roast until tender.

Prick the pastry bases all over with a fork and bake until golden.

Smooth the cheese filling with the back of a spoon dipped in hot water.

CARAMELISED ONION, MUSHROOM AND GOATS CHEESE TART

Preparation time: 40 minutes +
   35 minutes refrigeration
Total cooking time: 1 hour 35 minutes
Serves 6

2 cups (250 g/8 oz) plain flour
125 g (4 oz) butter, chilled and cubed
$^1/_2$ cup (125 g/4 oz) ricotta cheese
2 tablespoons iced water

FILLING
50 g (1$^3/_4$ oz) butter
3 onions, thinly sliced
200 g (6$^1/_2$ oz) button mushrooms,
   sliced
100 g (3$^1/_2$ oz) goats cheese,
   crumbled
$^1/_2$ cup (125 g/4 oz) ricotta cheese
1 tablespoon fresh thyme leaves

1 Put the flour, butter and ricotta in a food processor and process for 15 seconds, or until well mixed. Add the water. Process in short bursts until the mixture just comes together, adding a little more water if necessary. Turn out onto a floured surface and gather into a ball. Wrap in plastic and refrigerate for at least 15 minutes.
2 To make the filling, heat the butter in a large pan, add the onion and cook over low heat, stirring frequently, for 40–45 minutes, or until golden brown. Add the mushrooms and stir over the heat for a further 10 minutes. Drain and leave to cool. Stir through the crumbled goats cheese, ricotta and thyme leaves.
3 Roll out the pastry on a sheet of baking paper to a 32 cm (13 inch) circle and place on a large, greased pizza tray. Turn over the outside edge to make a small rim, pressing to seal. Prick the base all over with a fork, cover and refrigerate for 20 minutes.
4 Preheat the oven to 200°C (400°F/ Gas 6). Bake the base for 15 minutes and then reduce the oven to 180°C (350°F/Gas 4). Add the filling and bake for 25 minutes.

NUTRITION PER SERVE
Protein 15 g; Fat 35 g; Carbohydrate 35 g; Dietary Fibre 3 g; Cholesterol 105 mg; 2050 kJ (490 cal)

Cook the onion slowly, until caramelised, then add the mushroom.

Turn over a small rim on the outer edge of the pastry base.

Pricking the pastry base all over prevents it rising unevenly during cooking.

SALAMI, EGGPLANT AND ARTICHOKE TART

Preparation time: 20 minutes +
   30 minutes refrigeration
Total cooking time: 50 minutes
Serves 4–6

1 cup (125 g/4 oz) plain flour
60 g (2 oz) butter, chilled and cubed
1 egg yolk
1–2 tablespoons iced water

FILLING
2 tablespoons oil
250 g (8 oz) eggplant, cubed
1/2 cup (110 g/3 1/2 oz) quartered
   marinated artichokes

125 g (4 oz) piece salami, cubed
1 tablespoon chopped chives
1 tablespoon chopped fresh parsley
1 egg, lightly beaten
1/4 cup (60 ml/2 fl oz) cream

1 Put the flour and butter in a food processor and process for 15 seconds, or until crumbly. Add the egg yolk and water and process in short bursts until the mixture just comes together, adding a little more water if necessary. Turn the mixture out onto a floured surface and gather together into a ball. Wrap in plastic and refrigerate for at least 20 minutes. Preheat the oven to 200°C (400°F/Gas 6). Grease a shallow 20 cm (8 inch) loose-based tart tin.
2 Roll out the pastry on a sheet of baking paper to line the tin and trim off any excess. Refrigerate for 10 minutes. Prick the pastry with a fork and bake for 10 minutes, or until lightly browned. Cool.
3 Heat the oil and toss the eggplant over high heat until it begins to brown and soften; drain on paper towels. Mix the eggplant, artichokes, salami and herbs and press firmly into the pastry case. Pour over the combined egg and cream and bake for 35 minutes, or until browned and set.

NUTRITION PER SERVE (6)
Protein 8 g; Fat 25 g; Carbohydrate 15 g;
Dietary Fibre 2 g; Cholesterol 75 mg;
1300 kJ (310 cal)

Cut the salami and eggplant into cubes. You can use plain or flat-leaf parsley.

Toss the eggplant over high heat until it begins to brown and soften.

Press the filling firmly into the base and pour over the egg and cream.

FRESH HERB TART

Preparation time: 40 minutes +
   30 minutes refrigeration
Total cooking time: 1 hour 10 minutes
Serves 4–6

1¼ cups (150 g/5 oz) plain flour
100 g (3½ oz) butter, chilled and
   cubed
1–2 tablespoons iced water

250 g (8 oz) light sour cream
½ cup (125 ml/4 fl oz) thick cream
2 eggs, lightly beaten
1 tablespoon chopped fresh thyme
2 tablespoons chopped fresh parsley
1 tablespoon chopped fresh oregano

1 Put the flour and butter in a food processor and process for 15 seconds, or until the mixture resembles fine breadcrumbs. Add the water and process in short bursts until the mixture just comes together, adding a little more water if needed. Turn out onto a floured surface and gather into a ball. Cover with plastic wrap and refrigerate for at least 20 minutes. Roll out on a sheet of baking paper to line a 34 x 10 cm (14 x 4 inch) loose-based tart tin. Trim off the excess pastry. Refrigerate for 10 minutes. Preheat the oven to 200°C (400°F/Gas 6).
2 Cover the pastry shell with baking paper and fill evenly with baking beads or rice. Place on a baking tray and bake for 20 minutes. Remove the

paper and beads and reduce the oven to 180°C (350°F/Gas 4). Cook for 15–20 minutes, or until golden and dry. Cool.
3 Whisk together the sour cream, thick cream and eggs until smooth. Then stir in the herbs and season.
4 Place the pastry shell on a baking tray and pour in the filling. Bake for 25–30 minutes, or until set. Allow to stand for 15 minutes before serving.

NUTRITION PER SERVE (6)
Protein 6 g; Fat 25 g; Carbohydrate 20 g;
Dietary Fibre 1 g; Cholesterol 130 mg;
1340 kJ (320 cal)

If you don't have baking beads for blind baking, use dry rice or beans.

Put the sour cream, thick cream and eggs in a bowl and whisk together.

Put the pastry shell on a baking tray before cooking to catch any drips.

121

MUSHROOM AND RICOTTA FILO TART

Preparation time: 35 minutes
Total cooking time: 40 minutes
Serves 6

60 g (2 oz) butter
270 g (9 oz) field mushrooms, sliced
2 cloves garlic, crushed
1 tablespoon Marsala
1 teaspoon fresh thyme leaves
1/2 teaspoon chopped fresh rosemary
    leaves
pinch of freshly grated nutmeg
5 sheets filo pastry
75 g (2 1/2 oz) butter, melted

200 g (6 1/2 oz) ricotta cheese
2 eggs, lightly beaten
1/2 cup (125 g/4 oz) sour cream
1 tablespoon chopped fresh parsley

1 Preheat the oven to 180°C (350°F/Gas 4). Melt the butter in a frying pan and add the mushrooms. Cook over high heat for a few minutes, until they begin to soften. Add the garlic and cook for another minute. Stir in the Marsala, thyme, rosemary and nutmeg. Remove the mushrooms from the pan and drain off any liquid.

2 Work with 1 sheet of filo pastry at a time, keeping the rest covered with a damp tea towel to stop them drying out. Brush the sheets with melted butter and fold in half. Place on top of each other to line a shallow 23 cm (9 inch) loose-based tart tin, allowing the edges to overhang.

3 Beat the ricotta, eggs and sour cream together and season to taste. Spoon half the mixture into the tin, then add the mushrooms. Top with the rest of the ricotta mixture. Bake for 35 minutes, or until firm. Sprinkle with the chopped parsley.

NUTRITION PER SERVE
Protein 9 g; Fat 35 g; Carbohydrate 9 g;
Dietary Fibre 2 g; Cholesterol 160 mg;
1515 kJ (360 cal)

Remove the mushrooms from the pan, draining off as much liquid as possible.

Brush the filo with melted butter, fold in half and layer into the tin.

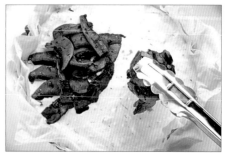

Layer half the ricotta filling into the pastry, then the mushroom mixture.

SPICY CHICKEN TARTS

Preparation time: 50 minutes
Total cooking time: 50 minutes
Makes 8

2 large onions, finely chopped
400 g (13 oz) eggplant, cubed
2 cloves garlic, crushed
2 x 410 g (13 oz) cans chopped
    tomatoes
1 tablespoon tomato paste
3 teaspoons soft brown sugar
1 tablespoon red wine vinegar
3 tablespoons chopped fresh parsley
4 sheets shortcrust pastry
2 teaspoons ground cumin seeds

2 teaspoons ground coriander
1 teaspoon paprika
400 g (13 oz) chicken breast fillets
sour cream and coriander leaves, to
    serve

1 Fry the onion in a little oil until golden. Add the eggplant and garlic and cook for a few minutes. Stir in the tomatoes, tomato paste, sugar and vinegar. Bring to the boil, reduce the heat, cover and simmer for 20 minutes. Uncover and simmer for 10 minutes, or until thick. Add the parsley and season. Preheat the oven to 190°C (375°F/Gas 5).
2 Grease eight 7.5 cm (3 inch) pie tins, line with the pastry and decorate the edges with a spoon. Prick the bases with a fork. Bake for 15 minutes, or until golden.
3 Mix the cumin, coriander and paprika on greaseproof paper. Coat the chicken pieces in the spices. Heat some oil in a frying pan and cook the chicken until brown and cooked through. Cut diagonally. Fill the pie shells with the eggplant mixture and add the chicken, sour cream and coriander leaves.

NUTRITION PER TART
Protein 20 g; Fat 35 g; Carbohydrate 45 g
Dietary Fibre 5 g; Cholesterol 65 mg;
2315 kJ (550 cal)

Simmer the tomato mixture uncovered to reduce the liquid, then add the parsley.

It is quick and simple to decorate the edge of the pastry case with a spoon.

Detach the tenderloin from the breast as it will cook much more quickly.

SMOKED SALMON BREAD BASKETS

Preparation time: 20 minutes + cooling
Total cooking time: 10 minutes
Makes 24

250 g (8 oz) smoked salmon
1 loaf white sliced bread
1/4 cup (60 ml/2 fl oz) olive oil
1/3 cup (90 g/3 oz) whole-egg
    mayonnaise
2 teaspoons extra virgin olive oil
1 teaspoon white wine vinegar
1 teaspoon finely chopped fresh dill
3 teaspoons horseradish cream
3 tablespoons salmon roe

1 Preheat the oven to 180°C (350°F/ Gas 4). Cut the salmon into strips. Flatten the bread to 1 mm (1/16 inch) with a rolling pin. Cut out 24 rounds with a 7 cm (2³/4 inch) cutter. Brush both sides of the rounds with olive oil and push into the holes of two 12-hole flat-based patty tins. Bake for 10 minutes, or until crisp. Cool.

2 Stir the mayonnaise in a bowl with the extra virgin olive oil, vinegar, dill and horseradish until combined.

3 Arrange folds of salmon in each cooled bread case and top each with 1 teaspoon of mayonnaise mixture. Spoon 1/2 teaspoon of salmon roe on top of each before serving.

NUTRITION PER TART
Protein 6 g; Fat 6 g; Carbohydrate 14 g; Dietary Fibre 1 g; Cholesterol 15 mg; 530 kJ (125 cal)

NOTE: The bread cases can be made a day in advance and, when completely cold, stored in an airtight container. If they soften, you can crisp them on a baking tray in a moderate oven for 5 minutes. Cool before filling.

Gently push the oiled circles of bread into the patty tin holes.

Fold the strips of salmon to fit into the cooled bread cases.

PUMPKIN TARTS

Preparation time: 20 minutes +
    30 minutes refrigeration
Total cooking time: 30 minutes
Serves 6

2 cups (250 g) plain flour
125 g (4 oz) butter, chilled and cubed
1/2 cup (125 ml/4 fl oz) iced water

FILLING
1.2 kg (2 lb 7 oz) pumpkin, cut into
    chunks
1/2 cup (125 g/4 oz) sour cream or
    cream cheese
sweet chilli sauce, to serve

1 Sift the flour and a pinch of salt into a large bowl and add the butter. Rub into the flour with your fingertips until it resembles fine breadcrumbs. Make a well in the centre, add the water and mix with a flat-bladed knife, using a cutting action, until the mixture comes together in beads. Gently gather the dough together and lift out onto a lightly floured work surface. Press together into a ball, wrap in plastic and refrigerate for 30 minutes.
2 Preheat the oven to 200°C (400°F/ Gas 6). Divide the pastry into six balls and roll each one out to fit a 10 cm (4 inch) pie dish. Trim the edges and prick the bases all over. Place on a baking tray and bake for 15 minutes, or until lightly golden, pressing down any pastry that puffs up. Cool, then remove from the tins.
3 To make the filling, steam the pumpkin pieces for about 15 minutes, or until tender.
4 Place a tablespoon of sour cream in the middle of each tart and pile the pumpkin pieces on top. Season and drizzle with sweet chilli sauce to taste. Return to the oven for a couple of minutes to heat through.

NUTRITION PER SERVE
Protein 9 g; Fat 26 g; Carbohydrate 44 g;
Dietary Fibre 4 g; Cholesterol 80 mg;
1876 kJ (448 cal)

VARIATION: Instead of steaming, roast the pumpkin with garlic, olive oil and fresh thyme.

Fit the pastry into the pie dishes, trim to fit, then prick the bases.

Pile the steamed pumpkin pieces on top of the sour cream.

GOATS CHEESE AND SWEET POTATO TART

Preparation time: 30 minutes +
    30 minutes refrigeration
Total cooking time: 40 minutes
Serves 2–3

2 teaspoons fine semolina
1 cup (125 g/4 oz) self-raising flour
60 g (2 oz) butter, chilled and cubed
1 egg yolk
2 tablespoons iced water

FILLING
2 tablespoons olive oil
1 small leek, chopped
50 g (1³/₄ oz) goats cheese, crumbled
1 egg, lightly beaten
2 tablespoons cream
150 g (5 oz) orange sweet potato,
    thinly sliced
¹/₂ teaspoon cumin seeds

1 Lightly grease a 25 cm (10 inch) pizza tray or baking tray and sprinkle with the semolina.
2 Put the flour and butter in a food processor and process for 15 seconds, or until the mixture resembles fine breadcrumbs. Add the egg yolk and water. Process in short bursts until the mixture just comes together, adding a little more water if necessary. Turn out onto a floured surface and gather together into a ball. Wrap in plastic and chill for 20 minutes.
3 Roll out the dough to a 20 cm (8 inch) circle. Lift onto the tray and roll over the outside edge to make a small rim; pinch this decoratively with your fingers. Prick the base with a fork and refrigerate for 10 minutes. Preheat the oven to 200°C (400°F/Gas 6). Bake for 12 minutes, or until just brown.

4 Heat half the oil in a pan, add the leek and cook until soft, then allow to cool. Spread the leek over the base of the pastry case, top with the cheese and season. Pour over the combined egg and cream and lay the sweet potato on top. Brush with the remaining oil and add the cumin seeds. Bake for 20–25 minutes, or until the filling is set. Leave for 5 minutes before cutting.

NUTRITION PER SERVE (3)
Protein 15 g; Fat 45 g; Carbohydrate 40 g;
Dietary Fibre 3 g; Cholesterol 200 mg;
2475 kJ (590 cal)

Peel the orange sweet potato and slice very thinly.

Turn over the edge of the pastry circle to make a small rim.

Pinch the rim between your fingers to make a decorative edging.

ROASTED TOMATO AND GARLIC TART

Preparation time: 40 minutes
Total cooking time: 1 hour 10 minutes
Serves 4

4 Roma tomatoes, halved
1 tablespoon olive oil
1 teaspoon balsamic vinegar
1 teaspoon salt
5–10 cloves garlic, unpeeled
2 sheets puff pastry
1 egg, lightly beaten
10 bocconcini, halved
small fresh basil leaves, to garnish

1 Preheat the oven to 200°C (400°F/ Gas 6). Put the tomatoes, cut-side-up, on a baking tray and drizzle with the olive oil, balsamic vinegar and salt. Bake for 20 minutes. Add the garlic and bake for a further 15 minutes. Cool and squeeze or peel the garlic from its skin.
2 Grease a 34 x 10 cm (14 x 4 inch) loose-based fluted tart tin. Lay a sheet of pastry over each end of the tin, so that they overlap the edges and each other. Seal the sheets together with egg and trim the edges. Cover with baking paper and baking beads. Bake for 15 minutes. Remove the paper and beads and bake for 10 minutes.

3 Place the roasted tomatoes along the centre of the tart and fill the gaps with the garlic and halved bocconcini. Bake for a further 10 minutes and serve with basil leaves.

NUTRITION PER SERVE
Protein 25 g; Fat 40 g; Carbohydrate 30 g; Dietary Fibre 3 g; Cholesterol 115 mg; 2580 kJ (615 cal)

Place the tomatoes on a baking tray and drizzle with oil, vinegar and salt.

Let the roasted garlic cloves cool, then squeeze or peel them from their skins.

Place a sheet of pastry over each end of the tin, so they overlap in the middle.

127

RED CAPSICUM, TOMATO AND ONION TART

Preparation time: 35 minutes +
    20 minutes refrigeration
Total cooking time: 1 hour 10 minutes
Serves 6

1 cup (125 g/4 oz) plain flour
1/2 cup (75 g/21/2 oz) wholemeal plain
    flour
100 g (31/2 oz) butter, chilled and
    cubed
1 tablespoon sesame seeds
1 egg, lightly beaten

FILLING
500 g (1 lb) tomatoes, finely chopped
2 tablespoons tomato paste
1 teaspoon dried oregano
1/2 teaspoon sugar
1 tablespoon olive oil
3 red onions, sliced
1 teaspoon chopped fresh thyme
3 red capsicums
1/3 cup (35 g/11/4 oz) grated
    Parmesan

1 Process the flours, butter and sesame seeds for about 15 seconds, or until the mixture resembles fine breadcrumbs. Add the egg and process in short bursts until the mixture just comes together. Add a little cold water if necessary. Turn out onto a lightly floured surface and gather into a ball. Wrap in plastic and refrigerate for at least 20 minutes. Preheat the oven to 200°C (400°F/Gas 6) and grease a shallow 19 x 28 cm (71/2 x 11 inch) loose-based fluted tart tin.
2 Roll out the pastry on a sheet of baking paper until large enough to line the tin. Press well into the sides

and trim away the excess. Prick the pastry all over with a fork and bake for 12 minutes, or until just brown and dry. Allow to cool.
3 Heat the tomatoes, tomato paste, oregano and sugar in a pan. Bring to the boil, then reduce the heat and simmer for 15–20 minutes, or until thick. Allow to cool. Season well.
4 Heat the oil in a pan and add the onion and thyme. Cook until the onion is soft and transparent.
5 Quarter the capsicums and remove the seeds and membrane. Grill, skin-side-up, until the skins have blistered. Cool in a plastic bag. Remove the skins and cut into quarters.
6 Spread the onion evenly over the base of the pastry shell and top with the tomato sauce. Sprinkle with cheese then top with the capsicum. Bake for 30 minutes, or until heated through and the pastry is crisp. Serve hot.

NUTRITION PER SERVE
Protein 10 g; Fat 20 g; Carbohydrate 30 g;
Dietary Fibre 5 g; Cholesterol 80 mg;
1485 kJ (355 cal)

STORAGE: The pastry can be made in advance and kept in the freezer for up to 3 months; or in the fridge for a day. Make sure it is well covered. Allow enough time to bring the pastry to room temperature before rolling it out.

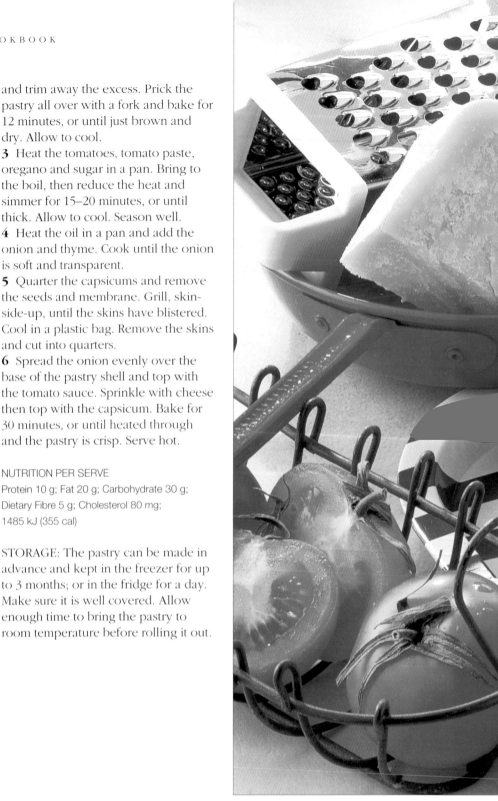

Slice the red onions into large pieces to add texture to the tart filling.

Place the flours, butter and sesame seeds in a food processor.

Lift the pastry into the prepared tin and press it well into the sides.

Heat the tomatoes, tomato paste, oregano and sugar in a pan.

Remove the blistered skin from the capsicums and cut them into pieces.

Spread the onions over the pastry shell and top with the tomato sauce.

129

FRIED GREEN TOMATO TART

Preparation time: 35 minutes +
    15 minutes refrigeration
Total cooking time: 30 minutes
Serves 6

4 green tomatoes
1 tablespoon olive oil
20 g (³/4 oz) butter
1 teaspoon ground cumin
2 cloves garlic, crushed
1 sheet puff pastry
¹/4 cup (60 g/2 oz) sour cream
1 tablespoon chopped fresh basil
2 tablespoons chopped fresh parsley
¹/2 cup (60 g/2 oz) grated Cheddar

1 Cut the tomatoes into thin slices.
Heat the oil and butter in a frying pan
and fry the cumin and garlic for
1 minute. Fry the tomatoes in batches
for 2–3 minutes, until slightly softened.
Drain on paper towels.
2 Cut a 24 cm (9¹/2 inch) round from
the puff pastry and place on a greased
baking tray. Make a 2 cm (³/4 inch)
border by scoring gently around the
edge. Make small cuts inside the
border. Refrigerate for 15 minutes.

Preheat the oven to 200°C (400°F/
Gas 6) and bake for 10–15 minutes.
3 Combine the sour cream, basil and
1 tablespoon of parsley. Sprinkle the
cheese over the centre of the pastry.
Arrange 1 layer of tomatoes around
the inside edge of the border and add
the rest. Bake for 10 minutes. Place the
cream mixture in the middle and add
the remaining chopped parsley.

NUTRITION PER SERVE
Protein 5 g; Fat 20 g; Carbohydrate 10 g;
Dietary Fibre 2 g; Cholesterol 40 mg;
1025 kJ (245 cal)

Lightly fry the tomatoes in batches until they are
slightly softened.

Using the tip of a knife, make small cuts in the
area inside the border.

Arrange the tomatoes around the inside edge of
the border.

ASPARAGUS AND CRISPY PROSCIUTTO TARTS

Preparation time: 40 minutes
Total cooking time: 40 minutes
Serves 8

32 fresh asparagus spears
30 g (1 oz) butter
1 leek, sliced
8 slices prosciutto
2 sheets puff pastry
1 tablespoon wholegrain mustard
shaved Parmesan
1 egg, lightly beaten, to glaze

1 Preheat the oven to moderately hot 200°C (400°F/Gas 6). Break the woody ends from the asparagus. Melt 20 g (3/4 oz) of butter in a large frying pan and cook the leek over low heat until soft. Remove from the pan. Melt the remaining butter in the pan, add the asparagus and toss over low heat for 1 minute. Drain on a paper towel.
2 Grill the prosciutto until crispy, then break into pieces when cool.
3 Cut the pastry sheets into quarters. Spread the centre of each with 1/2 teaspoon of mustard. Divide the leek between the pastry sheets and top with four pieces of asparagus. Lay the prosciutto and Parmesan on top.
4 Fold two side corners up to meet and overlap, sealing with some beaten egg. Lay on a greased baking tray. Brush again with beaten egg and bake for 25 minutes, or until golden.

NUTRITION PER SERVE
Protein 10 g; Fat 15 g; Carbohydrate 15 g;
Dietary Fibre 2 g; Cholesterol 60 mg;
1035 kJ (245 cal)

To remove the woody ends from the asparagus, hold at both ends and bend gently.

When it is cool, break the crispy prosciutto into pieces.

Arrange four pieces of asparagus on the pastry square and top with prosciutto.

FRENCH SHALLOT TATIN

Preparation time: 45 minutes +
  20 minutes refrigeration
Total cooking time: 1 hour
Serves 4–6

750 g (1¹/₂ lb) French shallots
50 g (1³/₄ oz) butter
2 tablespoons olive oil
¹/₃ cup (60 g/2 oz) soft brown sugar
3 tablespoons balsamic vinegar

PASTRY
1 cup (125 g/4 oz) plain flour
60g (2 oz) butter, chilled and cubed
2 teaspoons wholegrain mustard
1 egg yolk
1–2 tablespoons iced water

1 Peel the shallots, leaving the bases intact and tips exposed (see HINT).
2 Heat the butter and olive oil in a large pan. Cook the shallots for 15 minutes over low heat, then remove. Add the sugar, vinegar and 3 tablespoons of water to the pan and stir to dissolve the sugar. Add the shallots and simmer over low heat for 15–20 minutes, turning occasionally.
3 Preheat the oven to 200°C (400°F/ Gas 6). To make the pastry, process the flour and butter until crumbly. Add the mustard, egg yolk and water. Process in short bursts until the mixture comes together. Turn out onto a floured surface and gather into a ball. Wrap in plastic wrap and refrigerate for 20 minutes.
4 Grease a shallow 20 cm (8 inch) round sandwich tin. Pack the shallots tightly into the tin and pour over any syrup from the pan. Roll out the pastry on a sheet of baking paper to a circle, 1 cm (¹/₂ inch) larger than the tin. Lift the pastry into the tin and lightly push it down so it is slightly moulded over the shallots. Bake for 20–25 minutes, or until golden brown. Cool for 5 minutes on a wire rack. Place a plate over the tin and turn the tart out.

NUTRITION PER SERVE (6)
Protein 5 g; Fat 25 g; Carbohydrate 25 g; Dietary Fibre 2 g; Cholesterol 75 mg; 1360 kJ (325 cal)

HINT: Put the unpeeled shallots in boiling water for 30 seconds to make them easier to peel.

Return the shallots to the brown sugar and balsamic vinegar mixture in the pan.

Arrange the shallots over the base of the tin so that they are tightly packed.

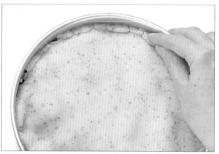

Lightly push the edges of the pastry down so that it moulds over the shallots.

ROAST CAPSICUM RISOTTO TARTS

Preparation time: 45 minutes
Total cooking time: 1 hour 15 minutes
Serves 6

20 g (³/4 oz) butter
¹/2 cup (95 g/3 oz) wild rice
1 cup (220 g/7 oz) short-grain brown
   rice
1 litre vegetable stock
2 eggs, beaten
¹/2 cup (50 g/1³/4 oz) grated
   Parmesan
2 green capsicums
2 red capsicums
2 yellow capsicums
150 g (5 oz) Camembert cheese,
   thinly sliced
2 tablespoons fresh oregano leaves

1 Melt the butter in a large pan, add the rice and stir over low heat until the rice is well coated. In a separate pan, heat the stock. Add ¹/2 cup (125 ml/4 fl oz) of stock to the rice, stirring well. Increase the heat to medium and add the remaining stock 1 cup (250 ml/8 fl oz) at a time, stirring until it has been absorbed. This will take about 30–40 minutes. Remove from the heat and cool. Add the eggs and Parmesan and season.
2 Grease 6 loose-based 10 cm (4 inch) fluted tart tins. Divide the risotto among the tins and press into the base and side. Allow to cool completely.
3 Cut the capsicums into large flat pieces and grill, skin-side-up, until the skins have blackened and blistered. Cool in a plastic bag, remove the skins and slice.
4 Preheat the oven to 200°C (400°F/ Gas 6). Place the Camembert slices in the bottom of the lined tins and divide the capsicum evenly between the tarts. Bake for 30 minutes. Sprinkle with oregano leaves and serve hot.

NUTRITION PER SERVE
Protein 15 g; Fat 15 g; Carbohydrate 40 g;
Dietary Fibre 3 g; Cholesterol 100 mg;
1515 kJ (360 cal)

Cool the risotto before adding the egg and Parmesan to prevent the egg scrambling.

Using a spoon, press the risotto into the base and side of the flan tins.

Remove the seeds and membrane and cut the capsicums into large flat pieces.

Divide the slices of Camembert between the lined flan tins.

PESTO AND ANCHOVY TART

Preparation time: 35 minutes
Total cooking time: 30 minutes
Serves 6

PESTO
1¹/₂ cups (75 g/2¹/₂ oz) fresh basil
    leaves, firmly packed
2 cloves garlic
¹/₂ cup (50 g/1³/₄ oz) grated
    Parmesan
¹/₂ cup (80 g/2³/₄ oz) pine nuts,
    toasted
¹/₄ cup (60 ml/2 fl oz) olive oil

375 g (12 oz) block puff pastry
1 egg yolk, lightly beaten
45 g (1¹/₂ oz) can anchovies, drained
¹/₃ cup (50 g/1³/₄ oz) grated
    mozzarella cheese
¹/₃ cup (35 g/1¹/₄ oz) grated
    Parmesan

1 To make the pesto, put the basil, garlic, Parmesan and pine nuts in a food processor and chop finely. With the motor running, add the oil and process until well combined.
2 Preheat the oven to 200°C (400°F/ Gas 6). Roll the pastry into a rectangle 18 x 35 cm (7 x 14 inches), and 5 mm (¹/₄ inch) thick. Cut a 2 cm (³/₄ inch) strip from all the way round the edge of the pastry. Combine the lightly beaten egg yolk with 1 teaspoon of water. Use this to brush the edge of the pastry. Trim the pastry strips to fit around the rectangle and attach them to form a crust. Place on a lightly floured baking tray and, using the tip of a sharp knife, make small cuts all over the base. Bake for 15 minutes. Press the centre of the pastry down

with the back of a spoon and bake for a further 5 minutes, or until lightly golden. Allow to cool.
3 Spread the pesto evenly over the base of the pastry. Cut the anchovies into thin strips and arrange over the pesto. Sprinkle the grated mozzarella

and Parmesan over the top and bake for 10 minutes, or until golden.

NUTRITION PER SERVE
Protein 15 g; Fat 40 g; Carbohydrate 25 g;
Dietary Fibre 2 g; Cholesterol 70 mg;
2155 kJ (515 cal)

Add the olive oil to the chopped basil, garlic, Parmesan and pine nuts.

Attach the strips of pastry around the edge of the rectangle to make a crust.

Spread the pesto evenly into the shaped pastry base.

VOL-AU-VENTS

Preparation time: 20 minutes +
  15 minutes refrigeration
Total cooking time: 30 minutes
Makes 4

250 g (8 oz) puff pastry
1 egg, lightly beaten

SAUCE AND FILLING
40 g (1¼ oz) butter
2 spring onions, finely chopped
2 tablespoons plain flour
1½ cups (375 ml/12 fl oz) milk
your choice of filling (see NOTE)

1 Preheat the oven to 220°C (425°F/Gas 7). Line a baking tray with baking paper. Roll out the pastry to a 20 cm (8 inch) square. Cut four circles of pastry with a 10 cm (4 inch) cutter. Place the rounds onto the tray and score 6 cm (2½ inch) circles into the centre of the rounds with a cutter, taking care not to cut right through the pastry. Refrigerate for 15 minutes.
2 Using a floured knife blade, knock up the sides of each pastry round by indenting with a knife every 1 cm (½ inch) around the circumference. This will help the cases rise evenly. Carefully brush the pastry with the egg, avoiding the edge as any glaze spilt on the side will stop the pastry from rising.
3 Bake for 15–20 minutes, or until the pastry has risen and is golden brown and crisp. Cool on a wire rack. Remove the centre from each pastry circle and pull out and discard any partially cooked pastry from the centre. The pastry can be returned to the oven for 2 minutes to dry out if the centre is undercooked. The pastry

cases are now ready to be filled with a hot filling before serving.
4 For the sauce, melt the butter in a saucepan, add the spring onion and stir over low heat for 2 minutes, or until soft. Add the flour and stir for 2 minutes, or until lightly golden. Gradually add the milk, stirring until smooth. Stir constantly over medium heat for 4 minutes, or until the mixture boils and thickens. Season well. Remove and stir in your choice of filling before spooning into the cases to serve.

NUTRITION PER VOL-AU-VENT
Protein 9 g; Fat 27 g; Carbohydrate 31 g; Dietary Fibre 1 g; Cholesterol 100 mg; 1680 kJ (400 cal)

NOTE: Add 350 g (11 oz) of any of the following to your white sauce: sliced, cooked mushrooms; peeled, cooked prawns; chopped, cooked chicken breast; poached, flaked salmon; dressed crab meat; oysters; steamed asparagus spears.
STORAGE: The cases can be made up to the 'knocking up' stage and then frozen.

Cut out four circles from the puff pastry with a 10 cm (4 inch) cutter.

Score circles part of the way through the pastry with a cutter.

Make indentations around the outside of the pastry with a knife.

MIXED POTATO TARTS

Preparation time: 30 minutes +
  30 minutes refrigeration
Total cooking time: 45 minutes
Makes 6

2 cups (250 g/8 oz) plain flour
1 teaspoon salt
125 g (4 oz) butter, chilled and cubed
1/2 cup (125 ml/4 fl oz) iced water

FILLING
50 g (1³/₄ oz) butter, melted
4 tablespoons oil
2 cloves garlic, crushed
1 tablespoon chopped fresh parsley
4 leeks, thinly sliced
1/4 cup (60 g/2 oz) sour cream
2 tablespoons chopped fresh herbs
250 g (8 oz) potatoes, unpeeled
250 g (8 oz) orange sweet potato,
    peeled
chopped chives, to garnish

1 Mix the flour, salt and butter in a food processor for 30 seconds, or until fine crumbs form. Add most of the water and process briefly until the mixture comes together. Add more water if the mixture is too dry. Turn out onto a lightly floured surface and bring together to form a smooth dough. Wrap in plastic and refrigerate for 30 minutes.
2 To make the filling, mix the melted butter and 2 tablespoons of the oil with the garlic and parsley to make a garlic butter. Heat the remaining oil and 1 tablespoon of the garlic butter in a large frying pan, add the leek and cook over medium heat until the leek begins to turn golden. Set aside.
3 Preheat the oven to 200°C (400°F/ Gas 6). Divide the pastry into six and roll each piece out to fit a shallow 10 cm (4 inch) diameter lightly greased pie tin. Trim the edges and decorate with a fork. Prick the bases lightly and bake for 15 minutes, or until lightly golden. Allow to cool and then remove the pastry cases from the tins.
4 Mix together the sour cream and chopped fresh herbs and set aside. Thinly slice the potato and orange sweet potato. Heat a frying or chargrill pan and cook the slices, in batches,

until tender, lightly brushing with the garlic butter as you go.
5 Pile the leek into the pastry cases, then overlap the potato and sweet potato over the leek. Top with herbed cream and chives. Serve warm or cold.

NUTRITION PER TART
Protein 8 g; Fat 30 g; Carbohydrate 45 g;
Dietary Fibre 5 g; Cholesterol 90 mg;
1950 kJ (465 cal)

Press the pastry into the tins, trim the edges and decorate with a fork.

Pile the leek into the pastry cases and top with the potato and sweet potato slices.

SWEET POTATO, POTATO AND ONION TART

Preparation time: 45 minutes +
 15 minutes refrigeration
Total cooking time: 1 hour 10 minutes
Serves 4–6

1 cup (125 g/4 oz) plain flour
90 g (3 oz) butter, chilled and cubed
1–2 tablespoons iced water

FILLING
500 g (1 lb) orange sweet potato,
 peeled
500 g (1 lb) potatoes, peeled
1 large onion, thinly sliced
1 cup (250 ml/8 fl oz) cream
2 eggs
1 tablespoon wholegrain mustard

1 To make the pastry, mix the flour and butter in a food processor until the mixture resembles fine breadcrumbs. Add the water and process for 5 seconds to combine. Turn out onto a lightly floured surface and gather into a smooth ball.
2 Roll out the pastry on a sheet of baking paper large enough to fit the base and sides of a 23 cm (9 inch) tart tin. Trim away the excess and chill for 15 minutes. Preheat the oven to 190°C (375°F/Gas 5).
3 Cover the pastry with a piece of baking paper, fill with baking beads or uncooked rice and bake for 10 minutes. Discard the paper and rice and bake for another 10 minutes. Cool.
4 Thinly slice the sweet potato and potato. Cook in a steamer for 15 minutes, or until just tender. Drain off any liquid, cover and set aside.
5 Layer the sweet potato and potato in the pastry shell, in an overlapping pattern, with the onion, gently pushing the layers in to compact them, finishing with onion. Combine the cream, egg and mustard, season and pour over the tart. Bake for 35 minutes, or until golden.

NUTRITION PER SERVE (6)
Protein 9 g; Fat 30 g; Carbohydrate 40 g;
Dietary Fibre 4 g; Cholesterol 155 mg;
2035 kJ (485 cal)

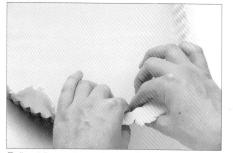

Roll out the pastry and use to line the base and side of the tin.

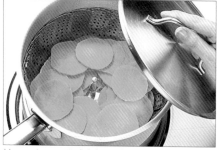

Use a steamer to lightly cook the vegetables, or simmer until just tender.

Build up the layers of potato and onion, pressing them together.

Mix together the cream, egg and mustard and pour over the tart.

POTATO AND ZUCCHINI TART

Preparation time: 25 minutes +
 15 minutes refrigeration
Total cooking time: 1 hour 20 minutes
Serves 6

1½ cups (185 g/6 oz) plain flour
125 g (4 oz) butter, chilled and cubed
1 egg yolk
1–2 tablespoons iced water

FILLING
450 g (14 oz) floury potatoes, peeled
 and roughly chopped
1/3 cup (40 g/1¼ oz) plain flour
125 g (4 oz) Jarlsberg cheese, grated
1/3 cup (80 ml/2¾ fl oz) cream
2 eggs, separated
2–3 small zucchini, thinly sliced
 lengthways
4 sprigs fresh thyme, to garnish

1 Grease a 25 cm (10 inch) loose-based flan tin.
2 To make the pastry, put the flour in a bowl with ½ teaspoon of salt. Rub in the butter with your fingertips, until the mixture resembles fine crumbs. Add the egg yolk and water and mix with a knife to form a rough dough. Turn out onto a lightly floured surface and work into a smooth ball, then wrap in plastic and refrigerate for 15 minutes. Preheat the oven to 190°C (375°F/Gas 5).
3 On a lightly floured surface, roll out the dough large enough to fit the tin. Trim off the excess pastry. Cover with baking paper and fill with baking beads or rice. Bake for 10 minutes and discard the paper and beads. Bake for another 5–10 minutes.
4 To make the filling, boil or steam the potato until tender. Drain, cool for 5 minutes and mash. Mix in the flour and cheese, stir in 2/3 cup (170 ml/5½ fl oz) of water and, when loosely incorporated, add the cream. Whisk until smooth, add the egg yolks and combine well. Season with salt and white pepper. Beat the egg whites in a small bowl until stiff peaks form, fold into the potato mixture and gently pour into the pie crust.

5 Arrange the zucchini over the pie in a decorative pattern. Decorate with thyme and bake for 35–45 minutes, until set and golden brown. Serve hot or at room temperature.

NUTRITION PER SERVE
Protein 15 g; Fat 30 g; Carbohydrate 40 g; Dietary Fibre 3 g; Cholesterol 185 mg; 2105 kJ (500 cal)

The easiest way to line the tin with pastry is to lift the pastry over the rolling pin.

Blind bake the pastry base before filling it with the potato mixture.

Arrange the thin slices of zucchini over the pie in a decorative pattern.

CARROT AND LEEK SOY TART

Preparation time: 35 minutes +
  40 minutes chilling
Total cooking time: 1 hour 35 minutes
Serves 6–8

200 g (6½ oz) russet potatoes,
  quartered
1 tablespoon soy milk
1 cup (150 g/5 oz) wholemeal flour
½ cup (50 g/1¾ oz) soy flour
150 g (5 oz) soy spread or margarine
450 g (14 oz) carrots, diced
2 leeks (450 g/14 oz), thinly sliced
1 cup (250 ml/8 fl oz) vegetable stock
½ teaspoon sugar
1 tablespoon tomato paste
3 eggs
200 g (6½ oz) plain soy yoghurt
1 small carrot, extra
1 small leek, extra
1 tablespoon soy spread or
  margarine, extra

1 Boil the potato in salted water for 8–10 minutes, or until tender. Drain well, return to the pan, add the soy milk and season. Mash until smooth, then cool.
2 Place the flours in a bowl and rub in 100 g (3½ oz) of the soy spread until the mixture resembles fine bread-crumbs. Add the potato and bring together to form a ball. Cool, then wrap in plastic. Refrigerate for at least 30 minutes.
3 Preheat the oven to 200°C (400°F/ Gas 6). Roll out the dough to line a 23 cm (9 inch) loose-based tart tin and trim off the excess pastry. Chill for 10 minutes. Line the pastry with baking paper and fill with baking beads or rice. Bake for 15 minutes.

Remove the baking paper and beads and bake for 5 minutes, or until slightly golden. Reduce the oven to 180°C (350°F/Gas 4).
4 Melt the remaining soy spread in a saucepan. Add the carrot, leek and 2 tablespoons water and cook gently for 10 minutes, or until the liquid has evaporated. Add the stock and sugar and cook for 20 minutes, or until the vegetables are tender and all the liquid has been absorbed. Cool slightly, then add the tomato paste, eggs and yoghurt. Mix in a food processor until smooth. Season. Pour into the pastry

case and bake for 20–25 minutes, or until set and lightly golden on top.
5 Peel the extra carrot into thin ribbons with a vegetable peeler. Slice the extra leek lengthways into thin ribbons. Melt the extra soy spread in a frying pan and cook the carrot and leek for 8 minutes, or until soft. Pile in the centre of the tart and serve.

NUTRITION PER SERVE (8)
Protein 6 g; Fat 24 g; Carbohydrate 17 g; Dietary Fibre 4.5 g; Cholesterol 68 mg; 1266 kJ (302 cal)

Combine the flours and soy spread with your fingers until the mixture resembles breadcrumbs.

Bring the dough together to form a ball, then wrap and refrigerate.

Cook the carrot, leek, stock and sugar until all the liquid has been absorbed.

SPICY PUMPKIN AND CASHEW TARTS

Preparation time: 1 hour + 20 minutes refrigeration
Total cooking time: 1 hour
Serves 4

2 cups (250 g/8 oz) plain flour
100 g (3¹/₂ oz) butter, chilled and cubed
1¹/₂ tablespoons coriander seeds, lightly crushed
1 egg
2 teaspoons iced water

CASHEW NUT TOPPING
¹/₄ cup (40 g/1¹/₄ oz) roasted cashews, chopped
¹/₄ teaspoon paprika
1 teaspoon cumin seeds
1 teaspoon sesame seeds

SPICY PUMPKIN FILLING
600 g (1¹/₄ lb) butternut pumpkin
1 tablespoon oil
1 onion, thinly sliced
1 clove garlic, crushed
¹/₄ teaspoon ground cumin
¹/₄ teaspoon ground coriander
¹/₂ teaspoon garam masala
¹/₄ teaspoon chilli flakes
1 tablespoon honey
1 tablespoon soy sauce
200 g (6¹/₂ oz) ricotta cheese

1 Place the flour, butter, coriander seeds and a pinch of salt in a food processor and process for 15 seconds, or until the mixture resembles fine breadcrumbs. Add the egg and water. Process in short bursts until the mixture just comes together, adding a little more water if necessary. Turn out onto a floured surface and gather together into a ball. Wrap in plastic and refrigerate for at least 20 minutes.
2 Preheat the oven to 200°C (400°F/ Gas 6). Grease 4 shallow 11 cm (4¹/₂ inch) loose-based tart tins. Divide the pastry into quarters and roll out on baking paper to line the tins, pressing well into the base and side. Trim off the excess pastry with a sharp knife or by rolling a rolling pin over the top of the tin. Prick all over the bases with a fork and bake for 18–20 minutes, or until browned. Set aside to cool. Reduce the oven to 180°C (350°F/ Gas 4).
3 To make the cashew nut topping, mix the cashews and paprika. Place the cumin and sesame seeds in a dry frying pan and stir over low heat until lightly toasted, add to the cashew mixture and set aside to cool.
4 To make the spicy pumpkin filling, cut the pumpkin into 2.5 cm (1 inch) pieces. Heat the oil in a pan, add the pumpkin, onion, garlic and spices and cook, stirring, over medium heat, until the onion is soft and translucent. Add the honey and 2 tablespoons of water. Bring to the boil, then reduce the heat and simmer, covered, for 10–15 minutes, or until the pumpkin is tender. Stir in the soy sauce.
5 Place a quarter of the ricotta cheese into the base of each pastry shell. Spoon the spicy pumpkin filling and its liquid over the cheese and then sprinkle with the cashew nut topping. Place the tarts in the oven to reheat for 10 minutes. Serve warm.

NUTRITION PER SERVE
Protein 20 g; Fat 40 g; Carbohydrate 70 g; Dietary Fibre 6 g; Cholesterol 135 mg; 2955 kJ (705 cal)

Lightly crush the coriander seeds in a mortar and pestle.

Lift the coriander pastry into the tin, pressing into the base and sides.

Chop the roasted cashew nuts and then mix with the paprika in a bowl.

Trim off the excess pastry and then prick all over the base of the pastry case.

Lightly toast the cumin and sesame seeds in a dry frying pan.

Add the honey and water and then bring the pumpkin filling to the boil.

ROAST VEGETABLE TART

Preparation time: 30 minutes
Total cooking time: 1 hour 45 minutes
Serves 4–6

2 slender eggplants, halved and cut
   into thick slices
350 g (11 oz) pumpkin, cut into large
   pieces
2 zucchini, halved and cut into thick
   slices
1–2 tablespoons olive oil
1 large red capsicum, chopped
1 teaspoon olive oil, extra
1 red onion, cut into thin wedges
1 tablespoon Korma curry paste
plain yoghurt, to serve

PASTRY
1¹/₂ cups (185 g/6 oz) plain flour
125 g (4 oz) butter, chilled and cubed
²/₃ cup (100 g/3¹/₂ oz) roasted
   cashews, finely chopped
1 teaspoon cumin seeds
2–3 tablespoons iced water

1 Preheat the oven to 200°C (400°F/
Gas 6). Put the eggplant, pumpkin and
zucchini on a lined oven tray, then
brush with oil and bake for
30 minutes. Turn, add the capsicum
and bake for 30 minutes. Cool.
2 Meanwhile, heat the extra oil in a
frying pan and cook the onion for
2–3 minutes, or until soft. Add the
curry paste and cook, stirring, for
1 minute, or until fragrant and well
mixed. Cool. Reduce the oven to 180°C
(350°F/Gas 4).
3 To make the pastry, sift the flour
into a large bowl and add the butter.
Rub in with your fingertips until the
mixture resembles fine breadcrumbs.
Stir in the cashews and cumin seeds.
Make a well in the centre and add the
water. Mix with a flat-bladed knife,
using a cutting action, until the
mixture comes together in beads.

Gather the dough together and lift out
onto a sheet of baking paper. Flatten
to a disc, then roll out to a circle about
35 cm (14 inches) in diameter.
4 Lift onto an oven tray and spread
the onion mixture over the pastry,
leaving a 5 cm (2 inch) border.
Arrange the other vegetables over the
onion, piling them in the centre.
Working your way around, fold the
edge of the pastry in pleats over the
vegetables. Bake for 45 minutes, or
until the pastry is golden. Serve
immediately with plain yoghurt.

NUTRITION PER SERVE (6)
Protein 9 g; Fat 34 g; Carbohydrate 33 g;
Dietary Fibre 5 g; Cholesterol 54 mg;
1959 kJ (470 cal)

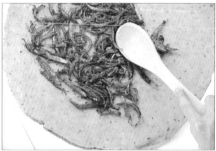
Spread the onion mixture over the pastry, leaving a clear border.

Fold the edge of the pastry over the vegetables in rough pleats.

CHICKEN TARTS WITH PUMPKIN, SPINACH AND HALOUMI

Preparation time: 20 minutes
Total cooking time: 55 minutes
Serves 4

430 g (14 oz) pumpkin, thinly sliced
3 tablespoons olive oil
2 chicken breast fillets
120 g (4 oz) haloumi cheese
1 sheet puff pastry, cut into four 12 cm
    (5 inch) squares
35 g (1 oz) baby English spinach
    leaves

1 Preheat the oven to 200°C (400°F/ Gas 6). Put the pumpkin on a baking tray and brush with 1 tablespoon oil. Season with pepper. Bake in the oven for 15–20 minutes, or until soft.
2 Heat 1 tablespoon oil in a frying pan and cook the chicken for 5 minutes on each side, or until cooked through. Cut each breast into 8 slices to give 16 pieces. Cut the haloumi into 8 slices and cut each slice in half to get 16.
3 Put the pastry squares on a lined oven tray. Lay the pieces of pumpkin over the base of the tarts, leaving a small border. Place the spinach leaves over the top, then the chicken pieces and the haloumi. Brush with the remaining oil. Bake for 25 minutes, or until the pastry is puffed and cooked and the top is golden.

NUTRITION PER SERVE
Protein 48 g; Fat 35 g; Carbohydrate 22 g;
Dietary Fibre 2 g; Cholesterol 110 mg;
2428 kJ (580 cal)

Brush the pumpkin slices with a little oil and then bake until soft.

Slice the haloumi thinly into eight pieces and then cut each piece in half.

Arrange the pumpkin slices on the bottom, then the spinach and finally the chicken and cheese.

Tartlets

These savoury tartlet recipes are simplicity itself and will provide you with ideas for very quick lunch or first course dishes. Most can be ready in under half an hour.

You can use either home-made or bought puff pastry to make any of the following tartlets. Puff pastry can be bought in frozen sheets, making the recipes even simpler. The tartlets can all be made as four individual serves or shaped into two rectangles to serve 4 people as a light meal.

You will need 500 g (1 lb) puff pastry. The pastry should be divided into two and each portion rolled out between two sheets of baking paper. If you are making four tartlets, cut out two 12 cm (5 inch) circles of pastry from each portion. If you are making two long tartlets, roll each portion of pastry into a rectangle 12 x 25 cm (5 x 10 inches). Arrange your choice of topping over the pastry, leaving a 1.5 cm (1/2 inch) clear border. The tartlets are then baked in the top half of a preheated 200°C (400°F/Gas 6) oven. The tartlets are all best served warm or hot.

TAPENADE AND ANCHOVY TARTLETS

Spread 1/2 cup (125 g/4 oz) tapenade evenly over the pastry, leaving a 1.5 cm (1/2 inch) border. Drain a 45 g (1 1/2 oz) can of anchovies, cut them into thin strips and arrange them over the top of the tapenade. Sprinkle 1/3 cup (35 g/1 1/4 oz) grated Parmesan and 1/2 cup (75 g/2 1/2 oz) grated mozzarella over the top and bake for 10 minutes, or until risen and golden.

MUSHROOM, ASPARAGUS AND FETA TARTLETS

Heat 2 tablespoons oil in a frying pan and cook 400 g (13 oz) sliced button mushrooms and 100 g (3½ oz) thin asparagus spears until softened. Remove from the heat, add 2 table-spoons chopped fresh parsley and 200 g (6½ oz) chopped feta. Spoon onto the pastry bases and bake for 10–15 minutes, until risen and brown.

FRIED GREEN TOMATO TARTLETS

Thinly slice 2 green tomatoes. Heat 1 tablespoon oil in a frying pan, add ½ teaspoon cumin and 1 crushed clove garlic and cook for 1 minute. Add the tomatoes in two batches and cook for 2–3 minutes each batch, until

slightly softened. Drain on paper towels. Mix ⅓ cup (90 g/3 oz) sour cream, 2 tablespoons chopped fresh basil and 2 tablespoons chopped fresh parsley. Sprinkle 1 cup (125 g/4 oz) grated Cheddar over the centre of the pastry bases. Arrange the tomato over the cheese and bake for 10 minutes. Place a dollop of cream mixture in the middle and sprinkle the tarts with shredded fresh basil.

SUMMER TARTLETS

Heat 2 tablespoons olive oil in a pan over low heat and cook 2 sliced red onions for 10 minutes, stirring occasionally. Add 1 tablespoon each of balsamic vinegar and soft brown sugar and cook for 10 minutes, or until soft and lightly browned. Cool and stir in 1 tablespoon chopped fresh thyme.

Spread over the pastry and bake for 10 minutes. Drain a 170 g (5½ oz) jar of quartered, marinated artichokes and arrange over the onion. Fill the spaces between with 24 pitted black olives and 6 quartered slices of prosciutto, lightly rolled. Drizzle with a little extra virgin olive oil and garnish with fresh thyme.

CHERRY TOMATO AND PESTO TARTLETS

Spread ½ cup (125 g/4 oz) pesto over the pastry. Top with about 375 g (12 oz) cherry tomatoes and 2 finely sliced spring onions. Season and bake for 10 minutes, or until golden. Drizzle with extra virgin olive oil and garnish with sliced spring onion.

TARTLETS, FROM LEFT: Tapenade and anchovy (top); Mushroom, asparagus and feta (below); Fried green tomato; Summer; Cherry tomato and pesto

Quiches

TOMATO AND THYME QUICHE

Preparation time: 35 minutes +
  30 minutes refrigeration
Total cooking time: 45 minutes
Serves 8

1¹/₂ cups (185 g/6 oz) plain flour
125 g (4 oz) butter, chilled and cubed
1 egg yolk
2–3 tablespoons iced water

FILLING
425 g (14 oz) can tomatoes
4 eggs
300 g (10 oz) sour cream
¹/₄ cup (25 g/³/₄ oz) grated Parmesan
2 spring onions, finely chopped
1–2 tablespoons chopped fresh
  thyme

1 Preheat the oven to 210°C (415°F/Gas 6–7). Sift the flour into a bowl and rub in the butter until the mixture resembles fine breadcrumbs. Add the combined egg yolk and water and mix to a soft dough. Turn out onto a lightly floured surface and gather into a ball.

Wrap in plastic and refrigerate for 30 minutes.

2 Roll out the pastry to line a shallow 23 cm (9 inch) tart tin, trimming off the excess. Cover with baking paper and spread with a layer of baking beads or rice. Bake for 10 minutes, then discard the paper and beads and cook for a further 5 minutes or until golden.

3 Drain the tomatoes and halve lengthways. Place, cut-side-down, on paper towels to drain. Beat together the eggs and sour cream and stir in the cheese and spring onion.

4 Pour the filling into the pastry shell. Arrange the tomatoes, cut-side-down, over the filling. Sprinkle with thyme and pepper. Reduce the oven to 180°C (350°F/Gas 4) and bake for 30 minutes or until the filling is set and golden.

NUTRITION PER SERVE
Protein 9 g; Fat 25 g; Carbohydrate 20 g;
Dietary Fibre 2 g; Cholesterol 105 mg;
1345 kJ (320 cal)

STORAGE: The pastry shell can be blind baked a day in advance and stored in an airtight container.

Drain the canned tomatoes and cut them in half lengthways. Put on paper towel to drain further.

Blind bake the pastry shell until it is dry and golden before pouring in the filling.

ZUCCHINI AND PROSCIUTTO QUICHE

Preparation time: 35 minutes +
    20 minutes refrigeration
Total cooking time: 1 hour 15 minutes
Serves 6

2 sheets shortcrust pastry
2 tablespoons olive oil
150 g (5 oz) prosciutto
1 onion, chopped
4 zucchini, thinly sliced
4 eggs
2/3 cup (170 ml/5½ fl oz) cream
¼ cup (60 ml/2 fl oz) milk
¼ cup (25 g/¾ oz) grated Parmesan

1 Place the two sheets of pastry together, slightly overlapping. Roll out the pastry until large enough to line a shallow 25 cm (10 inch) loose-based fluted tart tin. Trim off the excess pastry and refrigerate for 20 minutes. Preheat the oven to 200°C (400°F/ Gas 6). Cover the pastry shell with baking paper and spread with a layer of baking beads or rice. Bake for 15 minutes. Remove the paper and beads and bake for 10 minutes, or until the pastry is lightly golden. Cool on a wire rack.
2 To make the filling, heat the olive oil in a frying pan. Cut the prosciutto into thin strips and cook until it is crisp. Remove from the pan with a slotted spoon and drain on paper towels. Cook the onion until soft and remove from the pan. Cook the zucchini and, when almost cooked, season well. Remove from the heat.
3 Mix together the eggs, cream, milk and most of the Parmesan.
4 Lay the prosciutto, onion and zucchini in the pastry shell, then pour in the egg and milk mixture. Sprinkle with the remaining Parmesan. Bake for 35–40 minutes, until the filling has set and is golden.

NUTRITION PER SERVE
Protein 15 g; Fat 40 g; Carbohydrate 30 g; Dietary Fibre 2 g; Cholesterol 195 mg; 2215 kJ (525 cal)

Trim the excess pastry from the side of the tin with a sharp knife.

Remove the crisp prosciutto from the pan with a slotted spoon.

When almost cooked, season the zucchini with salt and black pepper.

SMOKED SALMON AND CAPER QUICHE

Preparation time: 25 minutes
+ 40 minutes refrigeration
Total cooking time: 1 hour 10 minutes
Serves 6–8

1¹/₂ cups (185 g/6 oz) plain flour
90 g (3 oz) butter, chilled and cubed
2 teaspoons cracked black pepper
1 egg yolk
2 tablespoons iced water

FILLING
1 tablespoon olive oil
1 small leek, chopped
¹/₂ teaspoon sugar
8 slices smoked salmon
¹/₃ cup (50 g/1³/₄ oz) frozen peas
2 tablespoons capers, chopped
75 g (2¹/₂ oz) cream cheese
2 eggs
2 teaspoons Dijon mustard
³/₄ cup (185 ml/6 fl oz) cream

1 Process the flour and butter for 15 seconds until crumbly. Add the peppercorns, egg yolk and water. Process in short bursts until the mixture comes together. Turn onto a floured surface and gather into a ball. Cover with plastic wrap and chill for 30 minutes. Preheat the oven to 200°C (400°F/Gas 6). Grease a 17 cm (7 inch) deep loose-based fluted tart tin.
2 Lay the pastry in the tin, place on a baking tray and refrigerate for 10 minutes. Prick the base with a fork and bake for 12 minutes.
3 To make the filling, heat the oil in a pan and cook the leek and sugar over low heat for 15 minutes. Cool, then spoon into the pastry. Scrunch up the salmon slices and lay around the edge. Put the peas and capers in the centre.
4 Process the cream cheese, eggs and mustard until smooth. Add the cream and pour into the pastry shell. Bake for 40 minutes, or until set.

NUTRITION PER SERVE (8)
Protein 10 g; Fat 25 g; Carbohydrate 20 g;
Dietary Fibre 2 g; Cholesterol 150 mg;
1485 kJ (355 cal)

Turn the pastry dough onto a floured surface and gather into a ball.

Prick all over the base of the pastry shell with a fork to prevent it rising up.

Scrunch up the salmon slices and arrange them around the edge of the quiche.

Process the cream cheese, eggs and mustard, then add the cream.

MUSHROOM QUICHE WITH PARSLEY PASTRY

Preparation time: 30 minutes +
  50 minutes refrigeration
Total cooking time: 1 hour
Serves 4–6

1¼ cups (155 g/5 oz) plain flour
¼ cup (15 g/½ oz) chopped fresh
  parsley
90 g (3 oz) butter, chilled and cubed
1 egg yolk
2 tablespoons iced water

FILLING
30 g (1 oz) butter
1 red onion, chopped
175 g (6 oz) button mushrooms, sliced
1 teaspoon lemon juice
⅓ cup (20 g/¾ oz) chopped fresh
  parsley
⅓ cup (20 g/¾ oz) chopped chives
1 egg, lightly beaten
⅓ cup (80 ml/2¾ oz) cream

1 Process the flour, parsley and butter for 15 seconds, or until crumbly. Add the egg yolk and water. Process in short bursts until the mixture comes together. Add a little more water if needed. Turn out onto a floured surface and gather into a ball. Cover with plastic wrap and refrigerate for at least 30 minutes.
2 Roll out the pastry between two sheets of baking paper until large enough to fit a 35 x 10 cm (14 x 4 inch) loose-based tart tin. Trim away the excess pastry. Refrigerate for 20 minutes. Preheat the oven to 190°C (375°F/Gas 5). Cover the pastry with baking paper and spread with a layer of baking beads or rice. Bake for 15 minutes. Remove the paper and

beads and bake for 10 minutes, or until the pastry is dry. Reduce the oven to 180°C (350°F/Gas 4).
3 To make the mushroom filling, melt the butter in a pan and cook the onion for 2–3 minutes until soft. Add the mushrooms and cook, stirring, for 2–3 minutes until soft. Stir in the lemon juice and herbs. Mix the egg and cream together and season.

4 Spread the mushroom filling into the pastry shell and pour over the egg and cream. Bake for 25–30 minutes, or until the filling has set.

NUTRITION PER SERVE (6)
Protein 6 g; Fat 25 g; Carbohydrate 20 g;
Dietary Fibre 2 g; Cholesterol 130 mg;
1350 kJ (320 cal)

Place the flour and parsley in a food processor and add the butter.

The easiest way to line the tin with pastry is to roll the pastry over the rolling pin to lift it.

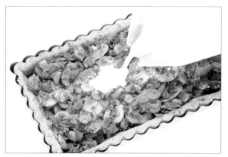

Pour the combined egg and cream over the mushroom filling.

PRAWN, CRAB AND CHEESE QUICHES

Preparation time: 45 minutes +
 30 minutes refrigeration
Total cooking time: 40 minutes
Serves 4

2 cups (250 g/8 oz) plain flour
125 g (4 oz) butter, chilled and cubed
2 egg yolks
3–4 tablespoons iced water

FILLING
170 g (5$\frac{1}{2}$ oz) can crab meat,
 drained and squeezed dry
4 spring onions, chopped
2 eggs, lightly beaten
1 cup (250 ml/8 fl oz) cream
1 cup (125 g/4 oz) finely grated
 Cheddar
2 tablespoons chopped fresh dill
1 teaspoon grated lemon rind
200 g (6$\frac{1}{2}$ oz) small prawns,
 cooked and peeled

1 Process the flour and butter for 15 seconds, or until the mixture resembles fine breadcrumbs. Add the egg yolks and water. Process in short bursts until the mixture comes together. Add a little more water if needed. Turn out onto a floured surface and gather into a ball. Cover with plastic wrap and refrigerate for at least 15 minutes.
2 Grease eight 8 cm (3 inch) loose-based tart tins. Divide the pastry into eight equal pieces and roll out until large enough to fit the tins. Trim off any excess pastry. Cover and refrigerate for 15 minutes. Preheat the oven to 190°C (375°F/Gas 5). Cover the pastry shells with baking paper and spread with a layer of baking beads or

rice. Bake for 10 minutes. Remove the paper and beads and bake for a further 10 minutes.
3 To make the filling, mix together the crab meat, spring onions, beaten eggs, cream, cheese, dill and lemon rind. Divide the prawns among the pastry shells. The crab filling will be quite

thick, so use a fork to spread it over the prawns. Bake for 15–20 minutes, or until the filling is golden brown.

NUTRITION PER SERVE
Protein 15 g; Fat 35 g; Carbohydrate 25 g;
Dietary Fibre 1 g; Cholesterol 255 mg;
1990 kJ (475 cal)

Squeeze small amounts of crab meat with your hands to get out a lot of the moisture.

Roll out the pastry until it is large enough to fit the tins, then trim away the excess.

Use a fork to help you spread the crab mixture into the pastry shells.

POTATO, LEEK AND SPINACH QUICHE

Preparation time: 1 hour + 50 minutes
  refrigeration
Total cooking time: 2 hours
Serves 6–8

2 cups (250 g/8 oz) plain flour
125 g (4 oz) butter, chilled and cubed
2–3 tablespoons iced water

FILLING
3 potatoes
30 g (1 oz) butter
2 tablespoons oil
2 cloves garlic, crushed
2 leeks, sliced
500 g (1 lb) English spinach
1 cup (125 g/4 oz) grated Cheddar
4 eggs
1/2 cup (125 ml/4 fl oz) cream
1/2 cup (125 ml/4 fl oz) milk

1 Place the flour in a food processor, add the butter and process for about 15 seconds until the mixture is crumbly. Add the water and process in short bursts until the mixture just comes together when you squeeze a little between your fingers. Add a little more water if necessary. Turn out onto a floured surface and bring together into a ball. Wrap in plastic and refrigerate for at least 30 minutes. Roll out between two sheets of baking paper until large enough to line a 21 cm (8 1/2 inch) loose-based fluted deep tart tin. Place on a baking tray and refrigerate for 20 minutes.
2 Peel and thinly slice the potatoes. Melt the butter and oil together in a frying pan; add the garlic and sliced potatoes. Gently turn the potatoes until they are coated, then cover and cook for 5 minutes over low heat. Remove the potatoes with a slotted spoon, drain on paper towels and set aside. Add the leeks to the pan and cook until they are softened, then remove from the heat. Wash the spinach and put in a large saucepan with just the water clinging to the leaves. Cover and cook for 2 minutes, or until just wilted. When cool, squeeze out the water with your hands, then spread out on paper towel or a tea towel to dry.
3 Preheat the oven to 180°C (350°F/Gas 4). Cover the pastry shell with baking paper and spread with a layer of baking beads or rice. Bake for 15 minutes. Remove the paper and beads and bake for 15 minutes.
4 Spread half the cheese over the bottom of the pastry base, top with half the potatoes, half the spinach and half the leeks. Repeat these layers again. Mix together the eggs, cream and milk and pour over the filling. Bake for 1 hour 20 minutes, or until firm. Serve warm or cold.

NUTRITION PER SERVE (8)
Protein 15 g; Fat 35 g; Carbohydrate 35 g;
Dietary Fibre 5 g; Cholesterol 180 mg;
2150 kJ (510 cal)

NOTE: Spinach can be very gritty, so wash thoroughly in a few changes of water. Squeeze out all the moisture after cooking and dry well on paper towels or a tea towel so that the water does not make the filling too moist.

Squeeze a little of the pastry with your fingers—it should stick together.

Roll the pastry out between two sheets of baking paper.

Remove the potatoes with a slotted spoon and drain on paper towels.

Cook the spinach for 2 minutes, or until it has just wilted.

Use your hands to squeeze out the excess water from the cooled spinach.

Layer half of the cheese, potato, spinach and leek over the pastry base.

TOMATO AND BACON QUICHE

Preparation time: 45 minutes + 1 hour
  refrigeration
Total cooking time: 1 hour 10 minutes
Serves 6

1½ cups (185 g/6 oz) plain flour
pinch of cayenne pepper
pinch of mustard powder
125 g (4 oz) butter, chilled and cubed
1/3 cup (40 g/1¼ oz) grated Cheddar
1 egg yolk

FILLING
25 g (3/4 oz) butter
100 g (3½ oz) lean bacon, chopped
1 small onion, finely sliced
3 eggs
3/4 cup (185 ml/6 fl oz) cream
1/2 teaspoon salt
2 tomatoes, peeled, seeded and
  chopped into chunks
3/4 cup (90 g/3 oz) grated Cheddar

1 Mix the flour, pepper, mustard and butter in a food processor until crumbly. Add the cheese and egg yolk and process in short bursts until the mixture comes together. Add 1–2 tablespoons of cold water if needed. Turn out onto a floured surface and gather into a ball. Wrap in plastic and refrigerate for 30 minutes. Grease a 23 cm (9 inch) loose-based deep tart tin.
2 To make the filling, melt the butter in a frying pan and cook the bacon for a few minutes until golden. Add the onion and cook until soft. Remove from the heat. Lightly beat the eggs, cream and salt together. Add the bacon and onion, then fold in the tomato and Cheddar.

3 Roll out the pastry on a floured surface until large enough to fit the tin. Trim the excess pastry and refrigerate for 30 minutes. Preheat the oven to 180°C (350°F/Gas 4). Cover the pastry with baking paper and spread with a layer of baking beads or rice. Bake for 10 minutes. Remove the paper and

beads and bake for 10 minutes.
4 Pour the filling into the pastry shell and bake for 35 minutes until golden.

NUTRITION PER SERVE
Protein 15 g; Fat 45 g; Carbohydrate 25 g;
Dietary Fibre 2 g; Cholesterol 255 mg;
2405 kJ (570 cal)

Remove the rind and excess fat from the bacon and chop the meat.

Cook the bacon in a little butter until golden and then add the onion.

Fold the tomato chunks and Cheddar into the egg and cream mixture.

CARAMELISED ONION QUICHE

Preparation time: 45 minutes +
  20 minutes refrigeration
Total cooking time: 1 hour 45 minutes
Serves 6

1¹/₂ cups (185 g/6 oz) plain flour
125 g (4 oz) butter, chilled and cubed
1 egg yolk
1–2 tablespoons iced water

FILLING
800 g (1 lb 10 oz) onions, thinly sliced
75 g (2¹/₂ oz) butter
1 tablespoon soft brown sugar
³/₄ cup (185 g/6 oz) sour cream
2 eggs
40 g (1¹/₄ oz) prosciutto, cut into strips
40 g (1¹/₄ oz) grated Cheddar
2 teaspoons fresh thyme leaves

1 Process the flour and butter until crumbly. Add the egg yolk and water. Process in short bursts until the mixture comes together. Add more water if needed. Turn out and gather into a ball. Wrap in plastic and refrigerate for 20 minutes.

2 Blanch the onion in boiling water for 2 minutes, then drain. Melt the butter in a pan and cook the onion over low heat for 25 minutes, or until soft. Stir in the sugar and cook for 15 minutes, stirring occasionally. Preheat the oven to 200°C (400°F/ Gas 6). Grease a 23 cm (9 inch) loose-based tart tin.

3 Roll out the pastry until large enough to fit the tin and trim off the excess. Cover with baking paper and spread with baking beads or rice. Bake for 15 minutes. Remove the paper and beads and bake for 5 minutes.

4 Lightly beat the sour cream and eggs together. Add the prosciutto, cheese and thyme. Stir in the onion. Pour into the pastry shell. Bake for 40 minutes, or until set. If the pastry starts to overbrown, cover with foil.

NUTRITION PER SERVE
Protein 10 g; Fat 45 g; Carbohydrate 30 g; Dietary Fibre 3 g; Cholesterol 230 mg; 2450 kJ (585 cal)

Add the egg yolk to the crumbly mixture of processed flour and butter.

Blanch the onion in a large saucepan filled with boiling water.

Stir the soft brown sugar through the softened onion to help it caramelise.

ARTICHOKE AND PROVOLONE QUICHES

Preparation time: 40 minutes +
    30 minutes refrigeration
Total cooking time: 35 minutes
Makes 6

2 cups (250 g/8 oz) plain flour
125 g (4 oz) butter, chilled and cubed
1 egg yolk
3 tablespoons iced water

FILLING
1 small eggplant, sliced
6 eggs, lightly beaten
3 teaspoons wholegrain mustard
150 g (5 oz) provolone cheese, grated
200 g (6¹/₂ oz) marinated artichokes,
    sliced
125 g (4 oz) semi-dried tomatoes

1 Process the flour and butter in a processor for about 15 seconds until crumbly. Add the egg yolk and water. Process in short bursts until the mixture comes together. Add a little more water if needed. Turn out onto a floured surface and gather into a ball. Wrap in plastic and refrigerate for at least 30 minutes.
2 Preheat the oven to 190°C (375°F/ Gas 5) and grease six 11 cm (4¹/₂ inch) oval pie tins.
3 To make the filling, brush the eggplant with olive oil and grill until golden. Mix together the eggs, mustard and cheese.
4 Roll out the pastry to line the tins. Trim the excess pastry and decorate the edges. Place one eggplant slice in each tin and top with artichokes and tomatoes. Pour the egg mixture over the top and bake for 25 minutes, or until golden.

NUTRITION PER QUICHE
Protein 20 g; Fat 30 g; Carbohydrate 35 g; Dietary Fibre 4 g; Cholesterol 290 mg; 2025 kJ (480 cal)

Gather the pastry into a ball and then wrap in plastic to refrigerate.

Brush each slice of eggplant with a little olive oil and then grill until golden.

Place one slice of eggplant in the bottom of each tin, then top with artichokes and tomatoes.

SEAFOOD QUICHE

Preparation time: 20 minutes +
   20 minutes refrigeration
Total cooking time: 1 hour
Serves 4–6

2 sheets shortcrust pastry

FILLING
30 g (1 oz) butter
300 g (10 oz) mixed raw seafood
   (prawns, scallops, crab meat)
3/4 cup (90 g/3 oz) grated Cheddar
3 eggs
1 tablespoon plain flour
1/4 teaspoon salt
1/2 teaspoon black pepper
1/2 cup (125 ml/4 fl oz) cream
1/2 cup (125 ml/4 fl oz) milk
1 small fennel, finely sliced
1 tablespoon grated Parmesan

1 Place the sheets of pastry slightly overlapping and roll out until large enough to fit a 23 cm (9 inch) loose-based tart tin. Trim away the excess pastry. Refrigerate for 20 minutes. Preheat the oven to 190°C (375°F/Gas 5). Cover the pastry shell with baking paper and spread with a layer of baking beads or rice. Bake for 15 minutes. Remove the paper and beads and bake for 10 minutes, or until golden. Cool on a wire rack.
2 Heat the butter in a pan and cook the seafood for 2–3 minutes. Cool, then arrange in the pastry shell. Sprinkle with Cheddar.
3 Beat the eggs together and whisk in the flour, salt, pepper, cream and milk. Pour over the seafood filling. Sprinkle the fennel and Parmesan over the top.
4 Bake for 30–35 minutes. Leave to cool slightly before serving.

NUTRITION PER SERVE (6)
Protein 20 g; Fat 35 g; Carbohydrate 30 g;
Dietary Fibre 1 g; Cholesterol 220 mg;
2190 kJ (520 cal)

Fit the pastry into the flan tin, pressing it well into the sides.

Remove the baking paper and rice from the pastry shell.

Cook the seafood in the melted butter before putting into the pastry shell.

Sprinkle the Cheddar over the top of the seafood in the pastry shell.

GREEN PEPPERCORN AND GRUYERE QUICHES

Preparation time: 25 minutes +
  15 minutes refrigeration
Total cooking time: 35 minutes
Makes 4

2 sheets puff pastry (see NOTE)
100 g (3¹/₂ oz) Gruyère cheese, diced
¹/₂ small stick celery, finely chopped
1 teaspoon chopped fresh thyme
2 teaspoons green peppercorns,
  chopped
1 egg, lightly beaten
¹/₄ cup (60 ml/2 fl oz) cream
1 tablespoon fresh rosemary

1 Lightly grease four deep 8 cm
(3 inch) loose-based tart tins. Cut two
14 cm (5¹/₂ inch) rounds from each
sheet of pastry. Lift the pastry into the
tins and press it well into the sides.
Trim the excess pastry with a sharp
knife or by rolling the rolling pin
across the top of the tin. Prick the
bases with a fork. Refrigerate for at
least 15 minutes.
2 Preheat the oven to 220°C
(425°F/Gas 7). Bake the pastry shells
for about 12 minutes, or until they are
browned and puffed. Remove from the
oven and, as the pastry is cooling,
gently press down the bases if they
have puffed too high—this will make
room for the filling.
3 To make the filling, mix together the
cheese, celery, thyme and peppercorns. Spoon into the pastry cases,
then pour over the combined egg and
cream. Sprinkle with the rosemary.
Bake for 20 minutes, or until the filling
is puffed and set.

NUTRITION PER QUICHE
Protein 15 g; Fat 35 g; Carbohydrate 30 g;
Dietary Fibre 1 g; Cholesterol 115 mg;
2045 kJ (485 cal)

NOTE: If it is available, use butterpuff
pastry for this recipe.

Chop the Gruyère cheese, celery and thyme into
small pieces.

Use a bowl or plate as a guide to help you cut
out the pastry.

Gently press down the bases of the pastry shells
if they have puffed up too high.

Sprinkle the tops of the quiches with the
fresh rosemary.

SPICY SWEET POTATO QUICHE

Preparation time: 30 minutes +
  20 minutes refrigeration
Total cooking time: 1 hour 35 minutes
Serves 6

2 cups (250 g/8 oz) plain flour
125 g (4 oz) butter, chilled and cubed
1 egg yolk
2–3 tablespoons iced water

FILLING
30 g (1 oz) butter
1 onion, sliced
1 clove garlic, crushed
2 teaspoons black mustard seeds
2 teaspoons ground cumin
1 teaspoon soft brown sugar
450 g (14 oz) orange sweet potato,
  chopped
2 eggs, lightly beaten
1/4 cup (60 ml/2 fl oz) milk
1/4 cup (60 ml/2 fl oz) cream
2 tablespoons chopped fresh parsley
2 tablespoons chopped chives

1 Process the flour and butter for about 15 seconds until crumbly. Add the egg yolk and water. Process in short bursts until the mixture comes together. Add a little more water if needed. Turn out onto a floured surface and gather into a ball. Roll the pastry between two sheets of baking paper until large enough to line a shallow 23 cm (9 inch) loose-based fluted tart tin. Trim away the excess pastry. Refrigerate for 20 minutes.
2 Heat the butter in a large pan and cook the onion and garlic for 5 minutes, or until golden. Add the mustard seeds, cumin and brown sugar and stir for 1 minute. Add the sweet potato and cook for 10 minutes over low heat until it has softened slightly. Stir gently, or the sweet potato will break up.
3 Preheat the oven to 180°C (350°F/ Gas 4). Cover the pastry shell with baking paper and spread with a layer of baking beads or rice. Bake for 15 minutes, then remove the paper and beads and bake for a further 15 minutes.

4 Put the sweet potato mixture into the pastry shell. Mix together the eggs, milk, cream and herbs and pour over the sweet potato. Bake for 50 minutes, or until set.

NUTRITION PER SERVE
Protein 10 g; Fat 30 g; Carbohydrate 45 g; Dietary Fibre 4 g; Cholesterol 140 mg; 2015 kJ (480 cal)

Peel the sweet potato and cut into bite-size chunks for the filling.

Add the mustard seeds, cumin and brown sugar to the onion and garlic.

Pour the combined eggs, milk, cream and herbs over the sweet potato mixture.

FRESH SALMON AND DILL QUICHE

Preparation time: 35 minutes +
  30 minutes refrigeration
Total cooking time: 1 hour
Serves 4–6

1¹/₂ cups (185 g/6 oz) plain flour
125 g (4 oz) butter, chilled and cubed
1 teaspoon icing sugar
1–2 tablespoons iced water

FILLING
2 eggs
1 egg yolk
1 cup (250 ml/8 fl oz) cream
1 teaspoon finely grated lemon rind
2 tablespoons finely chopped spring
  onion
500 g (1 lb) fresh salmon fillet, bones
  and skin removed and cut into
  bite-size chunks
1 tablespoon chopped fresh dill

1 Process the flour, butter and icing sugar for about 15 seconds until crumbly. Add the water. Process in short bursts until the mixture just comes together. Add a little more water if needed. Turn out onto a floured surface and gather into a ball. Wrap in plastic and refrigerate for 15 minutes.
2 Roll the pastry between two sheets of baking paper until large enough to fit a 23 cm (9 inch) loose-based tart tin. Trim away the excess pastry and refrigerate for 15 minutes. Preheat the oven to 180°C (350°F/Gas 4).
3 To make the filling, lightly beat the eggs and egg yolk. Add the cream, lemon rind and spring onion and season well. Cover and set aside.
4 Prick the base of the pastry with a

fork. Cover with baking paper and spread with a layer of baking beads or rice. Bake for 15 minutes, or until lightly golden. Remove the paper and beads and arrange the salmon over the base. Scatter with the dill and then pour in the egg mixture. Bake for 40 minutes, or until the salmon is cooked and the filling has set. Serve warm or cool.

NUTRITION PER SERVE (6)
Protein 25 g; Fat 45 g; Carbohydrate 25 g;
Dietary Fibre 1 g; Cholesterol 255 mg;
2535 kJ (605 cal)

Cut the boned and skinned salmon fillet into bite-size chunks.

Cover the pastry shell with baking paper and fill evenly with baking beads or uncooked rice.

Scatter the chopped dill over the salmon in the pastry case.

BLUE CHEESE AND PARSNIP QUICHE

Preparation time: 45 minutes +
   25 minutes refrigeration
Total cooking time: 1 hour 10 minutes
Serves 4–6

1 cup (125 g/4 oz) plain flour
1 cup (150 g/5 oz) wholemeal plain
   flour
100 g (3½ oz) butter, chilled and
   cubed
1 egg yolk
3 tablespoons iced water

FILLING
1 tablespoon oil
1 onion, chopped
2 carrots, cut into small cubes
2 parsnips, cut into small cubes
2 teaspoons cumin seeds
2 tablespoons chopped fresh
   coriander
200 g (6½ oz) mild blue cheese
2 eggs, lightly beaten
²/₃ cup (185 ml/6 fl oz) cream

1 Process the flours and butter until crumbly. Add the egg yolk and water. Process in short bursts until the mixture comes together. Add more water if needed. Turn out onto a floured surface and gather into a ball. Wrap in plastic and refrigerate for 15 minutes. Preheat the oven to 200°C (400°F/Gas 6) and put a baking tray in the oven. Grease a deep 19 cm (7½ inch) loose-based fluted tart tin.
2 Roll the pastry between two sheets of baking paper until large enough to line the tin. Trim away the excess pastry. Prick the base with a fork and refrigerate for 10 minutes. Place the tart tin on the heated baking tray and bake for 12 minutes, or until the pastry is just browned and dry. Leave to cool.
3 To make the filling, heat the oil in a pan and cook the onion, carrot, parsnip and cumin seeds, stirring, until the onion is translucent. Stir in the coriander and season to taste. Remove from the heat and cool slightly.
4 Crumble the cheese into the pastry shell, then spoon in the vegetable filling. Mix together the eggs and cream and pour over the filling. Sprinkle with pepper. Bake for 45 minutes, or until set.

NUTRITION PER SERVE (6)
Protein 15 g; Fat 45 g; Carbohydrate 40 g;
Dietary Fibre 7 g; Cholesterol 210 mg;
2560 kJ (610 cal)

Roll out the pastry until it is large enough to fit the greased tart tin.

Blind bake the pastry shell and then leave on the baking tray to cool.

Spoon the vegetable filling over the cheese in the base of the quiche.

ASPARAGUS AND PARMESAN QUICHE

Preparation time: 25 minutes +
  50 minutes refrigeration
Total cooking time: 1 hour
Serves 4

1¹/₂ cups (185 g/6 oz) plain flour
125 g (4 oz) butter, chilled and cubed
1 egg yolk
2 tablespoons iced water

ASPARAGUS FILLING
¹/₂ cup (50 g/1³/₄ oz) grated
  Parmesan
30 g (1 oz) butter
1 small red onion, chopped
2 spring onions, chopped
1 tablespoon chopped fresh dill
1 tablespoon chopped chives
1 egg, lightly beaten
¹/₄ cup (60 ml/2 fl oz) sour cream
¹/₄ cup (60 ml/2 fl oz) cream
400 g (13 oz) canned asparagus,
  drained

1 Process the flour and butter for about 15 seconds until crumbly. Add the egg yolk and water. Process in short bursts until the mixture just comes together. Add a little more water if needed. Turn out onto a floured surface and gather into a ball. Wrap in plastic and refrigerate for 30 minutes.
2 Roll the pastry between two sheets of baking paper until it is large enough to fit a 35 x 10 cm (14 x 4 inch) loose-based tart tin. Trim away the excess pastry and refrigerate for 20 minutes. Preheat the oven to 190°C (375°F/Gas 5). Cover the pastry with baking paper and spread with a layer of baking beads or rice. Bake for

15 minutes. Remove the paper and beads and bake for 10 minutes, or until the pastry is dry and golden. Cool slightly, then sprinkle with half the Parmesan. Reduce the oven to 180°C (350°F/Gas 4).
3 To make the asparagus filling, melt the butter in a pan and cook the onion and spring onion for 2–3 minutes until soft. Stir in the herbs and cool. Whisk together the egg, sour cream, cream

and remaining Parmesan and season.
4 Spread the onion mixture over the pastry, lay the asparagus spears over the top and add the egg mixture. Bake for 25–30 minutes, or until golden.

NUTRITION PER SERVE
Protein 15 g; Fat 50 g; Carbohydrate 35 g;
Dietary Fibre 4 g; Cholesterol 240 mg;
2800 kJ (665 cal)

Trim the excess pastry from the edge of the tin with a sharp knife.

Whisk together the egg, sour cream, cream and remaining Parmesan.

Arrange the asparagus decoratively over the top of the quiche.

LEEK AND HAM QUICHE WITH POLENTA PASTRY

Preparation time: 45 minutes +
  50 minutes refrigeration
Total cooking time: 1 hour 15 minutes
Serves 6

1 cup (125 g/4 oz) plain flour
1/2 cup (75 g/2 1/2 oz) polenta
90 g (3 oz) butter, chilled and cubed
90 g (3 oz) cream cheese, chilled and
  cubed

LEEK AND HAM FILLING
50 g (1 3/4 oz) butter
2 leeks, thinly sliced
2 eggs, lightly beaten
1 cup (250 ml/8 fl oz) cream
1/2 teaspoon ground nutmeg
100 g (3 1/2 oz) ham, chopped
75 g (2 1/2 oz) Swiss cheese, grated

1 Process the flour and polenta briefly to mix together. Add the butter and cream cheese and process for about 15 seconds until the mixture comes together. Add 1–2 tablespoons of water if needed. Turn out onto a floured surface and gather into a ball. Wrap in plastic wrap and refrigerate for 30 minutes.
2 To make the filling, heat the butter in a pan and cook the leeks, covered, stirring often, for 10–15 minutes, or until soft but not brown. Cool. Mix together the beaten eggs, cream and nutmeg and season with pepper.
3 Grease a shallow 21 x 28 cm (8 1/2 x 11 inch) loose-based tart tin with melted butter. Roll the pastry between two sheets of baking paper until large enough to fit the tin. Trim off any excess pastry and refrigerate for 20 minutes. Preheat the oven to

190°C (375°F/Gas 5). Cover the pastry shell with baking paper and spread with a layer of baking beads or rice. Bake for 15 minutes. Remove the paper and beads and bake for a further 15 minutes, or until the pastry is golden and dry. Reduce the oven to 180°C (350°F/Gas 4).
4 Spread the leek over the pastry shell

and sprinkle with the ham and cheese. Pour in the cream mixture. Bake for 30 minutes, or until golden and set.

NUTRITION PER SERVE
Protein 15 g; Fat 50 g; Carbohydrate 25 g; Dietary Fibre 2 g; Cholesterol 210 mg; 2495 kJ (595 cal)

Add the chopped butter and cream cheese to the flour and polenta in the processor.

Cook the leek, stirring frequently, until it is soft but not brown.

Spread the leek over the pastry shell and sprinkle with ham and Swiss cheese.

163

FETA, BASIL AND OLIVE QUICHE

Preparation time: 40 minutes +
25 minutes refrigeration
Total cooking time: 40 minutes
Serves 6

1¼ cups (150 g/5 oz) self-raising
flour, sifted
90 g (3 oz) butter, melted and cooled
¼ cup (60 ml/2 fl oz) milk

FILLING
250 g (8 oz) feta cheese, cubed
¼ cup (15 g/½ oz) fresh basil leaves,
shredded
¼ cup (30 g/1 oz) sliced black olives
3 eggs, lightly beaten
⅓ cup (80 ml/2¾ fl oz) milk
⅓ cup (90 g/3 oz) sour cream

1 Grease a 23 cm (9 inch) loose-based tart tin. Place the flour in a large bowl and make a well in the centre. Add the butter and milk and stir until the mixture comes together to form a dough. Turn out onto a floured surface and gather into a ball. Refrigerate for 5 minutes. Roll out the pastry and place in the tin, pressing it well into the sides. Trim off any excess pastry. Refrigerate for 20 minutes. Preheat the oven to 200°C (400°F/Gas 6).
2 To make the filling, spread the feta evenly over the base of the pastry and top with the shredded basil and olives.
3 Whisk the eggs, milk and sour cream until smooth, then pour into the pastry shell. Bake for 15 minutes, reduce the oven to 180°C (350°F/Gas 4) and cook for a further 25 minutes, or until the filling is firmly set. Serve at room temperature.

NUTRITION PER SERVE
Protein 15 g; Fat 35 g; Carbohydrate 20 g;
Dietary Fibre 2 g; Cholesterol 180 mg;
1750 kJ (415 cal)

Cut the feta into cubes and shred the fresh basil leaves.

Add the melted butter and milk to the well in the centre of the flour.

Sprinkle the shredded basil and sliced olives over the quiche.

ASPARAGUS AND ARTICHOKE QUICHES

Preparation time: 40 minutes +
  30 minutes refrigeration
Total cooking time: 40 minutes
Makes 6

1¼ cups (150 g/5 oz) plain flour
90 g (3 oz) butter, chilled and cubed
½ cup (60 g/2 oz) grated Cheddar
2–3 tablespoons iced water

FILLING
1 bunch (155 g/5 oz) asparagus,
  trimmed, cut into bite-size pieces
2 eggs
⅓ cup (80 ml/2¾ fl oz) cream
⅓ cup (40 g/1¼ oz) grated Gruyère
  cheese
150 g (5 oz) marinated artichoke
  hearts, quartered

1 Process the flour and butter for about 15 seconds until crumbly. Add the cheese and water. Process in short bursts until the mixture comes together. Add a little more water if needed. Turn out onto a floured surface and gather into a ball. Wrap in plastic and refrigerate for 30 minutes.
2 Preheat the oven to 190°C (375°F/ Gas 5). Grease six 8.5 cm (3¼ inch) loose-based fluted tart tins. Roll out the pastry to fit the tins, trimming off the excess. Prick the pastry bases with a fork, place on a baking tray and bake for 10–12 minutes, or until the pastry is light and golden.
3 To make the filling, blanch the asparagus pieces in boiling salted water. Drain and refresh in iced water. Lightly beat the eggs, cream and half the cheese together and season with salt and black pepper.

4 Divide the artichokes and asparagus among the pastry shells, pour the egg and cream mixture over the top and sprinkle with the remaining cheese. Bake for 25 minutes, or until the filling is set and golden. If the pastry is overbrowning, cover with foil.

NUTRITION PER QUICHE
Protein 10 g; Fat 30 g; Carbohydrate 20 g;
Dietary Fibre 2 g; Cholesterol 150 mg;
1665 kJ (395 cal)

Cut the marinated artichoke hearts into quarters.

Process in short bursts until the mixture just comes together.

Divide the artichoke and asparagus evenly among the pastry shells.

SPINACH AND RED CAPSICUM QUICHES WITH CHIVE PASTRY

Preparation time: 40 minutes +
   45 minutes refrigeration
Total cooking time: 1 hour
Makes 4

1³/₄ cups (215 g/7 oz) plain flour
2 tablespoons chopped chives
125 g (4 oz) butter, chilled and cubed
1 egg yolk
3 tablespoons iced water

FILLING
1 bunch (500 g/1 lb) English spinach
30 g (1 oz) butter
6 spring onions, finely sliced
1–2 cloves garlic, finely chopped
1 small red capsicum, finely chopped
2 eggs, lightly beaten
1 cup (250 ml/8 fl oz) cream
100 g (3¹/₂ oz) firm Camembert or
   Brie, cut into 8 slices

1 Place the flour and chives in a food processor, add the butter and process for about 15 seconds until the mixture is crumbly. Add the egg yolk and water. Process in short bursts until the mixture just comes together. Add a little more water if necessary. Turn out onto a floured surface and gather into a ball. Wrap in plastic and refrigerate for at least 30 minutes.
2 To make the filling, wash the spinach thoroughly and put in a pan with just the water clinging to the leaves. Cover and cook for 5 minutes, or until wilted. Drain and allow to cool. Using your hands, squeeze as much moisture from the spinach as possible. Chop roughly.

3 Heat the butter in a pan and cook the spring onion, garlic and capsicum for 5–7 minutes, stirring frequently. Stir in the spinach and cool. Combine the eggs and cream and season well.
4 Grease four 11 cm (4¹/₂ inch) loose-based fluted tart tins. Divide the pastry into four and roll out to fit the tins. Trim the excess pastry, cover the tins and refrigerate for 15 minutes. Preheat the oven to 190°C (375°F/Gas 5). Cover the pastry shells with baking paper and spread with a layer of baking beads or rice. Bake for 10 minutes. Remove the paper and beads and bake for a further 10 minutes.
5 Divide the spinach filling evenly among the pastry shells. Pour the combined cream and egg mixture over the filling. Place 2 slices of the cheese on top of each quiche. Bake for 25–30 minutes, or until the filling is golden brown and set.

NUTRITION PER QUICHE
Protein 15 g; Fat 45 g; Carbohydrate 30 g;
Dietary Fibre 4 g; Cholesterol 230 mg;
2440 kJ (580 cal)

VARIATION: You can replace the Camembert or Brie with mature Cheddar, mozzarella or fontina (a semi-firm, creamy cheese).

Use a large, sharp knife to finely chop the spring onions and garlic.

Cut the firm Camembert or Brie into 8 slices—two per quiche.

Turn the dough out onto a floured surface and gather into a ball.

Using your hands to squeeze as much moisture from the spinach as possible.

Cook the spring onion, garlic and capsicum, stirring frequently.

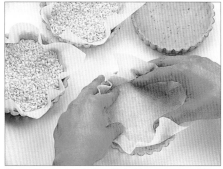

Cover the pastry shells with baking paper and fill evenly with rice.

MEDITERRANEAN QUICHE

Preparation time: 50 minutes +
 15 minutes refrigeration
Total cooking time: 1 hour 25 minutes
Serves 6–8

2 sheets shortcrust pastry
3 tablespoons olive oil
2 cloves garlic, crushed
1 onion, diced
1 small fresh chilli, seeded and finely
 chopped
1 red capsicum, chopped into
 bite-size pieces
1 yellow capsicum, chopped into
 bite-size pieces
400 g (13 oz) can tomatoes, drained
 and chopped
2 tablespoons chopped fresh oregano
4 eggs, lightly beaten
1/3 cup (35 g/1 1/4 oz) grated
 Parmesan

1 Grease a 23 cm (9 inch) loose-based fluted tart tin. Place the sheets of pastry so that they are slightly overlapping and roll out until large enough to fit the tin. Press well into the sides and trim off the excess pastry. Cover and refrigerate for 15 minutes. Preheat the oven to 190°C (375°F/Gas 5). Cover the pastry shell with baking paper and spread with a layer of baking beads or rice. Bake for 10 minutes. Remove the paper and beads and bake for 10 minutes, or until golden. Cool on a wire rack.
2 Heat the oil and fry the garlic and onion until soft. Add the chilli, red and yellow capsicum and cook for 6 minutes. Stir in the tomatoes and oregano and simmer, covered, for 10 minutes. Remove the lid and cook until the liquid has evaporated. Remove from the heat and cool.
3 Stir the eggs and Parmesan into the tomato mixture and spoon into the pastry shell. Bake for 35–45 minutes, or until the filling has set.

NUTRITION PER SERVE (8)
Protein 9 g; Fat 25 g; Carbohydrate 20 g;
Dietary Fibre 2 g; Cholesterol 105 mg;
1345 kJ (320 cal)

Lift out the baking paper and beads or rice and bake the pastry again without them.

Add the finely chopped chilli and cubed red and yellow capsicum.

Cook the vegetable filling until all the liquid has evaporated. Leave to cool.

Spoon the tomato and capsicum filling into the baked pastry case.

MUSTARD CHICKEN AND ASPARAGUS QUICHE

Preparation time: 25 minutes +
　40 minutes refrigeration
Total cooking time: 1 hour 20 minutes
Serves 8

2 cups (250 g/8 oz) plain flour
100 g (3¹/₂ oz) butter, chilled and
　cubed
1 egg yolk
3 tablespoons iced water

FILLING
150 g (5 oz) asparagus, chopped
25 g (³/₄ oz) butter
1 onion, chopped
¹/₄ cup (60 g/2 oz) wholegrain
　mustard
200 g (6¹/₂ oz) soft cream cheese
¹/₂ cup (125 ml/4 fl oz) cream
3 eggs, lightly beaten
200 g (6¹/₂ oz) cooked chicken,
　chopped
¹/₂ teaspoon black pepper

1 Process the flour and butter until crumbly. Add the egg yolk and water. Process in short bursts until the mixture comes together. Add a little more water if needed. Turn onto a floured surface and gather into a ball. Wrap in plastic and refrigerate for 30 minutes. Grease a deep 19 cm (7¹/₂ inch) loose-based tart tin.
2 Roll out the pastry and line the tin. Trim off any excess. Place the tin on a baking tray and chill for 10 minutes. Preheat the oven to 200°C (400°F/ Gas 6). Cover the pastry with baking paper and spread with a layer of baking beads or rice. Bake for 10 minutes. Remove the paper and beads and bake for 10 minutes, until

the pastry is lightly browned and dry. Cool. Reduce the oven to 180°C (350°F/Gas 4).
3 To make the filling, boil or steam the asparagus until tender. Drain and pat dry with paper towels. Heat the butter in a pan and cook the onion until translucent. Remove from the heat and add the mustard and cream cheese, stirring until the cheese has melted. Cool. Add the cream, eggs,

chicken and asparagus and mix well.
4 Spoon the filling into the pastry shell and sprinkle with the pepper. Bake for 50 minutes–1 hour, or until puffed and set. Cool for at least 15 minutes before cutting.

NUTRITION PER SERVE
Protein 15 g; Fat 30 g; Carbohydrate 25 g; Dietary Fibre 2 g; Cholesterol 190 mg; 1860 kJ (440 cal)

When the mixture is crumbly add the egg yolk and enough iced water to bring it together.

Dry the asparagus well to avoid excess moisture in the filling.

Add the mustard and cream cheese and stir until the cheese has melted.

HAM AND CORN PARTY QUICHES

Preparation time: 25 minutes
Total cooking time: 25 minutes
Makes 30

20 g (3/4 oz) butter
4 spring onions, finely chopped
100 g (3 1/2 oz) leg ham, cut into thin strips
270 g (9 oz) can corn kernels, drained
2 eggs, lightly beaten
2 tablespoons chopped chives

1/2 cup (125 ml/4 fl oz) cream
1/2 cup (125 ml/4 fl oz) milk
10 sheets filo pastry
oil or melted butter, for brushing

1 Preheat the oven to 200°C (400°F/ Gas 6). Melt the butter in a pan and cook the spring onion for 2 minutes, or until soft. Transfer to a bowl and add the ham, corn, egg and chives. Mix the cream and milk and stir into the onion mixture.
2 Work with 5 sheets of pastry at a time, keeping the rest covered with baking paper and a damp tea towel.

Brush each sheet of pastry with oil or melted butter and pile them up into a stack. Using an 8 cm (3 inch) round cutter, cut 15 circles from the stack.
3 Put the pastry circles in greased shallow 6 cm (2 1/2 inch) round patty tins. Fill each circle of pastry with a tablespoon of filling. Repeat with the remaining sheets of filo. Bake for 15–20 minutes, or until golden.

NUTRITION PER QUICHE
Protein 2 g; Fat 4 g; Carbohydrate 4 g;
Dietary Fibre 0 g; Cholesterol 20 mg;
255 kJ (60 cal)

Stir the combined cream and milk into the spring onion and ham mixture.

Cover the pastry with baking paper and a damp tea towel to prevent it drying out.

Fill each circle of layered filo pastry with a tablespoon of filling.

FRESH HERB QUICHE

Preparation time: 30 minutes +
  50 minutes refrigeration
Total cooking time: 1 hour
Serves 4–6

1¹/₂ cups (185 g/6 oz) plain flour
¹/₄ cup (15 g/¹/₂ oz) chopped fresh
  parsley
125 g (4 oz) butter, chilled and cubed
1 egg yolk
1 tablespoon iced water

FILLING
30 g (1 oz) butter
1 small leek, thinly sliced
1–2 cloves garlic, crushed
4 spring onions, chopped
¹/₄ cup (15 g/¹/₂ oz) chopped fresh
  parsley
2 tablespoons chopped chives
2 tablespoons chopped fresh dill
2 tablespoons fresh oregano leaves
3 eggs
1 cup (250 ml/8 fl oz) cream
¹/₄ cup (60 ml/2 fl oz) milk
1 cup (125 g/4 oz) grated Cheddar

1 Process the flour, parsley and butter until crumbly. Add the egg yolk and water. Process in short bursts until the mixture comes together. Add a little extra water if needed. Turn out onto a floured surface and gather into a ball. Wrap in plastic and refrigerate for 30 minutes.

2 Grease a 24 cm (9¹/₂ inch) loose-based tart tin. Roll out the pastry, line the tin and trim off any excess. Chill the lined tin for 20 minutes. Preheat the oven to 190°C (375°F/Gas 5). Cover the pastry with baking paper and spread with a layer of baking beads or rice. Bake for 15 minutes. Remove the paper and beads and bake for a further 10 minutes. Reduce the oven to 180°C (350°F/Gas 4).

3 To make the filling, heat the butter in a pan. Cook the leek, garlic and spring onion for 10 minutes, stirring often. Add the herbs and cool.

4 Beat the eggs, cream and milk and season with pepper. Spread the leek and herb mixture in the pastry base. Pour over the egg mixture and sprinkle with the Cheddar. Bake for 25–30 minutes, or until golden.

NUTRITION PER SERVE (6)
Protein 15 g; Fat 45 g; Carbohydrate 25 g;
Dietary Fibre 2 g; Cholesterol 220 mg;
2300 kJ (545 cal)

When the mixture is crumbly, add the egg yolk and iced water.

When the leek is cooked, stir through the fresh herbs.

Pour the mixed egg and cream over the filling and then sprinkle with Cheddar cheese.

MINI SALMON AND CAMEMBERT QUICHES

Preparation time: 30 minutes + 1 hour
  refrigeration + cooling
Total cooking time: 30 minutes
Makes 24

2 cups (250 g/8 oz) plain flour
150 g (5 oz) butter, chilled and cubed
2 egg yolks, lightly beaten
1/2 teaspoon paprika
1 teaspoon iced water

FILLING
1 tablespoon olive oil
2 small leeks, finely sliced
75 g smoked salmon, thinly sliced
80 g Camembert, chopped
2 eggs, lightly beaten
1/2 cup (125 ml/4 fl oz) cream
2 teaspoons grated lemon rind
1 teaspoon chopped fresh dill
1 tablespoon finely chopped
    fresh chives, for serving

1 Sift the flour into a large bowl and rub in the butter with your fingertips until the mixture resembles fine breadcrumbs. Make a well, add the egg, paprika and water and mix with a flat-bladed knife until the mixture comes together in beads. Turn out onto a lightly floured work surface and gather together into a ball. Wrap in plastic and refrigerate for 30 minutes.
2 Grease two 12-hole patty tins. Divide the pastry into four pieces. Roll each between two sheets of baking paper to 2 mm (1/8 inch) thick. Cut 24 rounds with a 7 cm (2 3/4 inch) fluted cutter. Lift into the patty tins, pressing into shape but being careful not to stretch the pastry. Refrigerate for 30 minutes.

3 Preheat the oven to 180°C (350°F/ Gas 4). Bake the pastry for 5 minutes, or until lightly golden. If the pastry has puffed up, press down lightly with a tea towel.
4 For the filling, heat the oil in a frying pan and cook the leek for 2–3 minutes, or until soft. Remove from the pan and cool. Divide the leek, smoked salmon and Camembert pieces evenly among the pastry cases.
5 Whisk the eggs, cream, lemon rind and dill together and pour into the pastry cases. Bake for 15–20 minutes, or until lightly golden and set. Serve sprinkled with chives.

NUTRITION PER QUICHE
Protein 3.5 g; Fat 10 g; Carbohydrate 8 g; Dietary Fibre 0.5 g; Cholesterol 57.5 mg; 570 kJ (135 cal)

NOTE: You can substitute crab meat or small prawns for the salmon.

Cut the rounds and lift into the patty tins, gently pressing into shape.

Bake the pastry rounds for 5 minutes, or until lightly golden.

Pour some of the egg, cream, lemon rind and dill mixture into each pastry case.

BLUE CHEESE AND ONION QUICHE

Preparation time: 40 minutes +
  20 minutes refrigeration
Total cooking time: 1 hour 40 minutes
Serves 8

2 tablespoons olive oil
1 kg (2 lb) red onions, very thinly sliced
1 teaspoon soft brown sugar
2 cups (250 g/8 oz) plain flour
100 g (3½ oz) butter, chilled and
    cubed
1–2 tablespoons iced water
¾ cup (185 ml/6 fl oz) cream
3 eggs
100 g (3½ oz) blue cheese, crumbled
1 teaspoon chopped fresh thyme

1 Heat the oil in a pan over low heat and cook the onion and sugar, stirring regularly, for 45 minutes, or until the onion is soft and lightly golden.
2 Process the flour and butter in a food processor for 15 seconds or until crumbly. Add the water and process in short bursts until the mixture just comes together. Turn out onto a floured surface and gather into a ball. Wrap in plastic and refrigerate for 10 minutes.
3 Preheat the oven to 180°C (350°F/ Gas 4). Roll out the pastry thinly on a lightly floured surface to fit a greased 22 cm (8¾ inch) loose-based tart tin. Trim away the excess pastry. Chill for 10 minutes. Line the pastry with baking paper and spread with a layer of baking beads or rice. Put on a baking tray and bake for 10 minutes. Remove the paper and beads, then bake for 10 minutes, or until lightly golden and dry.
4 Cool, then gently spread the onion in the pastry shell. Whisk together the cream, eggs, blue cheese, thyme and pepper to taste. Pour into the base and bake for 35 minutes, or until firm.

NUTRITION PER SERVE
Protein 9 g; Fat 30 g; Carbohydrate 25 g;
Dietary Fibre 1.5 g; Cholesterol 145 mg;
1718 kJ (410 cal)

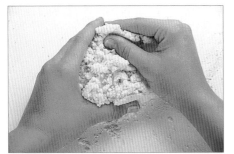
Turn the dough out onto a lightly floured surface and gather into a ball.

Roll the pastry out thinly and line the greased tart tin, trimming away any excess.

Spread the onion over the cooled pastry base, then pour in the cream mixture.

LOW-FAT ROAST VEGETABLE QUICHE

Preparation time: 45 minutes +
  25 minutes refrigeration
Total cooking time: 2 hours 30 minutes
Serves 6

1 large potato
400 g (13 oz) pumpkin
200 g (6½ oz) orange sweet potato
2 large parsnips
1 red capsicum
2 onions, cut into wedges
6 cloves garlic, halved
2 teaspoons olive oil
1¼ cups (150 g/5 oz) plain flour
40 g (1¼ oz) butter, chilled and cubed
45 g (1½ oz) ricotta
1 cup (250 ml/8 fl oz) skim milk
3 eggs, lightly beaten
¼ cup (30 g/1 oz) grated reduced-fat
  Cheddar
2 tablespoons chopped fresh basil

1 Preheat the oven to 180°C (350°F/ Gas 4). Lightly grease a 23 cm (9 inch) loose-based tart tin. Cut the potato, pumpkin, sweet potato, parsnips and capsicum into bite-size chunks, place in a baking dish with the onion and garlic and drizzle with the oil. Season and bake for 1 hour, or until tender. Leave to cool.
2 Mix the flour, butter and ricotta in a food processor until crumbly, then gradually add up to 3 tablespoons of the milk—enough to form a soft dough. Turn out onto a lightly floured surface and gather into a smooth ball. Cover and refrigerate for 15 minutes.
3 Roll the pastry out on a lightly floured surface, then ease into the tin, bringing it gently up the side. Trim the edge and refrigerate for another

10 minutes. Increase the oven to 200°C (400°F/Gas 6). Cover the pastry with baking paper and spread with a layer of baking beads or rice. Bake for 10 minutes, remove the paper and beads and bake for 10 minutes, or until golden brown and dry.
4 Place the vegetables in the pastry base and pour in the combined remaining milk, eggs, cheese and basil. Reduce the oven to 180°C

(350°F/Gas 4) and bake for 1 hour 10 minutes, or until set in the centre. Leave for 5 minutes before removing from the tin to serve.

NUTRITION PER SERVE
Protein 15 g; Fat 10 g; Carbohydrate 45 g; Dietary Fibre 5.5 g; Cholesterol 115 mg; 1440 kJ (345 cal)

Put the vegetables in a baking dish and drizzle with the olive oil.

Ease the pastry into the tart tin, bring it up the side and then trim the edge.

Mix the milk, eggs, cheese and basil and pour over the vegetables.

QUICHE LORRAINE

Preparation time: 35 minutes +
 35 minutes refrigeration
Total cooking time: 1 hour 5 minutes
Serves 4–6

1¹/₂ cups (185 g/6 oz) plain flour
90 g (3 oz) butter, chilled and cubed
1 egg yolk
2–3 tablespoons iced water

FILLING
20 g (³/₄ oz) butter
1 onion, chopped
4 rashers bacon, cut into thin strips
2 tablespoons chopped chives
2 eggs
³/₄ cup (185 ml/6 fl oz) cream
¹/₄ cup (60 ml/2 fl oz) milk
100 g (3¹/₂ oz) Swiss cheese, grated

1 Mix the flour and butter in a food processor for 15 seconds, or until crumbly. Add the egg yolk and water. Process in short bursts until the mixture just comes together. Add a little more water if needed. Turn out onto a floured surface and gather together into a ball. Wrap the dough in plastic and refrigerate for at least 15 minutes.

2 Roll the pastry between two sheets of baking paper until large enough to line a shallow 25 cm (10 inch) loose-based tart tin. Press well into the side of the tin and trim off any excess pastry. Refrigerate the pastry-lined tin for 20 minutes. Preheat the oven to 190°C (375°F/Gas 5).

3 Cover the pastry shell with baking paper, spread with a layer of baking beads or rice and bake for 15 minutes. Remove the paper and beads and bake the pastry shell for 10 minutes, or until the pastry is golden and dry. Reduce the oven temperature to 180°C (350°F/Gas 4).

4 To make the filling, heat the butter in a pan. Add the onion and bacon and cook for 10 minutes, stirring frequently, until the onion is soft and the bacon is cooked. Stir through the chives and leave to cool.

5 Beat together the eggs, cream and milk. Season with pepper. Spread the onion and bacon filling evenly into the pastry shell. Pour the egg mixture over the top and sprinkle with the cheese. Bake for 30 minutes, or until the filling is set and golden.

NUTRITION PER SERVE (6)
Protein 15 g; Fat 40 g; Carbohydrate 25 g;
Dietary Fibre 2 g; Cholesterol 210 mg;
2185 kJ (520 cal)

Roll out the pastry between two sheets of baking paper so it doesn't stick.

Pour the egg mixture over the onion and bacon in the base of the pastry shell.

MINI PUMPKIN AND CURRY QUICHES

Preparation time: 30 minutes +
    30 minutes refrigeration
Total cooking time: 40 minutes
Makes 8

1½ cups (185 g/6 oz) plain flour
125 g (4 oz) cream cheese, chilled and
    cubed
125 g (4 oz) butter, chilled and cubed

FILLING
1 tablespoon oil
2 onions, finely chopped
3 cloves garlic, crushed
1 teaspoon curry powder
3 eggs
½ cup thick cream
350 g (11 oz) pumpkin, cooked and
    mashed
2 teaspoons cumin seeds

1 Preheat the oven to 210°C (415°F/ Gas 6–7). Sift the flour into a bowl and rub in the cream cheese and butter until the mixture becomes crumbly, then gather into a ball.
2 Wrap the dough in plastic and refrigerate for 30 minutes. Grease 8 deep 10 cm (4 inch) tart tins. Roll out the pastry to line the tins and trim away the excess. Bake for 15 minutes or until lightly browned. Reduce the oven to 180°C (350°F/Gas 4).
3 Heat the oil in a pan and cook the onion and garlic over low heat for 5 minutes, or until soft. Add the curry powder and stir for 1 minute. Spread into the pastry bases.
4 Mix together the eggs, cream and pumpkin and beat well. Pour into the pastry cases and sprinkle with cumin seeds. Bake for 20 minutes or until the filling has set.

NUTRITION PER QUICHE
Protein 8 g; Fat 30 g; Carbohydrate 23 g; Dietary Fibre 2 g; Cholesterol 145 mg; 1620 kJ (390 cal)

STORAGE: These quiches can be cooked a day in advance and reheated in a moderate oven for 15 minutes.

Rub the butter and cream cheese into the flour and then gather into a ball.

Roll out the cream cheese pastry and use to line the deep flan tins.

Cook the onion and garlic until soft and then stir in the curry powder.

Pour the pumpkin filling over the onion in the pastry shells and sprinkle with cumin seeds.

SALAMI AND PESTO QUICHE

Preparation time: 35 minutes +
  30 minutes refrigeration
Total cooking time: 45 minutes
Serves 6

1 cup (125 g/4 oz) plain flour
90 g (3 oz) butter, chilled and cubed
1–2 tablespoons iced water

FILLING
2 tablespoons pesto
250 g (8 oz) mascarpone cheese
3 eggs

4 slices salami, finely chopped
2 tablespoons grated Parmesan

1 Preheat the oven to 210°C (415°F/
Gas 6–7). Sift the flour into a bowl and
rub in the butter with your fingertips
until the mixture resembles fine
breadcrumbs. Add the water and mix
with a flat-bladed knife until the
dough starts to come together. Turn
onto a lightly floured surface and
gather into a ball. Wrap in plastic and
refrigerate for 30 minutes.
2 Roll out the pastry between two
sheets of baking paper until large
enough to line a shallow 23 cm
(9 inch) tart tin. Line with baking

paper and spread with a layer of
baking beads or rice. Bake for
10 minutes, then remove the paper
and beads. Bake for another 5 minutes
or until lightly golden and dry. Reduce
the oven to 180°C (350°F/Gas 4).
3 Spread the pastry base with pesto.
Whisk together the mascarpone and
eggs until smooth and then pour over
the pesto. Scatter with salami and
sprinkle with cheese. Bake for
30 minutes or until set and golden.

NUTRITION PER SERVE
Protein 15 g; Fat 38 g; Carbohydrate 20 g;
Dietary Fibre 1 g; Cholesterol 190 mg;
2040 kJ (485 cal)

Mix in the water with a flat-bladed knife until the dough just starts to come together.

Blind bake the pastry base with a sheet of baking paper and a layer of baking beads or rice.

Pour the mascarpone and egg mixture over the pesto and then sprinkle with salami.

LEEK AND ROCKET QUICHE

Preparation time: 30 minutes +
   30 minutes refrigeration
Total cooking time: 1 hour
Serves 6

1½ cups (185 g/6 oz) plain flour
125 g (4 oz) butter, chilled and cubed
1–2 tablespoons iced water

FILLING
1 tablespoon oil
1 large leek, thinly sliced
2 cloves garlic, crushed
150 g (5 oz) rocket, finely sliced
2 eggs
½ cup (125 ml/4 fl oz) milk
½ cup (125 ml/4 fl oz) cream

1 Preheat the oven to 210°C (415°F/ Gas 6–7). Sift the flour into a bowl and rub in the butter with your fingertips until the mixture resembles fine breadcrumbs. Add the water and mix with a flat-bladed knife until the dough starts to come together. Turn onto a lightly floured surface and gather into a ball. Wrap in plastic and refrigerate for 30 minutes.
2 Roll out the pastry between two sheets of baking paper until large enough to line a shallow 23 cm (9 inch) tart tin. Line with baking paper and spread with a layer of baking beads or rice. Bake for 10 minutes, then remove the paper and beads. Bake for another 5 minutes or until lightly golden and dry. Reduce the oven to 180°C (350°F/Gas 4).
3 Heat the oil in a frying pan and cook the leek and garlic, stirring, over low heat for 5 minutes or until soft. Add the rocket and stir for 1 minute. Remove from the heat and leave to cool. Spread over the pastry shell. Whisk together the eggs, milk and cream and pour into the pastry shell. Bake for 50 minutes or until set.

NUTRITION PER SERVE
Protein 12 g; Fat 45 g; Carbohydrate 55 g;
Dietary Fibre 2 g; Cholesterol 150 mg;
1700 kJ (600 cal)

Wash the rocket and trim away the stems, then finely slice the leaves for the filling.

Turn out the dough onto a lightly floured surface and then gather into a ball.

Blind bake the pastry shell with a lining of baking paper and baking beads or rice.

Cook the leek and garlic, stirring, over low heat until the leek is soft.

CORN AND BACON CRUSTLESS QUICHES

Preparation time: 30 minutes
Total cooking time: 40 minutes
Makes 4

4 corn cobs
2 teaspoons olive oil
2 rashers bacon, cut into thin strips
1 small onion, finely chopped
3 eggs, lightly beaten
2 tablespoons chopped chives

2 tablespoons chopped fresh parsley
3/4 cup (60 g/2 oz) fresh white breadcrumbs
1/3 cup (80 ml/2³/4 fl oz) cream

1 Preheat the oven to 180°C (350°F/Gas 4). Lightly grease four 3/4 cup (185 ml/6 fl oz) ramekins. Remove the husks from the corn and, using a coarse grater, grate the corn kernels into a deep bowl—there should be about 1¹/2 cups corn flesh and juice.
2 Heat the oil in a pan and cook the bacon and onion for 3–4 minutes, or until the onion softens. Transfer to a bowl. Stir in the corn, eggs, chives, parsley, breadcrumbs and cream and season well. Spoon into the ramekins.
3 Put the ramekins in a large baking dish. Add enough hot water to come halfway up the sides of the ramekins. Lay foil loosely over the top. Bake for 25–30 minutes or until just set.

NUTRITION PER QUICHE
Protein 13 g; Fat 17 g; Carbohydrate 23 g; Dietary Fibre 3 g; Cholesterol 175 mg; 1230 kJ (295 cal)

Using the coarse side of the grater, grate the corn kernels into a bowl.

Mix together the cooked onion, bacon, corn, eggs, chives, parsley, breadcrumbs and cream.

Cook the quiches in a *bain-marie*, made by pouring water into a large baking dish.

OYSTER AND NUTMEG QUICHE

Preparation time: 20 minutes +
  20 minutes refrigeration
Total cooking time: 1 hour
Serves 4

1 sheet shortcrust pastry
2 eggs
2 teaspoons plain flour
1/4 teaspoon grated nutmeg
2 tablespoons cream
2 tablespoons milk
1/2 cup (65 g/2 1/4 oz) grated Gruyère
  cheese
1 dozen fresh oysters, shucked
20 g (3/4 oz) Parmesan, shaved

1 Use the pastry to line a shallow 19 cm (7 1/2 inch) loose-based tart tin, trimming away the excess. Refrigerate for 20 minutes. Preheat the oven to 180°C (350°F/Gas 4). Cover the pastry shell with baking paper and spread with a layer of baking beads or rice. Bake for 10 minutes. Remove the paper and beads and bake for a further 5 minutes, or until the pastry is lightly golden. Cool on a wire rack.
2 Beat the eggs, then whisk in the flour, nutmeg, cream, milk and a pinch of salt. Stir in the cheese and pour into the pastry shell.
3 Arrange the oysters in the pastry shell. Sprinkle with Parmesan and bake for 40–45 minutes. Cool slightly before serving.

NUTRITION PER SERVE
Protein 15 g; Fat 25 g; Carbohydrate 15 g;
Dietary Fibre 1 g; Cholesterol 150 mg;
1415 kJ (335 cal)

Cover the pastry shell with baking paper and fill evenly with baking beads.

Whisk the flour, nutmeg, cream, milk and salt into the beaten eggs.

Arrange the shucked oysters in the pastry base and then sprinkle with Parmesan.

ROASTED PUMPKIN AND SPINACH QUICHE

Preparation time: 20 minutes
Total cooking time: 1 hour 50 minutes
Serves 6

500 g (1 lb) butternut pumpkin
1 red onion, cut into small wedges
2 tablespoons olive oil
1 clove garlic, crushed
1 teaspoon salt
4 eggs
$^1/_2$ cup (125 ml/4 fl oz) cream
$^1/_2$ cup (125 ml/4 fl oz) milk
1 tablespoon chopped fresh parsley
1 tablespoon chopped fresh coriander
1 teaspoon wholegrain mustard
6 sheets filo pastry
50 g (1$^3/_4$ oz) English spinach,
    blanched
1 tablespoon grated Parmesan

1 Preheat the oven to 190°C (375°F/ Gas 5). Slice the pumpkin into 1 cm ($^1/_2$ inch) pieces, leaving the skin on. Place the pumpkin, onion, 1 table-spoon of the olive oil, garlic and salt in a baking dish. Roast for 1 hour, or until lightly golden and cooked.
2 Whisk together the eggs, cream, milk, herbs and mustard. Season with salt and pepper.
3 Grease a 23 cm (9 inch) loose-based fluted tart tin. Brush each sheet of filo pastry with oil and then line the flan tin with the six sheets. Fold the sides down, tucking them into the tin to form a crust.
4 Heat a baking tray in the oven for 10 minutes. Place the tart tin on the tray and arrange all the vegetables over the base. Pour the egg mixture over the vegetables and sprinkle with the Parmesan.
5 Bake for 35–40 minutes, or until the filling is golden brown and set.

NUTRITION PER SERVE
Protein 10 g; Fat 20 g; Carbohydrate 15 g; Dietary Fibre 2 g; Cholesterol 155 mg; 1200 kJ (285 cal)

Roast the pumpkin and red onion until lightly golden and cooked.

Brush the filo pastry with oil and then arrange in the tin.

Fold the sides of the filo pastry down and tuck them into the tin to form a crust.

Pour the egg and cream mixture over the roast vegetables in the lined tart tin.

SALMON AND SPRING ONION QUICHE

Preparation time: 20 minutes +
   20 minutes refrigeration
Total cooking time: 1 hour
Serves 6

2 cups (250 g/8 oz) self-raising flour
150 g (5 oz) butter, melted
1/2 cup (125 ml/4 fl oz) milk

FILLING
425 g (14 oz) can red salmon, drained
   and flaked
4 spring onions, sliced

1/3 cup (20 g/3/4 oz) chopped fresh
   parsley
4 eggs, lightly beaten
1/2 cup (125 ml/4 fl oz) milk
1/2 cup (125 ml/4 fl oz) cream
1/2 cup (60 g/2 oz) grated Cheddar

1 Grease a 26 cm (10 1/2 inch) loose-based fluted tart tin. Sift the flour into a large bowl and make a well in the centre. Pour in the melted butter and milk and mix until the mixture comes together and forms a dough. Refrigerate for 20 minutes. Preheat the oven to 200°C (400°F/Gas 6). Roll out the pastry and line the tin, trimming away the excess.

2 Cover the pastry with baking paper and spread with a layer of baking beads or rice. Bake for 15 minutes. Remove the paper and beads and bake for 10 minutes. Cool. Reduce the oven to 180°C (350°F/Gas 4).

3 Place the salmon in the pastry shell. Mix together the spring onions, parsley, eggs, milk, cream and cheese and pour into the pastry shell. Bake for 30 minutes, or until set.

NUTRITION PER SERVE
Protein 20 g; Fat 35 g; Carbohydrate 20 g;
Dietary Fibre 1 g; Cholesterol 210 mg;
1985 kJ (470 cal)

Break the drained canned red salmon into flakes with a fork.

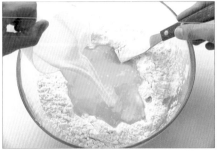

Pour the melted butter and milk into the well in the sifted flour.

Mix together the spring onions, parsley, eggs, milk, cream and cheese.

EGGPLANT AND SUN-DRIED CAPSICUM QUICHES

Preparation time: 30 minutes +
  45 minutes refrigeration
Total cooking time: 1 hour
Makes 6

1¹/2 cups (185 g/6 oz) plain flour
125 g (4 oz) butter, chilled and cubed
1 egg yolk
1 tablespoon iced water

FILLING
100 g (3¹/2 oz) eggplant, thinly sliced
30 g (1 oz) butter
4 spring onions, finely chopped
1–2 cloves garlic, crushed
¹/2 small red capsicum, finely chopped
¹/4 cup (40 g/1¹/4 oz) sun-dried
  capsicums, drained and chopped
2 eggs, lightly beaten
³/4 cup (185 ml/6 fl oz) cream

1 Process the flour and butter for about 15 seconds until crumbly. Add the egg yolk and water. Process in short bursts until the mixture comes together. Add a little extra water if needed. Turn out onto a floured surface and gather into a ball. Wrap in plastic and refrigerate for at least 30 minutes.
2 To make the filling, brush the eggplant slices with olive oil and grill for 3 minutes on each side, until browned. Heat the butter in a pan and cook the spring onion, garlic and capsicum, stirring frequently, for 5 minutes, or until soft. Add the sun-dried capsicum and leave to cool. Combine the egg and cream and season with salt and pepper.
3 Grease six 8 cm (3 inch) fluted tart tins. Roll out the pastry thinly to line the tins, trimming off any excess. Cover and refrigerate for 15 minutes. Preheat the oven to 190°C (375°F/Gas 5). Cover the pastry shells with baking paper and spread with a layer of baking beads or rice. Bake for 10 minutes. Remove the paper and beads and bake for 10 minutes.
4 Divide the filling mixture among the pastry shells, then top with the eggplant and pour in the cream and egg mixture. Bake for 25–30 minutes, or until set.

NUTRITION PER QUICHE
Protein 7 g; Fat 35 g; Carbohydrate 25 g;
Dietary Fibre 2 g; Cholesterol 200 mg;
1940 kJ (460 cal)

Cut the slender eggplant into thin slices on the diagonal.

Brush the sliced eggplant with olive oil and grill until browned.

Mix together the egg and cream and then pour into the pastry shells.

Mini Quiches

Popular for handing out with drinks, a favourite with kids, and quick and easy to make (especially if you use ready-rolled frozen pastry), mini quiches should be in every cook's list of party tricks.

SMOKED SALMON AND DILL QUICHES

Roll 2 sheets of shortcrust pastry into 27 cm (11 inch) squares. Using a 7 cm (2³/4 inch) plain or fluted cutter, cut 12 rounds from each sheet. Line 6 cm (2¹/2 inch) patty tins with the pastry. Cover the pastry-lined tins and refrigerate for 10–15 minutes. Chop 100 g (3¹/2 oz) smoked salmon and set aside one quarter. Mix the remaining salmon with 125 g (4 oz) light cream cheese, 2 lightly beaten eggs, 2 tablespoons mayonnaise, 1 tablespoon each of chopped fresh chives and dill and 1 teaspoon of finely grated lemon rind. Fill the pastry shells with the salmon mixture. Bake in a preheated 190°C (375°F/Gas 5) oven for 15–20 minutes, or until the quiches are golden. Divide the remaining salmon over the top and garnish with sprigs of dill.
Makes 24

CORN AND SEMI-DRIED TOMATO QUICHES

Roll 2 sheets of puff pastry into 27 cm (11 inch) squares. Using a 7 cm (2³/4 inch) plain or fluted cutter, cut 12 rounds from each. Line 6 cm (2¹/2 inch) patty tins with the pastry. Cover the pastry-lined tins and refrigerate for 10–15 minutes. Cut 12 semi-dried tomatoes in half and set aside. Fry 2 chopped rashers of bacon in 1 teaspoon of butter until cooked and crisp, then place in a bowl with 2 lightly beaten eggs, ¹/2 cup (125 g/4 oz) sour cream, 310 g (10 oz) can creamed corn and 1 tablespoon chopped fresh parsley. Fill each pastry shell with the corn mixture and top with a tomato half. Bake in a preheated 190°C (375°F/Gas 5) oven for 15–20 minutes, or until puffed and golden.
Makes 24

CRAB AND SPRING ONION QUICHES

Butter and stack 6 sheets of filo pastry. Using an 8 cm (3 inch) plain cutter, cut 15 rounds. Place the pastry in 6 cm (2¹/2 inch) patty tins. Drain two 170 g (5¹/2 oz) cans crab meat. Squeeze the meat dry with your hands. Cook 4 chopped spring onions in 1 teaspoon of butter until softened. Mix together the crab meat, spring onions, 2 beaten eggs, ³/4 cup (185 ml/6 fl oz) cream, 1 tablespoon plain flour and 60 g (2 oz) grated Gruyère cheese. Fill each pastry case with the crab filling. Sprinkle with 30 g (1 oz) Gruyère cheese and place a sprig of fresh thyme over the top. Bake in a preheated 180°C (350°F/Gas 4) oven for 18–20 minutes, or until puffed and golden.
Makes 15

ZUCCHINI BOATS

Roll 3 sheets of shortcrust pastry into 27 cm (11 inch) squares. Cut each sheet into 6 rectangles and line eighteen 12 x 5.5 cm (5 x 2 inch) greased fluted pastry boats. Refrigerate for 10–15 minutes. Cook 1 diced small red onion and 2 crushed cloves garlic in 30 g (1 oz) butter until soft. Cool, then stir in 2 beaten eggs, $^1/_2$ cup (125 g/4 oz) sour cream, $^1/_3$ cup (30 g/1 oz) grated Parmesan and 1 thinly sliced small zucchini. Spoon into the pastry boats and bake at 190°C (375°F/Gas 5) for 15 minutes, or until puffed and golden.
Makes 18

MUSHROOM QUICHES

Cook 300 g (10 oz) diced mushrooms and 4 chopped spring onions in a little butter for 4–5 minutes, or until soft and dry. Add 1 tablespoon chopped fresh parsley. Cool. Add 2 beaten eggs and $^2/_3$ cup (170 ml/$5^1/_2$ fl oz) cream and season. Take 2 sheets shortcrust pastry and, using a 6 cm ($2^1/_2$ inch) fluted cutter, cut 12 circles from each sheet and use to line patty tins. Cover and refrigerate. Spoon in the filling and bake at 190°C (375°F/ Gas 5) for 15 minutes until puffed and golden.
Makes 24

SPINACH AND PROSCIUTTO BRIOCHE QUICHES

Roll 4 sheets of shortcrust pastry into 27 cm (11 inch) squares, then cut each sheet into quarters and use to line sixteen 8 cm (3 inch) diameter 3 cm ($1^1/_4$ inch) deep mini brioche tins. Cover the tins and refrigerate for 10–15 minutes. Finely chop 1 small red onion, thinly slice 4 slices of prosciutto and cook for 2–3 minutes in a little butter with 2 crushed cloves of garlic. Stir in 1 cup (200 g/$6^1/_2$ oz) wilted chopped English spinach, 1 cup (250 g/8 oz) ricotta cheese, 3 lightly beaten eggs, $^1/_2$ cup (125 ml/4 fl oz) cream, $^1/_2$ teaspoon nutmeg and season to taste. Spoon into the pastry cases and bake in a 200°C (400°F/ Gas 6) oven for 20 minutes, or until crisp and golden.
Makes 16

QUICHES, FROM LEFT: Smoked salmon and dill; Corn and semi-dried tomato; Crab and spring onion; Zucchini boats; Mushroom; Spinach and prosciutto brioche

Sweet Pies

RHUBARB PIE

Preparation time: 40 minutes +
    30 minutes refrigeration + cooling
Total cooking time: 1 hour
Serves 6

2 cups (250 g/8 oz) plain flour
30 g (1 oz) unsalted butter,
    chilled and cubed
70 g (2¼ oz) Copha (white vegetable
    shortening), chilled and cubed
2 tablespoons icing sugar
150 ml (5 fl oz) iced water

FILLING
1.5 kg (3 lb) rhubarb, trimmed and
    chopped
1 cup (250 g/8 oz) caster sugar
½ teaspoon ground cinnamon
2½ tablespoons cornflour
30 g (1 oz) unsalted butter, cubed
1 egg, lightly beaten
icing sugar, to dust

1 Grease a 20 cm (8 inch) ceramic pie dish. Sift the flour and ½ teaspoon salt into a large bowl and rub in the butter and Copha with your fingertips until the mixture resembles fine breadcrumbs. Stir in the icing sugar. Make a well, add almost all the water and mix with a flat-bladed knife, using a cutting action, until it comes together in beads. Add more water if necessary.

2 Gently gather the dough together and lift onto a lightly floured work surface. Press into a ball, flatten into a disc, wrap in plastic and refrigerate for 30 minutes.

3 Put the rhubarb, sugar, cinnamon and 2 tablespoons water in a saucepan and stir over low heat until the sugar is dissolved. Simmer, covered, for 5–8 minutes, stirring occasionally, until the rhubarb is tender. Mix the cornflour with ¼ cup (60 ml/2 fl oz) water and add to the pan. Bring to the boil, stirring until thickened. Allow to cool. Preheat the oven to 180°C (350°F/Gas 4) and heat a baking tray.

4 Roll out two-thirds of the dough to a 30 cm (12 inch) circle to line the pie dish. Spoon the rhubarb into the dish. Dot with butter.

5 Roll out the remaining pastry to form a lid. Moisten the pie rim with egg and press the top in place. Trim the edges and make a slit in the top. Decorate with pastry trimmings. Brush with egg and bake on the hot tray for 35–40 minutes, or until golden. Dust with icing sugar to serve.

NUTRITION PER SERVE
Protein 7.5 g; Fat 22 g; Carbohydrate 82 g;
Dietary Fibre 6 g; Cholesterol 55 mg;
2290 kJ (545 cal)

Simmer the rhubarb filling, stirring occasionally, until tender.

Moisten the rim of the pastry with egg and press the pastry top into place.

CHOCOLATE FUDGE PECAN PIE

Preparation time: 30 minutes +
    40 minutes refrigeration + cooling
Total cooking time: 1 hour 20 minutes
Serves 6

1¼ cups (150 g/5 oz) plain flour
2 tablespoons cocoa powder
2 tablespoons soft brown sugar
100 g (3½ oz) unsalted butter, chilled
    and cubed
2–3 tablespoons iced water

FILLING
2 cups (200 g/6½ oz) pecans,
    chopped
100 g (3½ oz) dark chocolate,
    chopped
½ cup (90 g/3 oz) soft brown sugar
⅔ cup (170 ml/2¾ fl oz) corn
    syrup
3 eggs, lightly beaten
2 teaspoons vanilla essence

1 Grease an 18 cm (7 inch) pie dish. Sift the flour, cocoa and sugar into a bowl and rub in the butter until the mixture resembles fine crumbs. Make a well, add the water and mix with a knife, adding more water if necessary.
2 Press the dough into a ball and refrigerate for 20 minutes. Roll out between two sheets of baking paper to fit the dish, trimming away the excess. Refrigerate for 20 minutes.
3 Preheat the oven to 180°C (350°F/ Gas 4). Cover the pastry with baking paper and spread with a layer of

baking beads or rice. Bake for 15 minutes. Remove the paper and beads and bake for 15–20 minutes, or until dry. Cool completely.
4 Put the dish on a tray. Spread the pecans and chocolate in the shell. Whisk the sugar, corn syrup, eggs and vanilla. Pour into the shell and bake for 45 minutes. Cool completely.

NUTRITION PER SERVE
Protein 11 g; Fat 45 g; Carbohydrate 82 g; Dietary Fibre 4 g; Cholesterol 132 mg; 3240 kJ (775 cal)

Use a rolling pin to help line the pie dish with the chocolate pastry.

Whisk together the sugar, corn syrup, eggs and vanilla with a fork.

MANGO AND PASSIONFRUIT PIES

Preparation time: 25 minutes +
  refrigeration
Total cooking time: 25 minutes
Makes 6

750 g (1¹/₂ lb) sweet shortcrust pastry
3 ripe mangoes, peeled and sliced or
  chopped, or 400 g (13 oz) can
  mango slices, drained
¹/₄ cup (60 g/2 oz) passionfruit pulp
1 tablespoon custard powder
¹/₃ cup (90 g/3 oz) caster sugar

1 egg, lightly beaten
icing sugar, to dust

1 Preheat the oven to 190°C (375°F/
Gas 5). Grease six 8 cm (3 inch) fluted
tart tins. Roll out two-thirds of the
pastry between two sheets of baking
paper until 3 mm (¹/₈ inch) thick. Cut
out six 13 cm (5 inch) circles. Line the
tins with the circles and trim the edges.
Refrigerate while you make the filling.
2 Mix together the mango, passionfruit, custard powder and sugar.
3 Roll out the remaining pastry
between two sheets of baking paper to
a thickness of 3 mm. Cut out six 11 cm

(4¹/₂ inch) circles. Re-roll the
trimmings and cut out small shapes
for decorations.
4 Fill the pastry cases with the mango
mixture and brush the edges with egg.
Top with the pastry circles and press
the edges to seal. Trim the edges and
decorate with the shapes. Brush the
tops with beaten egg and dust with
icing sugar. Bake for 20–25 minutes, or
until the pastry is golden brown.

NUTRITION PER PIE
Protein 11 g; Fat 29 g; Carbohydrate 85 g;
Dietary Fibre 6 g; Cholesterol 114 mg;
2685 kJ (640 cal)

Line the tins with the pastry circles and trim away
the excess pastry.

Spoon the mango and passionfruit filling into the
pastry cases.

Decorate the tops of the pies with shapes cut
from the pastry trimmings.

PUMPKIN PIE

Preparation time: 20 minutes +
  40 minutes refrigeration + cooling
Total cooking time: 1 hour 30 minutes
Serves 6–8

1¼ cups (150 g/5 oz) plain flour
100 g (3½ oz) unsalted butter, chilled
    and cubed
2 teaspoons caster sugar
4 tablespoons iced water

FILLING
750 g (1½ lb) butternut pumpkin,
    cubed
2 eggs, lightly beaten
1 cup (185 g/6 oz) soft brown sugar
⅓ cup (80 ml/2¾ fl oz) cream
1 tablespoon sweet sherry or brandy
½ teaspoon ground ginger
½ teaspoon ground nutmeg
1 teaspoon ground cinnamon

1 Sift the flour into a large bowl and rub in the butter with your fingertips until the mixture resembles fine breadcrumbs. Mix in the caster sugar. Make a well in the centre, add almost all the water and mix with a flat-bladed knife, using a cutting action, until the mixture comes together in beads, adding more water if needed.
2 Gather the dough together and lift out onto a lightly floured work surface. Press into a disc. Wrap in plastic and refrigerate for 20 minutes.
3 Roll out the pastry between two sheets of baking paper until large enough to line an 18 cm (7 inch) pie dish. Line the dish with pastry, trim away the excess and crimp the edges with a fork. Cover with plastic wrap and refrigerate for 20 minutes.
4 Preheat the oven to 180°C (350°F/Gas 4). Cook the pumpkin in boiling water until tender. Drain, mash, push through a sieve and leave to cool.
5 Line the pastry shell with baking paper and spread with a layer of baking beads or rice. Bake for 10 minutes, then remove the paper and beads and bake for 10 minutes, or until lightly golden. Set aside to cool.
6 Whisk the eggs and sugar together in a large bowl. Add the cooled pumpkin, cream, sherry and the spices and stir thoroughly. Pour into the pastry shell, smooth the surface and bake for 1 hour, or until set. If the pastry overbrowns, cover the edges with foil. Cool before serving.

NUTRITION PER SERVE (8)
Protein 6 g; Fat 16.5 g; Carbohydrate 45 g; Dietary Fibre 2 g; Cholesterol 90 mg; 1470 kJ (350 cal)

Bake the pastry for 10 minutes, then remove the paper and beads and cook until golden.

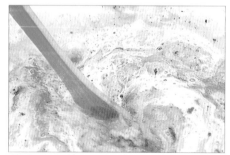
Stir the pumpkin, cream, sherry and spices into the egg and sugar mixture.

NUTTY FIG PIE

Preparation time: 40 minutes +
    20 minutes refrigeration
Total cooking time: 1 hour
Serves 8

375 g (12 oz) sweet shortcrust pastry
200 g (6¹/2 oz) hazelnuts
100 g (3¹/2 oz) pine nuts
100 g (3¹/2 oz) flaked almonds
100 g (3¹/2 oz) blanched almonds
150 ml (5 fl oz) cream
60 g (2 oz) unsalted butter
¹/4 cup (90 g/3 oz) honey
¹/2 cup (90 g/3 oz) soft brown sugar
150 g (5 oz) dessert figs, quartered

1 Preheat the oven to 200°C (400°F/ Gas 6) and grease an 18 cm (7 inch) pie tin. Roll the pastry out between two sheets of baking paper until large enough to line the tin, trimming away the excess. Prick the base several times with a fork. Score the edge with a fork. Refrigerate for 20 minutes, then bake for 15 minutes, or until dry and lightly golden. Allow to cool.
2 Meanwhile, bake the hazelnuts on a baking tray for 8 minutes, or until the skins start to peel away. Tip into a tea towel and rub to remove the skins. Place the pine nuts, flaked almonds and blanched almonds on a baking tray and bake for 5–6 minutes, or until lightly golden.

3 Place the cream, butter, honey and brown sugar in a saucepan and stir over medium heat until the sugar dissolves and the butter melts. Remove from the heat and stir in the nuts and figs. Spoon into the pastry case and bake for 30 minutes. Remove and cool until firm before slicing.

NUTRITION PER SERVE
Protein 11 g; Fat 57 g; Carbohydrate 44 g; Dietary Fibre 5.5 g; Cholesterol 57 mg; 3030 kJ (725 cal)

Roll out the pastry until large enough to line the pie tin, letting the excess hang over the edge.

Use a small, sharp knife to trim the excess pastry from the edge of the dish.

Spoon the nut and fig filling into the pastry-lined pie tin.

BRAMBLE PIE

Preparation time: 30 minutes +
  30 minutes refrigeration
Total cooking time: 40 minutes
Serves 4–6

1 cup (125 g/4 oz) self-raising flour
1 cup (125 g/4 oz) plain flour
125 g (4 oz) unsalted butter, chilled
  and cubed
2 tablespoons caster sugar
1 egg, lightly beaten
3–4 tablespoons milk

FILLING
2 tablespoons cornflour
2–4 tablespoons caster sugar, to taste
1 teaspoon grated orange rind
1 tablespoon orange juice
600 g (1¼ lb) brambles (see NOTE)
1 egg yolk, mixed with 1 teaspoon
  water, to glaze

1 Mix the flours, butter and sugar in a food processor for 30 seconds or until the mixture is fine and crumbly. Add the egg and almost all the milk; process for another 15 seconds or until the mixture comes together, adding more milk if needed. Turn onto a lightly floured surface and gather into a ball. Refrigerate for 30 minutes.
2 To make the filling, put the cornflour, caster sugar, orange rind and juice in a pan and mix well. Add half the brambles and stir over low heat for 5 minutes or until the mixture boils and thickens. Leave to cool, then add the remaining brambles. Pour into a 750 ml (24 fl oz) pie dish.
3 Preheat the oven to 180°C (350°F/ Gas 4). Divide the pastry dough in half and roll out one half until large enough to cover the dish, trimming away the excess. Roll out the other half and, using heart-shaped pastry cutters of various sizes, cut out enough hearts to cover the pie top. Brush the pie top with egg glaze. Bake for 35 minutes or until golden brown.

NUTRITION PER SERVE (6)
Protein 8 g; Fat 20 g; Carbohydrate 65 g;
Dietary Fibre 7 g; Cholesterol 115 mg;
1960 kJ (470 cal)

NOTE: Brambles include any creeping stem berries, such as boysenberries, blackberries, loganberries and youngberries. Use just one variety or a combination. You could use frozen or canned berries if you drain them well.

When the mixture has thickened, add the remaining brambles to the pan and stir.

Use small heart-shaped cutters to make shapes to decorate the top of the pie.

MULBERRY AND APPLE PIE

Preparation time: 30 minutes + refrigeration
Total cooking time: 45 minutes
Serves 4–6

2 cups (250 g/8 oz) plain flour
3 tablespoons caster sugar
1 teaspoon grated orange rind
185 g (6 oz) unsalted butter, chilled and cubed
2 egg yolks
2–3 tablespoons iced water

FILLING
410 g (13 oz) can pie apples
3 tablespoons caster sugar
1 tablespoon cornflour
500 g (1 lb) fresh mulberries or raspberries, stems removed
1 egg yolk, mixed with 1 teaspoon water, to glaze
1 egg white
2 tablespoons caster sugar, extra

1 Mix the flour, sugar, rind and butter in a food processor for 30 seconds or until fine and crumbly. Add the egg yolks and almost all the water and process for 20 seconds or until the mixture just comes together. Add more water if necessary. Turn onto a lightly floured surface and gather into a ball. Remove one quarter of the dough. Roll the larger portion out on a sheet of baking paper to a 25 cm (10 inch) circle. Roll the smaller portion into a rectangle. Refrigerate until required.
2 Put the apples, sugar and cornflour in a small pan and stir over low heat for 2–3 minutes until slightly thickened. Set aside to cool. Add the mulberries to the apples and gently fold through. Add more sugar to taste, if necessary. Spoon into a 23 cm (9 inch) pie dish. Brush the outer rim of the pie dish with egg glaze.
3 Preheat the oven to 210°C (415°F/Gas 6–7). Place the pastry circle over the pie and trim the edges. Using a pastry wheel, cut narrow strips from the remaining pastry and place them in a pattern on top of the pie. Cut a small circle to place in the centre.
4 Brush the pie with egg white and sprinkle with the extra caster sugar. Bake for 10 minutes, reduce the oven to 180°C (350°F/Gas 4) and bake the pie for 30 minutes or until golden.

NUTRITION PER SERVE (6)
Protein 9 g; Fat 28 g; Carbohydrate 70 g; Dietary Fibre 4 g; Cholesterol 163 mg; 2375 kJ (567 cal)

Using a pastry wheel, cut narrow strips of pastry to arrange in a pattern on the pie.

After brushing the pie top with egg white, sprinkle it generously with caster sugar.

BLACKBERRY PIE

Preparation time: 20 minutes +
    30 minutes refrigeration
Total cooking time: 40 minutes
Serves 6

500 g (1 lb) sweet shortcrust pastry
500 g (1 lb) blackberries
2/3 cup (160 g/5 1/2 oz) caster sugar
2 tablespoons cornflour
milk, to brush
1 egg, lightly beaten
caster sugar, extra, to sprinkle

1 Preheat the oven to 200°C (400°F/ Gas 6). Grease a 20 cm (8 inch) pie dish. Roll out two-thirds of the pastry between two sheets of baking paper until large enough to line the dish, pressing firmly into place and trimming away the excess.
2 Toss the blackberries, sugar and cornflour together in a bowl until well mixed, then transfer to the pie dish. Roll out the remaining pastry between two sheets of baking paper until large enough to cover the pie. Moisten the rim of the pie base with milk and press the pastry lid firmly into place. Trim and crimp the edges. Brush with egg and sprinkle with the extra sugar. Pierce the top of the pie with a knife.
3 Bake on the bottom shelf of the oven for 10 minutes. Reduce the oven to 180°C (350°F/Gas 4) and move the pie to the centre. Bake for another 30 minutes, or until golden on top. Cool before serving.

NUTRITION PER SERVE
Protein 8.5 g; Fat 20 g; Carbohydrate 75 g; Dietary Fibre 7 g; Cholesterol 87 mg; 2120 kJ (505 cal)

Press the pastry into the pie dish, trimming away the excess that hangs over the edge.

Spoon the blackberry filling into the pastry-lined pie dish.

After brushing the lid with beaten egg, sprinkle it with caster sugar.

SHAKER LEMON PIE

Preparation time: 20 minutes +
 20 minutes refrigeration
Total cooking time: 50 minutes
Serves 6–8

2 lemons
1/2 cup (60 g/2 oz) plain flour
2 cups (500 g/1 lb) caster sugar
40 g (11/4 oz) unsalted butter, melted
4 eggs, lightly beaten
1 egg, extra, lightly beaten, to glaze

PASTRY
3 cups (375 g/12 oz) plain flour
185 g (6 oz) unsalted butter, chilled
 and cubed
2 tablespoons caster sugar
4–5 tablespoons iced water

1 Finely grate 1 lemon to give
2 teaspoons of rind. Place this in
a large bowl. Cut the pith off both
lemons and discard. Thinly slice the
lemon flesh, discarding the seeds.
2 Sift the flour into the bowl with the
rind, then stir in the sugar and
a pinch of salt. Add the butter and egg
and stir until smooth. Gently fold in
the lemon slices.
3 Preheat the oven to 200°C (400°F/
Gas 6) and heat a baking tray. Grease
a 20 cm (8 inch) pie dish.
4 To make the pastry, sift the flour
and 1/4 teaspoon salt into a large bowl
and rub in the butter with your
fingertips until the mixture resembles
fine breadcrumbs. Mix in the sugar.
Make a well, add almost all the water
and mix with a flat-bladed knife, using
a cutting action, until the mixture
comes together in beads, adding more
water if necessary. Gather together on
a lightly floured surface and press into
a disc. Wrap in plastic and refrigerate
for 20 minutes.
5 Roll out two-thirds of the pastry
until large enough to fit the dish.
Spoon the filling into the pastry shell.
Roll out the remaining pastry until
large enough to cover the pie. Using a
sharp knife, cut out three small
triangles in a row across the centre of
the lid. Brush the rim of the pastry
base with beaten egg, then press the
lid in place. Trim off any excess.

Scallop the edges with your fingers,
then go around the open scallops and
mark with the tines of a narrow fork.
Brush the top with egg glaze.
6 Bake on the hot tray for 20 minutes.
Reduce the temperature to 180°C
(350°F/Gas 4), cover the pie with foil
and bake for 30 minutes, or until the
filling is set and the pastry golden.

NUTRITION PER SERVE (8)
Protein 9 g; Fat 26 g; Carbohydrate 106 g;
Dietary Fibre 2.5 g; Cholesterol 161 mg;
2880 kJ (690 cal)

Use a small sharp knife to remove all of the skin
and pith from the lemons.

Gently fold the lemon slices into the butter and
egg mixture.

FREEFORM BLUEBERRY PIE

Preparation time: 30 minutes +
    20 minutes refrigeration
Total cooking time: 30 minutes
Serves 6–8

1¹/₂ cups (185 g/6 oz) plain flour
100 g (3¹/₂ oz) unsalted butter, chilled
    and cubed
2 teaspoons grated orange rind
1 tablespoon caster sugar
2–3 tablespoons iced water

FILLING
¹/₃ cup (40 g/1¹/₄ oz) crushed amaretti
    biscuits or almond bread
¹/₂ cup (60 g/2 oz) plain flour
1 teaspoon ground cinnamon
¹/₃ cup (90 g/3 oz) caster sugar
500 g (1 lb) blueberries
milk, for brushing
2 tablespoons blueberry jam

1 Sift the flour into a large bowl and rub in the butter with your fingertips until the mixture resembles fine breadcrumbs. Stir in the orange rind and sugar. Make a well, add almost all the water and mix with a flat-bladed knife, using a cutting action, until the mixture comes together in beads. Add more water if necessary to bring the dough together. Turn out onto a lightly floured surface and gather into a ball. Wrap in plastic and refrigerate for 20 minutes.

2 Preheat the oven to 200°C (400°F/ Gas 6). Combine the biscuits, flour, cinnamon and 1¹/₂ tablespoons sugar. Roll the pastry out to a 36 cm (14 inch) circle and sprinkle with the biscuit mixture, leaving a 4 cm (1¹/₂ inch) border. Arrange the blueberries evenly over the biscuits, then bring up the edges of the pie to make a crust.

3 Brush the side of the pie with the milk. Sprinkle with the remaining sugar and bake for 30 minutes, or until the sides are crisp and brown.

4 Warm the jam in a saucepan over low heat and brush over the berries. Serve at room temperature.

NUTRITION PER SERVE (8)
Protein 4 g; Fat 13 g; Carbohydrate 51 g;
Dietary Fibre 3 g; Cholesterol 33 mg;
1370 kJ (325 cal)

Sprinkle the crushed biscuit mixture over the pastry circle, leaving a border.

Brush the blueberries with the warmed blueberry jam to glaze.

(center caption) Arrange the blueberries over the biscuit mixture, then bring up the edges of the pie.

LEMON MERINGUE PIE

Preparation time: 30 minutes
  + 20 minutes refrigeration
Total cooking time: 50 minutes
Serves 4–6

375 g (12 oz) sweet shortcrust pastry
$1/4$ cup (30 g/1 oz) plain flour
$1/4$ cup (30 g/1 oz) cornflour
1 cup (250 g/8 oz) caster sugar
$3/4$ cup (185 ml/6 fl oz) lemon juice
1 tablespoon grated lemon rind
50 g ($1^{1}/_2$ oz) unsalted butter,
  chopped
6 egg yolks

MERINGUE
6 egg whites
$1^{1}/_3$ cups (340 g/11 oz) caster sugar
pinch of cream of tartar

1 Lightly grease an 18 cm (7 inch) pie plate. Roll out the pastry between two sheets of baking paper into a 30 cm (12 inch) circle to line the pie plate,

trimming away the excess.
2 Re-roll the pastry trimmings and cut into three 10 x 2 cm (4 x $3/4$ inch) strips. Brush the pie rim with water, place the pastry strips around the top of the pastry rim and use your fingers to make a decorative edge. Prick all over the base with a fork. Cover and refrigerate for 20 minutes. Preheat the oven to 180°C (350°F/Gas 4).
3 Line the pastry with baking paper and spread with a layer of baking beads or rice. Bake for 15 minutes, then remove the paper and beads and bake for 15–20 minutes, or until dry. Leave to cool. Increase the oven to 200°C (400°F/Gas 6).
4 To make the lemon filling, put the flours, sugar, lemon juice and rind in a saucepan. Gradually add $1^{1}/_4$ cups (315 ml/10 fl oz) water and whisk over medium heat until smooth. Cook, stirring, for another 2 minutes, or until thickened. Remove from the heat and vigorously whisk in the butter and egg yolks. Return to low heat and stir for 2 minutes, or until very thick.

5 To make the meringue, beat the egg whites, sugar and cream of tartar in a clean, dry bowl with electric beaters, for 10 minutes until thick and glossy.
6 Spread the lemon filling into the cooled pastry base, then spread the meringue over the top, piling high in the centre and forming into peaks with a knife. Bake for 8–10 minutes, or until lightly browned.

NUTRITION PER SERVE (6)
Protein 11 g; Fat 28 g; Carbohydrate 133 g;
Dietary Fibre 1.5 g; Cholesterol 217 mg;
3385 kJ (810 cal)

Spread the meringue over the pie and then form into peaks with a knife.

DEEP-DISH APPLE PIE

Preparation time: 40 minutes +
  20 minutes refrigeration
Total cooking time: 50 minutes
Serves 6–8

2 teaspoons semolina
1¹/₂ cups (185 g/6 oz) plain flour
¹/₂ cup (60 g/2 oz) self-raising flour
125 g (4 oz) unsalted butter, chilled
  and cubed
¹/₄ cup (60 g/2 oz) caster sugar
1 egg
3–4 tablespoons iced water

FILLING
875 g (1 lb 13 oz) apples, peeled,
  cored, halved and thinly sliced
¹/₄ cup (60 g/2 oz) caster sugar
¹/₂ teaspoon ground cinnamon
¹/₄ teaspoon ground mixed spice
1 egg, separated
demerara sugar, to sprinkle

1 Grease a deep 19 cm (7¹/₂ inch) pie dish, then sprinkle it with semolina. Sift the flours and ¹/₄ teaspoon salt into a large bowl. Rub in the butter with your fingertips until the mixture resembles fine breadcrumbs. Mix in the sugar. Make a well in the centre, add the egg and most of the water and mix with a flat-bladed knife, using a cutting action, until the mixture comes together in beads, adding a little more water if necessary.
2 Turn out the dough onto a lightly floured work surface and gather into a smooth disc. Wrap in plastic and refrigerate for 20 minutes. Preheat the oven to 200°C (400°F/Gas 6).
3 Meanwhile, combine the apple, sugar and spices in a large bowl.
4 Roll out the dough between two sheets of baking paper to a rough-edged 40 cm (16 inch) circle and line the dish, leaving the excess pastry hanging over the edge. Brush the base with egg yolk. Pile the apple filling in the centre.
5 Bring the pastry edges up and over the filling, leaving a gap in the centre. Tuck and fold the pastry as necessary. Brush the pastry with egg white and sprinkle with the demerara sugar. Bake for 20 minutes, then reduce the

heat to 180°C (350°F/Gas 4). Bake for another 30 minutes, or until the pastry is crisp and golden. Cover with foil if the pastry is overbrowing. Serve hot or at room temperature.

NUTRITION PER SERVE (8)
Protein 5.5 g; Fat 15 g; Carbohydrate 51 g;
Dietary Fibre 3.5 g; Cholesterol 84.5 mg;
1470 kJ (350 cal)

Peel the apples, remove the cores and cut each in half, then thinly slice.

Brush the pastry with egg white and sprinkle with the demerara sugar.

ALMOND PIES

Preparation time: 20 minutes
Total cooking time: 25 minutes
Makes 8

50 g (1¹/₂ oz) flaked almonds
125 g (4 oz) unsalted butter, softened
1 cup (125 g/4 oz) icing sugar
125 g (4 oz) ground almonds
¹/₄ cup (30 g/1 oz) plain flour
2 eggs
1 tablespoon rum or brandy
¹/₂ teaspoon vanilla essence

4 sheets puff pastry
1 egg, lightly beaten
1 tablespoon sugar, to sprinkle

1 Preheat the oven to 200°C (400°F/ Gas 6). Toast the flaked almonds on a baking tray for 2–3 minutes, or until just golden. Remove and return the tray to the oven to keep it hot.
2 Beat together the butter, icing sugar, ground almonds, flour, eggs, rum and vanilla with electric beaters for 2–3 minutes, or until smooth and combined. Fold in the flaked almonds.
3 Cut out eight 10 cm (4 inch) rounds

and eight 11 cm (4¹/₂ inch) rounds from the puff pastry. Spread the smaller rounds with the filling, leaving a small border. Brush the borders with beaten egg and cover with the tops. Seal the edges with a fork. Pierce the tops to allow steam to escape. Brush with egg and sprinkle with sugar. Bake on the hot tray for 15–20 minutes, or until the pastry is puffed and golden.

NUTRITION PER PIE
Protein 12 g; Fat 46 g; Carbohydrate 50 g; Dietary Fibre 3 g; Cholesterol 128 mg; 2750 kJ (655 cal)

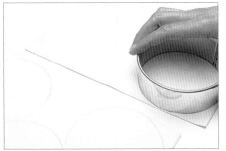

Use a 10 cm (4 inch) biscuit cutter to cut out the rounds of puff pastry.

Divide the almond filling equally among the eight puff pastry bases.

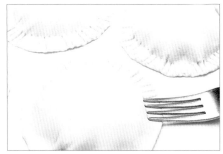

Seal the top pastry to the bottom by crimping the edges with a fork.

PEACH PIE

Preparation time: 35 minutes +
  20 minutes refrigeration
Total cooking time: 1 hour
Serves 6

500 g (1 lb) sweet shortcrust pastry
2 x 825 g (1 lb 11 oz) cans peach
  slices, drained
1/2 cup (125 g/4 oz) caster sugar
1/4 cup (30 g/1 oz) cornflour
1/4 teaspoon almond essence
20 g (3/4 oz) unsalted butter, chopped
1 tablespoon milk
1 egg, lightly beaten
1 tablespoon caster sugar, to sprinkle

1 Roll out two-thirds of the dough between two sheets of baking paper until large enough to line an 18 cm (7 inch) pie tin, pressing it firmly into the side and trimming away the excess. Refrigerate for 20 minutes.
2 Preheat the oven to 200°C (400°F/ Gas 6). Line the pastry with baking paper and spread with a layer of baking beads or rice. Bake for 10 minutes, remove the paper and beads and return to the oven for 5 minutes, until the base is dry and lightly golden. Allow to cool.
3 Mix the peaches, caster sugar, cornflour and almond essence and spoon into the pastry shell. Dot with butter and moisten the edge with milk.
4 Roll out the remaining dough to a 25 cm (10 inch) square. Using a fluted pastry cutter, cut the pastry into ten strips, each 2.5 cm (1 inch) wide. Lay the strips in a lattice pattern over the filling. Press firmly on the edges and trim. Brush the lattice with egg and sprinkle with sugar. Bake for 10 minutes, reduce the oven to 180°C (350°F/Gas 4) and bake for 30 minutes, or until the top is golden.

NUTRITION PER SERVE
Protein 7 g; Fat 25 g; Carbohydrate 70 g; Dietary Fibre 3 g; Cholesterol 62 mg; 2195 kJ (525 cal)

Combine the peaches with the caster sugar, cornflour and almond essence.

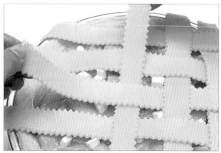
Lay the pastry strips in a lattice pattern over the top of the filling.

BANANA CREAM PIE

Preparation time: 25 minutes +
  20 minutes refrigeration
Total cooking time: 30 minutes
Serves 6–8

375 g (12 oz) shortcrust pastry
90 g (3 oz) dark chocolate chips
4 egg yolks
1/2 cup (125 g/4 oz) caster sugar
1/2 teaspoon vanilla essence
2 tablespoons custard powder
2 cups (500 ml/16 fl oz) milk
40 g (1 1/4 oz) unsalted butter, softened
1 teaspoon brandy or rum
3 large ripe bananas, thinly sliced
60 g (2 oz) dark chocolate, grated

1 Roll out the pastry between two sheets of baking paper to line an 18 cm (7 inch) pie tin, pressing it firmly into the side and trimming away the excess. Refrigerate for 20 minutes.
2 Preheat the oven to 190°C (375°F/ Gas 5). Line the pastry with baking paper and spread with baking beads or rice. Bake for 10 minutes, remove the paper and beads and bake for 10–12 minutes, until the pastry is dry and lightly golden.
3 While the pastry is still hot, place the chocolate chips in the base. Leave for 5 minutes to melt, then spread over the crust with the back of a spoon.
4 To make the filling, beat the egg yolks, sugar, vanilla and custard powder with electric beaters for 2–3 minutes, or until pale and thick. Bring the milk to boiling point in a small pan, then remove from the heat and gradually pour into the egg and sugar mixture, stirring well. Return to the pan and bring to the boil, stirring. Cook for 2 minutes, or until thickened. Remove from the heat and stir in the butter and brandy. Cool completely.
5 Arrange the banana over the chocolate, then pour the custard over the top. Refrigerate until ready to serve. Decorate with banana slices and the grated chocolate.

NUTRITION PER SERVE (8)
Protein 8 g; Fat 26 g; Carbohydrate 60 g;
Dietary Fibre 2 g; Cholesterol 124 mg;
2060 kJ (490 cal)

Beat the egg and sugar mixture until it is pale and thick.

Pour the custard into the pie shell over the banana slices.

APPLE PIE

Preparation time: 45 minutes +
  cooling time
Total cooking time: 50 minutes
Serves 6

6 large Granny Smith apples, peeled,
  cored and cut into wedges
2 tablespoons caster sugar
1 teaspoon finely grated lemon rind
pinch of ground cloves
2 tablespoons apricot jam
1 egg, lightly beaten
1 tablespoon sugar

PASTRY
2 cups (250 g/8 oz) plain flour
3 tablespoons self-raising flour
150 g (5 oz) butter, chilled and cubed
2 tablespoons caster sugar
4–5 tablespoons iced water

1 Put the apples in a large heavy-based pan with the sugar, lemon rind, cloves and 2 tablespoons water. Cover and simmer for 8 minutes, or until just tender, shaking the pan occasionally. Drain and cool.
2 To make the pastry, sift the flours into a bowl. Rub the butter into the flour with your fingertips until the mixture resembles fine breadcrumbs. Add the sugar, mix well and make a well in the centre. Add the water and mix with a flat-bladed knife, using a cutting action, until the mixture comes together in beads. Gather the pastry together on a floured surface. Divide into two, making one half a little bigger. Wrap in plastic and refrigerate for 20 minutes.
3 Preheat the oven to 200°C (400°F/ Gas 6). Roll out the larger piece of pastry between two sheets of baking paper to line a 23 cm (9 inch) pie plate, trimming away the excess pastry. Brush the jam over the base and spoon in the apple filling. Roll out the remaining piece of pastry between the baking paper until large enough to cover the pie. Brush a little water around the rim, to secure the top. Trim off the excess pastry, pinch the edges together and cut steam slits in the top.
4 Roll out the trimmings to make leaves to decorate the pie top. Brush the top lightly with egg and sprinkle with sugar. Bake for 20 minutes, then reduce the oven to 180°C (350°F/ Gas 4) and bake for 15–20 minutes, or until golden.

NUTRITION PER SERVE
Protein 7 g; Fat 20 g; Carbohydrate 60 g; Dietary Fibre 4 g; Cholesterol 95 mg; 1955 kJ (465 cal)

Roll out the pastry between two sheets of baking paper to prevent sticking.

Invert the pastry into the pie dish and peel off the baking paper.

Put the pastry lid on the pie and trim off any excess pastry.

KEY LIME PIE

Preparation time: 25 minutes
Total cooking time: 25 minutes +
  2 hours refrigeration
Serves 8

125 g (4 oz) sweet wheatmeal biscuits
90 g (3 oz) butter, melted
4 egg yolks
400 g (13 oz) can condensed milk
1/2 cup (125 ml/4 fl oz) lime juice
2 teaspoons finely grated lime rind
1 cup (250 ml/8 fl oz) cream, whipped
lime rind, to garnish

1 Finely crush the biscuits in a food processor for 30 seconds.
2 Transfer to a bowl, add the butter and mix thoroughly with the crumbs. Press into a 23 cm (9 inch) pie dish and refrigerate until firm. Preheat the oven to 180°C (350°F/Gas 4).
3 Beat the yolks, condensed milk, lime juice and rind with electric beaters for 1 minute. Pour into the crust and smooth the surface. Bake for 20–25 minutes, or until set.
4 Refrigerate the pie for 2 hours or until well chilled. Decorate with whipped cream and lime rind.

NUTRITION PER SERVE
Protein 9 g; Fat 19 g; Carbohydrate 47 g;
Dietary Fibre 1 g; Cholesterol 120 mg;
1615 kJ (385 cal)

Process the wheatmeal biscuits in a food processor until finely crushed.

Press the crumb base into a 23 cm (9 inch) diameter pie dish.

Beat the egg yolks, condensed milk, lime juice and rind until well combined.

Using a zester, make strips of lime rind to decorate the pie.

PEAR AND PECAN PIE

Preparation time: 25 minutes +
  40 minutes refrigeration + cooling
Total cooking time: 50 minutes
Serves 6

PASTRY

1¹/₂ cups (185 g/6 oz) plain flour
75 g (2¹/₂ oz) unsalted butter, chilled
  and cubed
50 g (1¹/₂ oz) Copha (white vegetable
  shortening), chilled and cubed
1 teaspoon caster sugar
2–3 tablespoons iced water

40 g (1¹/₄ oz) unsalted butter
¹/₂ cup (180 g/6 oz) golden syrup
2 tablespoons cornflour
¹/₄ teaspoon ground ginger
¹/₂ teaspoon grated lemon rind
¹/₂ teaspoon mixed spice
4 pears, peeled, cored and thinly
  sliced
1 cup (100 g/3¹/₂ oz) pecans,
  chopped
1 tablespoon caster sugar
1 tablespoon ground pecans
1 tablespoon sugar
1 egg, lightly beaten

1 To make the pastry, sift the flour and ¹/₄ teaspoon salt into a large bowl and rub in the butter and Copha with your fingertips until the mixture resembles fine breadcrumbs. Mix in the sugar. Make a well, add almost all the water and mix with a flat-bladed knife, using a cutting action, until the mixture comes together in beads, adding more water if necessary.
2 Gather the dough together and lift onto a lightly floured work surface. Press into a ball and flatten slightly into a disc. Cover in plastic wrap and refrigerate for 20 minutes.
3 Preheat the oven to 200°C (400°F/ Gas 6) and heat a baking tray. Grease an 18 cm (7 inch) pie dish. Roll out two-thirds of the pastry between two sheets of baking paper to line the dish, trimming away the excess. Cover and refrigerate for 20 minutes.
4 For the filling, heat the butter and golden syrup in a saucepan over medium heat for 2 minutes. Add the cornflour, ginger, rind and mixed spice and stir until smooth. Add the pears, then stir in half the chopped pecans and cook for 5 minutes, or until the pear is tender. Cool completely.
5 Combine the caster sugar and remaining chopped pecans and scatter over the pastry base. Add the filling.
6 Combine the ground pecans and sugar. Roll out the remaining pastry to form a pie lid. Brush with beaten egg. Cut long wide strips of paper and arrange over the pie lid in straight lines with wide gaps between. Scatter the nut and sugar mixture over the exposed pastry and roll lightly with the rolling pin to embed them. Lift off the paper strips, then position the lid on the pie, pinching the edges down to seal. Trim the rim.
7 Bake on the hot tray in the centre of the oven for 20 minutes. Reduce the oven to 180°C (350°F/Gas 4), cover the top with foil and bake for another 20 minutes. Cool in the tin. Serve warm or cold.

NUTRITION PER SERVE
Protein 7 g; Fat 34 g; Carbohydrate 69 g;
Dietary Fibre 5 g; Cholesterol 62 mg;
2485 kJ (595 cal)

Peel the pears, remove the cores and cut them into thin slices.

Add the cornflour, ginger, lemon rind and mixed spice and stir until smooth.

Spoon the pear filling over the base of the pastry shell.

Scatter the nut and sugar mixture over the pastry top, so that it forms stripes.

Carefully remove the paper strips from the pastry top without dislodging the nut topping.

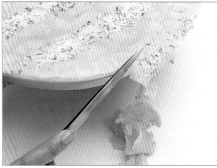

Position the deocorated lid on the pie and trim the edges neatly.

CHOCOLATE AND PEANUT BUTTER PIE

Preparation time: 30 minutes + 4 hours refrigeration
Total cooking time: 5 minutes
Serves 12

200 g (6½ oz) chocolate biscuits with cream centre, crushed
60 g (2 oz) unsalted butter, melted
1 cup (250 g/8 oz) cream cheese
⅔ cup (90 g/3 oz) icing sugar, sifted
½ cup (125 g/4 oz) smooth peanut butter
1 teaspoon vanilla essence
300 ml (10 fl oz) cream, whipped
¼ cup (60 ml/2 fl oz) cream, extra
3 teaspoons unsalted butter, extra
100 g (3½ oz) dark chocolate, grated
honey-roasted peanuts, to garnish

1 Mix the biscuit crumbs with the melted butter until thoroughly coated. Press the mixture into a deep 18 cm (7 inch) pie dish and refrigerate for 15 minutes, or until firm.
2 Beat the cream cheese and icing sugar with electric beaters until smooth. Add the peanut butter and vanilla and beat together well. Stir in a little of the whipped cream until the mixture is smooth, then very gently fold in the remaining whipped cream.
3 Pour two-thirds of the filling into the pie shell and smooth the top. Refrigerate the pie and the remaining filling for 2 hours, or until firm.
4 Put the extra cream and butter in a small saucepan and stir over medium heat until the butter is melted and the cream just comes to a simmer. Remove from the heat and add the grated chocolate. Stir until smooth and silky. Cool to room temperature, then pour over the top of the pie, smoothing if necessary with a spatula dipped in hot water. Refrigerate for another 2 hours, or until the topping is firm. Remove the extra filling from the fridge about 30 minutes before you serve.
5 Fill a piping bag with the softened filling and pipe rosettes or use two small spoons to decorate the edges of the pie. Top each rosette with a honey-roasted peanut. Serve in thin wedges as this pie is very rich.

NUTRITION PER SERVE
Protein 7 g; Fat 35 g; Carbohydrate 25 g; Dietary Fibre 1.5 g; Cholesterol 76 mg; 1820 kJ (435 cal)

Gently fold the whipped cream into the loosened peanut butter filling.

Pour the cooled chocolate over the top of the pie and smooth with a spatula.

WALNUT PIE WITH CARAMEL SAUCE

Preparation time: 40 minutes + cooling
Total cooking time: 40 minutes
Serves 8

2 cups (250 g/8 oz) plain flour
180 g (6 oz) unsalted butter, chilled
    and cubed
1/3 cup (40 g/1 1/4 oz) icing sugar
1 egg yolk
3–4 tablespoons iced water
1 egg yolk, lightly beaten, to glaze
icing sugar and walnuts, to garnish

FILLING
2 eggs
210 g (7 oz) caster sugar
150 g (5 oz) walnuts, finely chopped

CARAMEL SAUCE
40 g (1 1/4 oz) unsalted butter
1 1/4 cups (230 g/7 oz) soft brown
    sugar
2 teaspoons vanilla essence
200 ml (6 1/2 fl oz) cream

1 Sift the flour and 1/2 teaspoon salt into a large bowl and rub in the butter with your fingertips until the mixture resembles fine breadcrumbs. Mix in the icing sugar. Make a well, add the egg yolk and almost all the water and mix with a flat-bladed knife, using a cutting action, until the mixture comes together in beads.
2 Gather the dough together and lift onto a lightly floured work surface. Press together into a ball and flatten slightly into a disc. Wrap in plastic and refrigerate for 20 minutes.
3 Preheat the oven to 180°C (350°F/ Gas 4). Grease a fluted 36 x 11 cm (14 x 5 inch) pie tin. Beat the eggs and sugar with a spoon or whisk for 2 minutes. Stir in the walnuts.
4 Divide the dough into two portions, with one slightly larger than the other. Roll the larger portion out between two sheets of baking paper until large enough to line the base and sides of the pie tin. Refrigerate, covered in plastic wrap, while you roll out the remaining portion of pastry until it is large enough to cover the top of the tin.

5 Pour the walnut filling into the pastry case, brush the rim with the egg yolk and position the lid in place, pressing the edges to seal. Trim the edge. Make a steam hole in the top. Brush with egg yolk and bake for 30–35 minutes. Leave to cool for at least 1 hour (do not refrigerate).
6 To make the caramel sauce, place the butter, sugar, vanilla and cream in a saucepan and cook, stirring, for 5 minutes, or until thick. Dust the pie with the icing sugar and sprinkle with walnuts. Drizzle with the caramel sauce to serve.

NUTRITION PER SERVE
Protein 9 g; Fat 50 g; Carbohydrate 84 g; Dietary Fibre 2.5 g; Cholesterol 193 mg; 3345 kJ (800 cal)

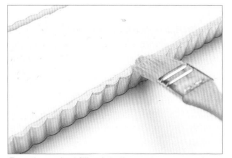
Pour the walnut filling into the pastry case and brush the rim with beaten egg yolk.

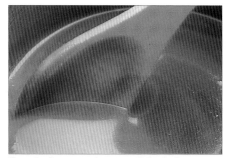
To make the caramel sauce, stir the butter, sugar, vanilla and cream over heat until thick.

QUINCE PIE WITH STICKY SYRUP

Preparation time: 50 minutes +
   20 minutes refrigeration
Total cooking time: 3 hours
Serves 8

2 cups (440 g/14 oz) demerara sugar
1 vanilla bean, split in half
6 cardamom pods, bruised
2 star anise
1 cinnamon stick
2 kg (4 lb) quinces, peeled, cored and
   cut into large wedges

PASTRY
100 g (3¹/2 oz) plain flour
100 g (3¹/2 oz) self-raising flour
100 g (3¹/2 oz) lard, chilled and grated
1–2 tablespoons iced water
2 tablespoons milk
¹/4 teaspoon ground cinnamon
2 teaspoons caster sugar

1 Place the sugar, vanilla bean, cardamom, star anise and cinnamon in a stockpot or very large saucepan with 1 litre water and stir over low heat until the sugar dissolves. Add the quinces and bring to the boil, then reduce the heat and simmer for 2 hours, or until orange and tender.
2 Remove the quinces with a slotted spoon and set aside. Strain the syrup into a bowl, then return it to the pan and boil for 10 minutes, or until reduced, thick and sticky.
3 Preheat the oven to 200°C (400°F/ Gas 6). Sift the flours and a little salt into a large bowl, add the lard and rub it into the flour with your fingertips until it resembles fine breadcrumbs. Make a well in the centre, add the water and mix with a flat-bladed knife, using a cutting action, until the mixture comes together in beads.
4 Gently gather the dough together and lift onto a lightly floured surface. Press together into a ball and flatten slightly into a disc. Wrap in plastic and refrigerate for 20 minutes.
5 Spoon the quince filling into a 20 cm (8 inch) pie plate and mix in ¹/2 cup (125 ml/4 fl oz) of the reserved syrup. Roll out the dough between two sheets of baking paper until large

enough to cover the pie, allowing any excess to hang over, and pinch the edges to seal. Trim away the excess pastry. Cut steam holes in the top and decorate with pastry trimmings. Brush the pastry with milk and sprinkle the combined cinnamon and sugar over the pie. Place on a baking tray and bake for 35–40 minutes, or until crisp and golden. Warm the remaining syrup and serve with the pie.

NUTRITION PER SERVE
Protein 4 g; Fat 13 g; Carbohydrate 67 g;
Dietary Fibre 12 g; Cholesterol 13 mg;
1645 kJ (395 cal)

Pour a small amount of syrup over the quince filling in the pie plate.

PEAR AND APPLE CRUMBLE PIE

Preparation time: 20 minutes +
  20 minutes refrigeration
Total cooking time: 1 hour 10 minutes
Serves 8

375 g (13 oz) shortcrust pastry
3 pears
4 Granny Smith apples
1/4 cup (60 g/2 oz) caster sugar
2 teaspoons grated orange rind
90 g (3 oz) raisins
3/4 cup (90 g/3 oz) plain flour
1/2 cup (90 g/3 oz) soft brown sugar
1/2 teaspoon ground ginger
90 g (3 oz) unsalted butter

1 Roll out the pastry between two sheets of baking paper until large enough to line an 18 cm (7 inch) pie dish, trimming away the excess. Wrap in plastic and refrigerate for 20 minutes.

2 Meanwhile, peel, core and slice the pears and apples and place in a large saucepan. Add the sugar, orange rind and 2 tablespoons water and cook over low heat, stirring occasionally for 20 minutes, or until the fruit is tender but still holding its shape. Remove from the heat, add the raisins and a pinch of salt, mix and leave to cool completely. Spoon into the pie dish.
3 Preheat the oven to 200°C (400°F/ Gas 6) and preheat a baking tray. To make the topping, put the flour, brown sugar and ginger in a bowl and rub in

the butter with your fingertips until the mixture resembles coarse breadcrumbs. Sprinkle over the fruit.
4 Put the dish on the hot baking tray, bake for 10 minutes, then reduce the oven to 180°C (350°F/Gas 4) and bake for 40 minutes, or until browned. Check after 20 minutes and cover with foil if the topping is overbrowing.

NUTRITION PER SERVE
Protein 5 g; Fat 22 g; Carbohydrate 72 g;
Dietary Fibre 5 g; Cholesterol 42 mg;
2055 kJ (490 cal)

Cook the pear and apple pieces, stirring occasionally, until tender.

Sprinkle the crumble mixture over the pear and apple filling.

RAISIN PIE

Preparation time: 15 minutes +
  20 minutes refrigeration
Total cooking time: 1 hour
Serves 8

600 g (1 1/4 lb) shortcrust pastry
1/3 cup (80 ml/2 3/4 fl oz) orange juice
2 tablespoons lemon juice
2 cups (320 g/11 oz) raisins
3/4 cup (150 g/5 oz) soft brown sugar
1/2 teaspoon mixed spice
1/4 cup (30 g/1 oz) cornflour
1 teaspoon finely grated lemon rind
1 teaspoon finely grated orange rind
1 egg, lightly beaten
1 tablespoon sugar, to sprinkle

1 Preheat the oven to 190°C (375°F/
Gas 5). Place a baking tray in the oven
to preheat. Grease an 18 cm (7 inch)
pie plate.

2 Roll out two-thirds of the pastry
between two sheets of baking paper to
line the dish, pressing firmly into the
side and trimming away the excess.
Refrigerate while you make the filling.
3 Combine the citrus juices, raisins
and 1 cup (250 ml/8 fl oz) water in a
small saucepan. Boil over high heat,
stirring occasionally, for 2 minutes.
Remove from the heat.
4 Mix the brown sugar, mixed spice
and cornflour in a bowl. Add 1/2 cup
(125 ml/4 fl oz) water and mix to a
smooth paste. Slowly stir into the
raisin mixture and return the saucepan
to high heat. Bring to the boil, stirring
regularly, then reduce the heat and
simmer, stirring occasionally, for
5 minutes, or until the mixture
thickens and reduces slightly. Stir in
the citrus rind and cool for 30 minutes.
5 Roll out the remaining pastry to
cover the pie. Fill the base with the
raisin mixture, brush the edge with

beaten egg and cover with the pastry
top, pinching the edges together and
making a few small holes with a
skewer. Decorate with pastry
trimmings. Brush with egg, sprinkle
with sugar and bake for 45 minutes, or
until golden. Serve warm or cold.

NUTRITION PER SERVE
Protein 6 g; Fat 20 g; Carbohydrate 76 g;
Dietary Fibre 3 g; Cholesterol 44 mg;
2095 kJ (500 cal)

Use a small ball of dough to press the pastry
base into the tin.

PLUM PIE

Preparation time: 15 minutes +
  20 minutes refrigeration
Total cooking time: 55 minutes
Serves 8

600 g (1¼ lb) sweet shortcrust pastry
14 large plums, halved, stoned
  and roughly chopped,
  or 2 x 825 g (1 lb 11 oz) tins
  plums, drained
½ cup (90 g/3 oz) soft brown sugar
1 teaspoon grated lemon rind
1 teaspoon grated orange rind
30 g (1 oz) unsalted butter, softened
2 tablespoons plain flour
½ teaspoon ground cinnamon
1 egg, lightly beaten
caster sugar, for sprinkling

1 Preheat the oven to 180°C (350°F/ Gas 4). Grease a 23 cm (9 inch) pie tin.
2 Roll out two-thirds of the pastry between two sheets of baking paper to line the tin, trimming away the excess pastry. Refrigerate with the remaining pastry for 20 minutes.
3 Combine the plums, brown sugar, citrus rind and butter in a large bowl. Sift the flour and cinnamon together over the plums and fold through. Place in the pie tin. Roll out the remaining pastry to cover the tin and trim the edge. Pinch the edges and make a small steam hole in the centre. Brush with egg and bake for 55 minutes, or until the pastry is golden. Sprinkle with caster sugar before serving.

NUTRITION PER SERVE
Protein 7 g; Fat 23 g; Carbohydrate 54 g; Dietary Fibre 5 g; Cholesterol 53 mg; 1870 kJ (445 cal)

Line the tin with the pastry and trim the edges with a small sharp knife.

Fold the sifted flour and cinnamon through the plum mixture.

Cover the pie with the pastry lid, trim the edges and pinch to seal.

MINCE PIES

Preparation time: 40 minutes +
  40 minutes refrigeration
Total cooking time: 25 minutes
Makes 24

2 cups (250 g/8 oz) plain flour
1/2 teaspoon ground cinnamon
125 g (4 oz) unsalted butter, chilled
  and cubed
1 teaspoon finely grated orange rind
1/4 cup (30 g/1 oz) icing sugar, sifted
1 egg yolk
3–4 tablespoons iced water

FILLING
1/3 cup (60 g/2 oz) raisins, chopped
1/3 cup (60 g/2 oz) soft brown sugar
1/4 cup (40 g/11/4 oz) sultanas
1/4 cup (45 g/11/2 oz) mixed peel
1 tablespoon currants
1 tablespoon chopped blanched
  almonds
1 small Granny Smith apple, grated
1 teaspoon lemon juice
1 teaspoon finely grated lemon rind
1 teaspoon finely grated orange rind
1/2 teaspoon mixed spice
1/4 teaspoon grated fresh ginger
pinch of ground nutmeg
25 g (3/4 oz) unsalted butter, melted
1 tablespoon brandy

1 Sift the flour, cinnamon and
1/4 teaspoon salt into a large bowl.
Add the butter and rub it into the flour
with your fingertips until it resembles
fine breadcrumbs. Stir in the orange
rind and icing sugar and mix. Make a
well in the centre and add the egg yolk
and water. Mix with a flat-bladed
knife, using a cutting action, until the
mixture comes together in beads,
adding more water if necessary.

Gather together, lift out onto a lightly
floured work surface and press
together into a disc, wrap in plastic
and refrigerate for 20 minutes. Mix
together all the filling ingredients.
2 Preheat the oven to 180°C (350°F/
Gas 4). Grease two 12-hole shallow
patty tins. Roll out two-thirds of the
pastry between two sheets of baking
paper until 3 mm (1/8 inch) thick. Use
an 8 cm (3 inch) round biscuit cutter to
cut out rounds to line the 24 patty tins.
3 Divide the filling among the patty
cases. Roll out the remaining pastry
and cut out 12 rounds with a 7 cm
(23/4 inch) cutter. Using a 2.5 cm
(1 inch) star cutter, cut a star from the
centre of each and use this small piece
to top 12 of the pies. Use the outside
part to top the other 12, pressing the
edges together to seal. Refrigerate for
20 minutes.
4 Bake for 25 minutes, or until the
pastry is golden. Leave in the tins for
5 minutes before cooling on a wire
rack. Dust with icing sugar to serve.

NUTRITION PER PIE
Protein 2 g; Fat 6 g; Carbohydrate 17 g;
Dietary Fibre 1 g; Cholesterol 23 mg;
535 kJ (130 cal)

NOTE: Any extra fruit mince can be
stored in a sterilised jar in a cool, dark
place for up to 3 months.

Use the fine side of the grater to grate the rind
from the orange.

Stir the orange rind and icing sugar into the butter
and flour mixture.

Mix the pastry using a cutting action until the
mixture comes together in beads.

Carefully spoon the fruit mince mixture into the patty tins.

Cut a star shape from the centre of 12 of the pastry circles.

Top 12 of the pies with stars and the rest with the outside parts.

REAL LEMON PIE

Preparation time: 25 minutes +
  overnight resting
Total cooking time: 50 minutes
Serves 10

LEMON FILLING
4 lemons
2 cups (500 g/16 oz) caster sugar
4 eggs

1³/₄ cups (220 g/7 oz) plain flour
150 g (5 oz) butter, chilled and cubed
2 tablespoons caster sugar
1–2 tablespoons iced water

1 Wash the lemons thoroughly and slice two of them very thinly (use a meat slicer if one is available), removing the seeds. Peel the remaining lemons and slice the flesh very thinly, removing the seeds and any white pith. Put the lemons in a bowl with the sugar and stir gently until all the slices are well coated. Cover and leave overnight.

2 Preheat the oven to 180°C (350°F/Gas 4). Mix the flour and a pinch of salt in a bowl. Rub in the butter until crumbly and stir in the sugar. Add the water, mixing with a knife. Press the dough together, divide in half and roll each portion into a 25 cm (10 inch)

circle. Lightly grease a 23 cm (9 inch) pie dish and line with one circle of pastry. Leave the other pastry circle flat, cover and refrigerate.

3 Beat the eggs and add to the lemon slices, mixing gently but thoroughly. Spoon into the pastry shell and cover with the other pastry circle, crimping the edges to seal. Brush the top with milk and then bake for 50–55 minutes, or until golden brown.

NUTRITION PER SERVE
Protein 3 g; Fat 14 g; Carbohydrate 55 g;
Dietary Fibre 1 g; Cholesterol 110 mg;
1476 kJ (353 cal)

Peel and remove the pith from two of the lemons and slice the flesh very thinly.

Divide the pastry in half and roll each portion into a 25 cm (10 inch) circle.

Use a ladle to spoon the lemon filling into the pastry shell.

FARMHOUSE RHUBARB PIE

Preparation time: 40 minutes + chilling
Total cooking time: 50 minutes
Serves 6

1¹/2 cups (185 g/6 oz) plain flour,
   sifted
125 g (4 oz) unsalted butter, chilled
   and cubed
2 tablespoons icing sugar
1 egg yolk
1 tablespoon iced water

FILLING
1 cup (250 g/8 oz) sugar
750 g (1¹/2 lb) chopped rhubarb
2 large apples, peeled, cored and
   chopped
2 teaspoons grated lemon rind
3 pieces preserved ginger, sliced
2 teaspoons sugar
sprinkle of ground cinnamon

1 Mix the flour, butter and icing sugar in a food processor until crumbly. Add the yolk and water and process until the dough comes together. Wrap in plastic and refrigerate for 15 minutes. Preheat the oven to 190°C (375°F/ Gas 5). Roll out the pastry to a rough 35 cm (14 inch) circle and line a greased 20 cm (8 inch) pie plate, leaving the extra pastry to hang over the edge. Refrigerate while you prepare the filling.
2 Heat the sugar and ¹/2 cup (125 ml/ 4 fl oz) water in a pan for 4–5 minutes or until syrupy. Add the rhubarb, apple, lemon rind and ginger, then cover and simmer for 5 minutes, until the rhubarb is cooked but still holds its shape.
3 Drain off the liquid and cool the rhubarb. Spoon into the pastry base and sprinkle with the sugar and cinnamon. Fold the overhanging pastry roughly over the fruit and bake for 40 minutes, or until golden.

NUTRITION PER SERVE
Protein 6 g; Fat 20 g; Carbohydrate 82 g;
Dietary Fibre 6 g; Cholesterol 83 mg;
2145 kJ (513 cal)

Add the egg yolk and iced water and process until the dough comes together.

Simmer until the rhubarb is tender but still holds its shape.

Fold the overhanging pastry roughly over the fruit so that there is an open area in the middle.

PLUM COBBLER

Preparation time: 25 minutes
Total cooking time: 40 minutes
Serves 6

750 g (1¹/₂ lb) plums
¹/₃ cup (90 g/3 oz) sugar
1 teaspoon vanilla essence

TOPPING
1 cup (125 g/4 oz) self-raising flour
60 g (2 oz) unsalted butter, chilled and
    cubed
¹/₄ cup (60 g/2 oz) soft brown sugar
¹/₄ cup (60 ml/2 fl oz) milk
1 tablespoon caster sugar

1 Preheat the oven to 200°C (400°F/ Gas 6). Cut the plums into quarters and remove the stones. Put the plums, sugar and 2 tablespoons water in a pan and bring to the boil, stirring, until the sugar dissolves.

2 Reduce the heat, then cover and simmer for 5 minutes, or until the plums are tender. Remove the skins if you prefer. Add the vanilla essence and spoon the mixture into a 3 cup (750 ml/24 fl oz) ovenproof dish.

3 To make the topping, sift the flour into a large bowl and add the butter. Rub in the butter with your fingertips until the mixture resembles fine breadcrumbs. Stir in the brown sugar and 2 tablespoons milk.

4 Stir with a knife to form a soft dough, adding more milk if necessary. Turn out onto a lightly floured surface and gather together to form a smooth dough. Roll out until 1 cm (¹/₂ inch) thick and cut into rounds with a 4 cm (1¹/₂ inch) cutter.

5 Overlap the rounds around the side of the dish over the filling. Lightly brush with milk and sprinkle with sugar. Bake on a tray for 30 minutes, or until the topping is golden and cooked through.

NUTRITION PER SERVE
Protein 3 g; Fat 9 g; Carbohydrate 50 g;
Dietary Fibre 3.5 g; Cholesterol 25 mg;
1245 kJ (295 cal)

Sift the flour into a bowl, then rub in the butter with your fingertips.

Stir with a flat-bladed knife, using a cutting action, to form a soft dough.

Roll out the dough to a thickness of 1 cm, then cut into rounds.

PECAN PIE

Preparation time: 30 minutes +
  20 minutes refrigeration
Total cooking time: 1 hour 10 minutes
Serves 6

1¹/₂ cups (185 g/6 oz) plain flour
125 g (4 oz) unsalted butter, chilled
  and cubed
2–3 tablespoons iced water

FILLING
200 g (6¹/₂ oz) pecans
3 eggs, lightly beaten
50 g (1³/₄ oz) unsalted butter, melted
  and cooled
³/₄ cup (140 g/4¹/₂ oz) soft brown
  sugar
²/₃ cup (170 ml/5¹/₂ fl oz) light corn
  syrup
1 teaspoon vanilla essence

1 Mix the flour and butter in a food processor for 20 seconds or until fine and crumbly. Add almost all the water and process briefly until the mixture comes together, adding more water if necessary. Turn out onto a lightly floured surface and gather into a ball.
2 Roll the pastry out to a large rectangle to line a fluted tart tin. Refrigerate for 20 minutes.
3 Preheat the oven to 180°C (350°F/ Gas 4). Cover the pastry with baking paper and spread with a layer of baking beads or rice. Bake for 15 minutes. Remove the paper and rice and bake for another 10 minutes, or until dry and golden. Cool completely.
4 Spread pecans over the pastry base. Whisk together the eggs, butter, brown sugar, corn syrup, vanilla and a pinch of salt, then pour carefully over the nuts. Decorate with pastry trimmings, put the tin on an oven tray and bake for 45 minutes. Allow to cool and serve at room temperature.

NUTRITION PER SERVE
Protein 10 g; Fat 53 g; Carbohydrate 42 g;
Dietary Fibre 5 g; Cholesterol 125 mg;
2850 kJ (676 cal)

Process the flour and butter in a food processor until the mixture comes together.

Line the tin with the pastry and trim off any excess before refrigerating.

After baking for 15 minutes, discard the paper and baking beads or rice.

Pour the whisked filling mixture carefully over the pecan nuts.

RASPBERRY LATTICE PIES

Preparation time: 50 minutes
Total cooking time: 25 minutes
Makes 8

125 g (4 oz) cream cheese
125 g (4 oz) unsalted butter
1 1/2 cups (185 g/6 oz) plain flour
1 egg, beaten
1 tablespoon caster sugar

FILLING
250 g (8 oz) raspberries
70 g (2 1/4 oz) unsalted butter, softened
1/3 cup (90 g/3 oz) caster sugar
1 egg
70 g (2 1/4 oz) ground almonds

1 Beat the cream cheese and butter until soft. Stir in the sifted flour with a knife and mix to a dough. Press together to form a ball. Lightly grease 8 small pie dishes or eight 1/2 cup (125 ml/4 fl oz) muffin tins. Roll out the pastry to 3 mm (1/8 inch) thick between two sheets of baking paper. Cut out 8 rounds with a 10 cm (4 inch) cutter and ease into the tins.
2 Divide the raspberries among the pastry cases. Cream together the butter and sugar and then beat in the egg. Fold in the almonds and spoon on top of the raspberries.
3 Preheat the oven to 180°C (350°F/ Gas 4). Roll out the pastry scraps and cut into 5 mm (1/4 inch) wide strips. Weave into a lattice on a board, lightly

press down with the palm of your hand and cut into rounds with the 10 cm (4 inch) Brush the pastry rims of the tartlets with beaten egg, put the lattice rounds on top and gently press down the edges to seal. Re-roll the scraps until all the tartlets are topped. Glaze with beaten egg, sprinkle with caster sugar and bake for 20–25 minutes, or until golden.

NUTRITION PER PIE
Protein 10 g; Fat 30 g; Carbohydrate 25 g; Dietary Fibre 4 g; Cholesterol 100 mg; 1677 kJ (400 cal)

Stir the sifted flour into the creamed mixture and mix to a dough with a knife.

Cut out rounds of pastry and then ease into the dishes or tins.

Brush the pastry edges with beaten egg and place the lattice on top.

CHERRY PIE

Preparation time: 25 minutes +
   15 minutes refrigeration
Total cooking time: 40 minutes
Serves 6–8

1¼ cups (155 g/5 oz) plain flour
¼ cup (30 g/1 oz) icing sugar
60 g (2 oz) ground almonds
100 g (3½ oz) unsalted butter, chilled
   and cubed
3 tablespoons iced water

2 x 700 g (1 lb 6 oz) jars pitted morello
   cherries, drained
1 egg, lightly beaten
caster sugar, to sprinkle

1 Sift the flour and icing sugar into a bowl and then stir in the ground almonds. Add the butter and rub in with your fingertips until the mixture resembles fine breadcrumbs. Add almost all the water and cut into the flour mixture with a knife until the mixture forms beads, adding the remaining water if necessary.
2 Turn the dough out onto a lightly floured surface and press together until smooth. Roll out the dough to a circle about 25 cm (10 inches). Cover with plastic wrap and refrigerate for about 15 minutes.
3 Preheat the oven to 200°C (400°F/ Gas 6). Spoon the cherries into a 23 cm (9 inch) round pie dish. Cover the pie dish with the pastry top and trim away the excess. Roll out the trimmings to make decorations. Brush the pastry top with beaten egg to secure the decorations on top. Sprinkle lightly with caster sugar. Place the pie dish on a baking tray to catch drips and cook for 35–40 minutes or until golden.

NUTRITION PER SERVE (8)
Protein 5 g; Fat 14 g; Carbohydrate 37 g;
Dietary Fibre 4 g; Cholesterol 54 mg;
1233 kJ (295 cal)

Rub the butter into the flour, using your fingertips until the mixture is fine and crumbly.

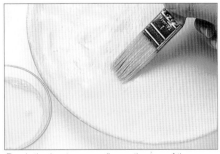

Brush the beaten egg all over the top of the pastry, using a pastry brush.

APPLE STRUDELS

Preparation time: 20 minutes
Total cooking time: 30 minutes
Serves 8

4 green cooking apples
30 g (1 oz) butter
2 tablespoons orange juice
1 tablespoon honey
3 tablespoons sugar
1/2 cup (90 g/3 oz) sultanas
2 sheets puff pastry
3 tablespoons ground almonds
1 egg, lightly beaten
2 tablespoons soft brown sugar
1 teaspoon ground cinnamon

1 Preheat the oven to 220°C (425°F/ Gas 7). Lightly grease two oven trays. Peel, core and thinly slice the apples. Heat the butter in a pan and cook the apples for 2 minutes until lightly golden. Add the orange juice, honey, sugar and sultanas and stir until the sugar dissolves and the apples are just tender. Leave to cool completely.
2 Place a sheet of pastry on a flat work surface. Fold in half and make small cuts in the folded edge of pastry at 2 cm (3/4 inch) intervals. Open out and sprinkle with half of the ground almonds. Drain the apple and place half of the apple in the centre of the pastry. Brush the edges with egg and fold together, pressing firmly.

3 Place the strudel on the tray, seam-side down. Brush with egg and sprinkle with half of the combined sugar and cinnamon. Make another strudel with the other sheet of pastry and remaining apple filling. Bake for 20–25 minutes or until the pastry is golden and crisp.

NUTRITION PER SERVE
Protein 5 g; Fat 18 g; Carbohydrate 45 g; Dietary Fibre 4 g; Cholesterol 42 mg; 1412 kJ (337 cal)

VARIATION: Many types of fruit or canned fruit, such as pears, cherries or apricots, can be used for strudel.

Stir the fruit over heat until the sugar has dissolved and the apple is tender.

Make small cuts in the folded edge of the pastry at intervals.

Put the strudel on the oven tray and sprinkle with the combined sugar and cinnamon.

APPLE AND PECAN FILO PIE

Preparation time: 25 minutes
Total cooking time: 30 minutes
Serves 8

¹/₂ cup (60 g/2 oz) pecans
50 g (1³/₄ oz) butter
3 tablespoons caster sugar
1 teaspoon finely grated lemon rind
1 egg, lightly beaten
2 tablespoons plain flour
3 green apples
10 sheets filo pastry
40 g (1¹/₄ oz) butter, melted
icing sugar, to dust

1 Preheat the oven to 180°C (350°F/ Gas 4). Lightly grease a 35 x 11 cm (14 x 5 inch) tin. Spread the pecans in a single layer on an oven tray and bake for 5 minutes to lightly toast. Leave to cool, then chop finely.
2 Beat the butter, sugar, lemon rind and egg with electric beaters until creamy. Stir in the flour and nuts.
3 Peel, core and thinly slice the apples. Layer 10 sheets of the filo pastry in the tin, brushing each sheet with melted butter before laying the next sheet on top. Spread the nut mixture evenly over the pastry base and lay the apple slices on top.
4 Fold the overhanging pastry over the filling and brush with butter. Trim one side of the pastry lengthways and crumple it over the top of the tart. Bake for 45 minutes, or until brown and crisp. Before serving, dust with icing sugar. Serve hot or cold.

NUTRITION PER SERVE
Protein 4 g; Fat 22 g; Carbohydrate 27 g; Dietary Fibre 3 g; Cholesterol 51 mg; 1300 kJ (313 cal)

STORAGE: This tart is best eaten on the day it is made.

VARIATION: Thinly sliced pears can be used instead of apples. Walnuts can replace the pecans. Toasting the nuts improves their flavour and makes them a little more crunchy.

Lightly toast the pecans in the oven to improve their flavour, before chopping.

Beat the butter, sugar, rind and egg and then stir in the flour and nuts.

Spread the nut mixture into the pastry base and then arrange the sliced apple on top.

Fold the overhanging pastry over the filling and brush with melted butter.

221

Sweet Tarts

DATE CUSTARD TART

Preparation time: 35 minutes +
   20 minutes refrigeration
Total cooking time:
   1 hour 40 minutes
Serves 8

1¼ cups (150 g/5 oz) plain flour
90 g (3 oz) unsalted butter, chilled and
   cubed
60 g (2 oz) ground walnuts
2 tablespoons iced water

FILLING
125 g (4 oz) fresh dates
1 cup (250 ml/8 fl oz) milk
½ vanilla bean
2 eggs
¼ cup (60 g/2 oz) caster sugar
icing sugar, for dusting

1 Sift the flour into a large bowl and add the butter. Rub the butter into the flour with your fingertips until it resembles fine breadcrumbs. Stir in the walnuts, then make a well in the centre. Add the iced water and mix with a flat-bladed knife, using a cutting action until the mixture comes together in small beads.
2 Gently gather the dough together into a ball and transfer to a sheet of baking paper. Roll out to fit a 22 cm (9 inch) loose-based fluted tart tin.

Line the tin with the pastry, trim the edges and refrigerate for 20 minutes.
3 Preheat the oven to 170°C (325°F/ Gas 3). Line the pastry shell with baking paper and spread with a layer of baking beads or rice. Bake for 15 minutes, remove the paper and beads, then bake for 20 minutes, or until the pastry is lightly golden and dry. Leave to cool.
4 To make the filling, cut the dates into quarters lengthways and discard the stones. Arrange, cut-side-down, in circles on the pastry base. Pour the milk into a saucepan. Split the vanilla bean lengthways, scrape the seeds into the milk and add the bean. Slowly heat the milk until almost boiling.
5 Whisk the eggs and sugar together. Slowly pour the hot milk onto the egg mixture, whisking gently as you pour. Discard the vanilla bean.
6 Place the tin on a flat baking tray. Gently pour the custard over the dates. Bake for 1 hour, or until the custard has set. Cool to room temperature, then dust with icing sugar to serve.

NUTRITION PER SERVE
Protein 6 g; Fat 16 g; Carbohydrate 35 g; Dietary Fibre 2.5 g; Cholesterol 70 mg; 1228 kJ (293 cal)

Arrange the quartered dates, cut-side-down, in the blind-baked pastry base.

Split the vanilla bean and scrape the seeds into the milk. Add the seed pod as well.

PEAR AND ALMOND FLAN

Preparation time: 15 minutes +
  2 hours 30 minutes chilling
Total cooking time: 1 hour 10 minutes
Serves 8

1¼ cups (155 g/5 oz) plain flour
90 g (3 oz) butter, chilled and cubed
¼ cup (60 g/2 oz) caster sugar
2 egg yolks
1 tablespoon iced water

FILLING
165 g (5½ oz) butter, softened
⅔ cup (160 g/5½ oz) caster sugar
3 eggs
1¼ cups (230 g/7½ oz) ground
  almonds
1½ tablespoons plain flour
2 ripe pears

1 Grease a shallow 24 cm (9½ inch) loose-based tart tin. Place the flour, butter and sugar in a food processor and process until the mixture resembles breadcrumbs. Add the egg yolks and water and mix until the dough just comes together. Turn out onto a lightly floured surface and gather into a ball. Wrap in plastic and refrigerate for 30 minutes. Preheat the oven to 180°C (350°F/Gas 4).
2 Roll the pastry between two sheets of baking paper until large enough to line the tin, trimming off any excess. Sparsely prick the base with a fork. Line with baking paper, spread with a layer of baking beads or rice and bake for 10 minutes. Remove the paper and beads and bake for 10 minutes.
3 To make the filling, mix the butter and sugar with electric beaters for 30 seconds (don't cream the mixture).

Add the eggs one at a time, beating after each addition. Fold in the ground almonds and flour and spread smoothly over the cooled pastry base.
4 Peel and halve the pears lengthways and remove the cores. Cut the pears crossways into 3 mm (⅛ inch) slices. Separate the slices slightly, then place each half on top of the tart to form a cross. Bake for about 50 minutes, or until the filling has set (the middle may still be a little soft). Cool in the tin, then refrigerate for at least 2 hours before serving.

NUTRITION PER SERVE
Protein 7 g; Fat 30 g; Carbohydrate 48 g;
Dietary Fibre 2 g; Cholesterol 165 mg;
2085 kJ (500 cal)

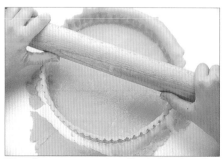

Trim off any excess pastry with a knife or by rolling the rolling pin over the tin.

Fold in the ground almonds and flour and mix until well combined.

Halve each pear lengthways and carefully remove the core.

STRAWBERRY AND MASCARPONE TART

Preparation time: 45 minutes +
   45 minutes refrigeration
Total cooking time: 30 minutes
Serves 6

PASTRY
1¹/₂ cups (185 g/6 oz) plain flour
125 g (4 oz) unsalted butter, chilled
   and cubed
¹/₃ cup (80 ml/2³/₄ fl oz)) iced water

FILLING
500 g (1 lb) strawberries, hulled and
   halved
2 teaspoons vanilla essence
50 ml (1¹/₂ fl oz) Drambuie
¹/₃ cup (60 g/2 oz) soft brown sugar
250 g (8 oz) mascarpone
300 ml (10 fl oz) thick cream
2 teaspoons finely grated orange rind

1 Sift the flour into a large bowl and add the butter. Rub the butter into the flour with your fingertips until it resembles fine breadcrumbs. Make a well in the centre, add almost all the water and mix with a flat-bladed knife, using a cutting action, until the mixture comes together in beads, adding the remaining water if needed. Gently gather the dough together and lift out onto a lightly floured surface.
2 Roll the dough out between two sheets of baking paper until large enough to line a lightly greased 23 cm (9 inch) loose-based tart tin. Trim away the excess then refrigerate the pastry-lined tin for 15 minutes. Preheat the oven to 200°C (400°F/Gas 6) and heat up a baking tray in the oven.
3 Line the pastry with baking paper and spread with a layer of baking beads or rice. Bake on the heated tray for 15 minutes. Remove the paper and beads and bake for 10–15 minutes, or until dry and golden. Cool completely.
4 Mix together the strawberries, vanilla, Drambuie and 1 tablespoon of the brown sugar in a bowl. In another bowl, mix the mascarpone, cream, orange rind and remaining brown sugar. Cover both bowls and refrigerate for 30 minutes, tossing the strawberries once or twice.
5 Whip half the mascarpone cream until firm, then evenly spoon it into the tart shell. Drain the strawberries, reserving the liquid. Pile the strawberries onto the tart. Serve slices of tart with a drizzle of the reserved strawberry liquid and the remaining mascarpone cream.

NUTRITION PER SERVE
Protein 9.5 g; Fat 53 g; Carbohydrate 37 g;
Dietary Fibre 3 g; Cholesterol 162 mg;
2729 kJ (652 cal)

Mix with a flat-bladed knife until the dough comes together in beads.

Remove the paper and baking beads from the pastry shell.

BERRY RICOTTA CREAM TARTLETS

Preparation time: 1 hour + 1 hour
  refrigeration
Total cooking time: 40 minutes
Serves 6

1¹/2 cups (185 g/6 oz) plain flour
¹/2 cup (90 g/3 oz) ground almonds
¹/3 cup (40 g/1¹/4 oz) icing sugar
125 g (4 oz) unsalted butter, chilled
  and cubed
1 egg, lightly beaten

FILLING
200 g (6¹/2 oz) ricotta
1 teaspoon vanilla essence
2 eggs
²/3 cup (160 g/5¹/2 oz) caster sugar
¹/2 cup (125 ml/4 fl oz) cream
¹/2 cup (60 g/2 oz) raspberries
¹/2 cup (80 g/2³/4 oz) blueberries
icing sugar, to dust

1 Sift the flour into a large bowl, then add the almonds and icing sugar. Rub the butter into the flour with your fingertips until it resembles fine breadcrumbs. Make a well in the centre and add the egg and mix with a flat-bladed knife, using a cutting action, until the mixture comes together in beads. Turn out onto a lightly floured work surface and gather into a ball. Wrap in plastic and refrigerate for 30 minutes.

2 Grease six 8 cm (3 inch) loose-based tart tins. Roll out the pastry between two sheets of baking paper to fit the base and side of the tins, trimming away the excess. Prick the bases with a fork, then refrigerate for 30 minutes. Preheat the oven to 180°C (350°F/Gas 4).

3 Line the pastry bases with baking paper and spread with a layer of baking beads or rice. Bake for 8–10 minutes and then remove the paper and beads.

4 Mix the ricotta, vanilla essence, eggs, sugar and cream in a food processor until smooth.

5 Divide the berries and filling among the tarts and bake for 25–30 minutes, or until the filling is just set—the top should be soft but not too wobbly. Cool. Dust with icing sugar to serve.

NUTRITION PER SERVE
Protein 14 g; Fat 42 g; Carbohydrate 62 g; Dietary Fibre 3.5 g; Cholesterol 187 mg; 2780 kJ (665 cal)

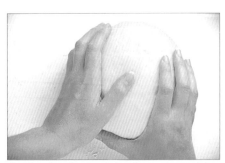

Gently gather the dough together and press into a ball. Wrap in plastic and refrigerate.

Roll out the pastry between two sheets of baking paper to prevent sticking.

Divide the berries among the pastry cases and then pour in the filling over the top.

CITRUS TART

Preparation time: 1 hour + 30 minutes
  refrigeration
Total cooking time: 1 hour 45 minutes
Serves 8

1 cup (125 g/4 oz) plain flour
75 g (2^1/$_2$ oz) unsalted butter, softened
1 egg yolk
2 tablespoons icing sugar, sifted

FILLING
3 eggs
2 egg yolks
^{3}/$_4$ cup (185 g/6 oz) caster sugar
^{1}/$_2$ cup (125 ml/4 fl oz) cream
^{3}/$_4$ cup (185 ml/6 fl oz) lemon juice
1^1/$_2$ tablespoons finely grated lemon
  rind
2 small lemons
^{2}/$_3$ cup (160 g/5^1/$_2$ oz) sugar

1 To make the pastry, sift the flour
and a pinch of salt into a large bowl.
Make a well in the centre and add the
butter, egg yolk and icing sugar. Work
together the butter, yolk and sugar
with your fingertips, then slowly
incorporate the flour. Bring together
into a ball—you may need to add a
few drops of iced water. Flatten the
ball slightly, wrap in plastic and
refrigerate for 20 minutes.
2 Preheat the oven to 200°C (400°F/
Gas 6). Lightly grease a shallow 21 cm
(8 inch) loose-bottomed flan tin.
3 Roll the pastry out between two
sheets of baking paper to about 3 mm
(^{1}/$_8$ inch) thick to fit the tin. Trim away
the excess pastry and refrigerate the
tin for 10 minutes. Line the pastry with
baking paper, spread with a layer of
baking beads or rice and bake for
10 minutes, or until cooked. Remove
the paper and beads and bake for
6–8 minutes, or until the pastry is
lightly golden and dry. Leave to cool.
4 Reduce the oven to 150°C (300°F/
Gas 2). Whisk the eggs, yolks and
sugar together, add the cream and
juice and mix well. Strain into a jug
and add the rind. Place the tin on a
baking sheet on the middle shelf of the
oven and carefully pour in the filling.
Bake for 40 minutes, or until just set—
the filling will wobble in the middle
when the tin is firmly tapped. Cool
before removing from the tin.
5 Wash and scrub the lemons well.
Slice very thinly. Combine the sugar
and 200 ml (6^1/$_2$ fl oz) water in a small
frying pan and stir over low heat until
the sugar has dissolved. Add the
lemon slices and simmer over low heat
for 40 minutes, or until the peel is very
tender and the pith looks transparent.
Lift out of the syrup and drain on
baking paper. Arrange over the top of
the tart.

NUTRITION PER SERVE
Protein 6 g; Fat 18 g; Carbohydrate 60 g;
Dietary Fibre 1 g; Cholesterol 180 mg;
1766 kJ (422 cal)

Work the butter, yolk and sugar together, then
slowly incorporate the flour.

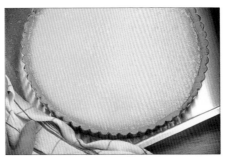
Bake the tart until the citrus filling is just set—it
should still wobble when you tap the tin.

Simmer the lemon peel until it is very tender and
the pith is transparent.

TARTE TATIN

Preparation time: 15 minutes
Total cooking time: 1 hour 10 minutes
Serves 6

100 g (3½ oz) unsalted butter
¾ cup (185 g/6 oz) sugar
6 large pink lady or fuji apples, peeled,
   cored and quartered (see NOTE)
1 sheet puff pastry

1 Preheat the oven to 220°C (425°F/
Gas 7). Lightly grease a 23 cm (9 inch)
shallow cake tin. Melt the butter in a
frying pan, add the sugar and cook,
stirring, over medium heat for
4–5 minutes, or until the sugar starts to
caramelise and turn brown. Continue
to cook, stirring, until the caramel
turns golden brown.
2 Add the apple to the pan and cook
over low heat for 20–25 minutes, or
until it starts to turn golden brown.
Carefully turn the apple over and cook
the other side until evenly coloured. If
much liquid comes out of the apple,
increase the heat until it has
evaporated—the caramel should be
sticky rather than runny. Remove from
the heat. Using tongs, arrange the hot
apple in circles in the tin and pour the
sauce over the top.
3 Place the pastry over the apple,
tucking the edge down firmly with
the end of a spoon. Bake for
30–35 minutes, or until the pastry is
cooked. Leave for 15 minutes before
inverting onto a serving plate. Remove
the paper before serving.

NUTRITION PER SERVE
Protein 2 g; Fat 20 g; Carbohydrate 47 g;
Dietary Fibre 1.5 g; Cholesterol 50 mg;
1544 kJ (370 cal)

NOTE: The moisture content of the
different apples varies quite a lot,
which affects the cooking time.
Golden delicious, pink lady or fuji are
good to use because they don't break
down during cooking.

Cook the butter and sugar until the caramel is
golden brown.

Remove the apple from the pan with tongs and
arrange in circles in the tin.

Arrange the pastry over the top of the apple in the
tin, to cover it completely, tucking down the edge.

PORTUGUESE CUSTARD TARTS

Preparation time: 40 minutes
Total cooking time: 40 minutes
Makes 12

1¼ cups (150 g/5 oz) plain flour
25 g (¾ oz) Copha (white vegetable
   shortening), softened
30 g (1 oz) unsalted butter, softened
1 cup (250 g/8 oz) sugar
2 cups (500 ml/16 fl oz) milk
3 tablespoons cornflour
1 tablespoon custard powder
4 egg yolks
1 teaspoon vanilla essence

1 Sift the flour into a large bowl and add about ³/₄ cup (185 ml/6 fl oz) water, or enough to form a soft dough. Gather together, then roll out on baking paper into a 24 x 30 cm (9¹/₂ x 12 inch) rectangle. Spread with the vegetable shortening. Roll up from the short edge to form a log.
2 Roll the dough out into a rectangle again, and spread with the butter. Roll up again into a roll and slice into 12 even pieces. Working from the centre, use your fingertips to press each round out until large enough to line twelve ¹/₃-cup (80 ml/2³/₄ fl oz) muffin holes. Refrigerate the tins.
3 Put the sugar and ¹/₃ cup (80 ml/ 2³/₄ fl oz) of water in a pan and stir

over low heat until the sugar dissolves.
4 Mix a little milk with the cornflour and custard powder to form a smooth paste, and add to the pan with the remaining milk, egg yolks and vanilla. Stir over low heat until thickened. Put in a bowl, cover and cool.
5 Preheat the oven to 220°C (425°F/ Gas 7). Divide the filling among the bases and bake for 25–30 minutes, or until the custard is set and the tops have browned. Cool in the tins, then transfer to a wire rack.

NUTRITION PER TART
Protein 3.5 g; Fat 7 g; Carbohydrate 35 g; Dietary Fibre 0.5 g; Cholesterol 75 mg; 892 kJ (215 cal)

Roll out the dough and spread with the white vegetable shortening.

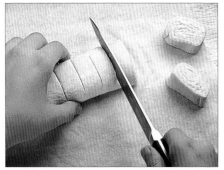
Slice the roll of dough into 12 even pieces with a sharp knife.

With your fingertips press each round out to a circle and press into the tin.

HONEY AND PINE NUT TART

Preparation time: 25 minutes +
  15 minutes refrigeration
Total cooking time: 1 hour
Serves 6

2 cups (250 g/8 oz) plain flour
1^1/$_2$ tablespoons icing sugar
115 g (4 oz) unsalted butter, chilled
  and cubed
1 egg, lightly beaten
2 tablespoons iced water

FILLING
1^1/$_2$ cups (235 g/7^1/$_2$ oz) pine nuts
^{1}/$_2$ cup (180 g/6 oz) honey
115 g (4 oz) unsalted butter, softened
^{1}/$_2$ cup (125 g/4 oz) caster sugar
3 eggs, lightly beaten
^{1}/$_4$ teaspoon vanilla essence
1 tablespoon almond liqueur
1 teaspoon finely grated lemon rind
1 tablespoon lemon juice
icing sugar, for dusting

1 Preheat the oven to 190°C (375°F/ Gas 5) and place a baking tray on the middle shelf. Lightly grease a 23 x 3.5 cm (9 x 1^1/$_2$ inch) deep-based tart tin. Sift the flour and icing sugar into a large bowl and add the butter. Rub in the butter with your fingertips until the mixture resembles fine breadcrumbs. Make a well in the centre and add the egg and water. Mix with a flat-bladed knife, using a cutting action, until the dough comes together in beads.
2 Turn out onto a lightly floured work surface and press together into a ball. Roll out to a circle 3 mm (^{1}/$_8$ inch) thick to line the tin and trim away any excess pastry. Prick the base all over with a fork and chill for 15 minutes. Cut out leaves from the trimmings for decoration. Cover and chill.
3 Line the pastry with baking paper and spread with a layer of baking beads or rice. Bake on the heated tray for 10 minutes, then remove.
4 Reduce the oven to 180°C (350°F/ Gas 4). To make the filling, spread the pine nuts on a baking tray and roast in the oven for 3 minutes, or until golden. Heat the honey in a small

saucepan until runny. Beat the butter and sugar in a bowl until smooth and pale. Gradually add the eggs, beating well after each addition. Mix in the honey, vanilla, liqueur, lemon rind and juice and a pinch of salt. Stir in the pine nuts, spoon into the pastry case and smooth the surface. Arrange the pastry leaves in the centre.
5 Place on the hot tray and bake for 40 minutes, or until golden and set. Cover the top with foil after

25 minutes. Serve warm, dusted with icing sugar, perhaps with crème fraîche or mascarpone cheese.

NUTRITION PER SERVE
Protein 14 g; Fat 63 g; Carbohydrate 83 g; Dietary Fibre 3.5 g; Cholesterol 217 mg; 3936 kJ (940 cal)

NOTE: The filling rises and cracks during baking but settles down as the tart cools.

Use a small ball of pastry to press the pastry into the base and side of the tin.

Arrange the pastry leaves over the smoothed pine nut filling.

LIME AND BLUEBERRY TART

Preparation time: 30 minutes +
  20 minutes refrigeration
Total cooking time: 1 hour
Serves 8

375 g (12 oz) sweet shortcrust pastry
3 eggs
1/2 cup (125 g/4 oz) caster sugar
1/4 cup (60 ml/2 fl oz) buttermilk
1 tablespoon lime juice
2 teaspoons finely grated lime rind
2 tablespoons custard powder
250 g (8 oz) blueberries

1 Roll out the pastry between two sheets of baking paper to line a 23 cm (9 inch) pie tin, trimming away the excess. Refrigerate for 20 minutes.
2 Preheat the oven to 200°C (400°F/ Gas 6). Line the pastry with baking paper and spread with baking beads or rice. Bake for 10 minutes, remove the paper and beads and bake for 4–5 minutes, or until the pastry is dry. Cool slightly. Reduce the oven to 180°C (350°F/Gas 4).
3 To make the filling, beat the eggs and caster sugar with electric beaters until thick and pale. Add the buttermilk, lime juice and rind, and sifted custard powder. Stir together, then spoon into the pastry shell. Bake for 15 minutes, then reduce the oven to 160°C (315°F/Gas 2–3) and cook for another 20–25 minutes, or until the filling has coloured slightly and is set. Leave to cool (the filling will sink a little), then top with the blueberries.

NUTRITION PER SERVE
Protein 5.5 g; Fat 14 g; Carbohydrate 38.5 g; Dietary Fibre 1 g; Cholesterol 81.5 mg; 1240 kJ (295 cal)

Bake the pastry, then remove the paper and beads and bake for another 5 minutes.

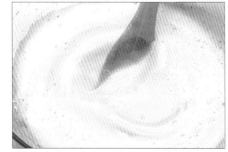
Stir the buttermilk, lime juice, rind and custard powder into the egg mixture.

CHOCOLATE TARTS

Preparation time: 30 minutes +
  20 minutes refrigeration
Total cooking time: 15 minutes
Makes 24

2 cups (250 g/8 oz) plain flour
2 tablespoons custard powder
125 g (4 oz) unsalted butter, chilled
  and cubed
1 egg yolk
2–3 tablespoons iced water

FILLING
250 g (8 oz) cream cheese, at room
  temperature
1/2 cup (125 g/4 oz) caster sugar
1 egg
125 g (4 oz) dark chocolate, melted
3 tablespoons ground almonds
100 g (3 1/2 oz) white chocolate,
  melted

1 Preheat the oven to 180°C (350°F/ Gas 4). Lightly grease two 12-cup shallow patty tins. Mix the flour, custard powder and butter in a food processor for 30 seconds, or until fine and crumbly. Add the egg yolk and almost all of the water and process for 20 seconds or until the mixture just comes together, adding the rest of the water if necessary. Turn out onto a lightly floured surface and gather into a smooth ball. Wrap in plastic and refrigerate for 20 minutes.

2 Divide the dough in two; wrap one portion and set aside. Roll the other half between two sheets of baking paper until 3 mm (1/8 inch) thick. Cut rounds with a 7 cm (2 3/4 inch) fluted cutter to line the tins. Repeat with the other portion of pastry. Refrigerate the trays while preparing the filling.

3 Beat the cream cheese and sugar until light and creamy. Add the egg and cooled melted chocolate. Beat until no streaks are visible. Stir in the almonds. Spoon into the pastry cases. Bake for 15 minutes or until just beginning to firm (the filling will set on standing.) Cool on a rack. Drizzle with white chocolate and leave to set.

NUTRITION PER TART
Protein 3 g; Fat 12 g; Carbohydrate 20 g;
Dietary Fibre 1 g; Cholesterol 40 mg;
827 kJ (200 cal)

Process the mixture for 30 seconds, or until it is fine and crumbly.

Cut out pastry rounds with a fluted pastry cutter and use to line the patty tins.

Spoon the chocolate filling into the pastry bases and then bake until just firm.

LITTLE LEMON TARTS

Preparation time: 40 minutes
Total cooking time: 15 minutes
Makes 24

2 cups (250 g/8 oz) plain flour
125 g (4 oz) unsalted butter, chilled
    and cubed
2 teaspoons caster sugar
1 teaspoon finely grated lemon rind
1 egg yolk
2–3 tablespoons iced water

FILLING
125 g (4 oz) cream cheese, softened
1/2 cup (125 g/4 oz) caster sugar
2 egg yolks

2 tablespoons lemon juice
1/2 cup (125 ml/4 fl oz) sweetened
    condensed milk

1 Preheat the oven to 180°C (350°F/
Gas 4). Lightly oil two 12-hole patty
tins. Sift the flour into a bowl. Rub in
the butter until the mixture resembles
fine breadcrumbs. Add the sugar, rind,
egg yolk and water and mix with a
knife, using a cutting action, until the
mixture forms beads. Turn out onto a
lightly floured surface and gather into
a smooth ball. Wrap in plastic and
refrigerate for 10 minutes.
2 Beat the cream cheese, sugar and
egg yolks until smooth and thickened.
Add the lemon juice and condensed
milk and beat together well.

3 Roll out the dough between two
sheets of baking paper until 3 mm
(1/8 inch) thick. Cut into rounds with a
7 cm (23/4 inch) fluted round cutter
and line the patty tins. Lightly prick
each base several times with a fork
and bake for 10 minutes, or until just
starting to turn golden. Spoon
2 teaspoons of filling into each case,
then bake for another 5 minutes, or
until the filling has set. Cool slightly
before removing from the tins.

NUTRITION PER TART
Protein 3 g; Fat 7 g; Carbohydrate 18 g;
Dietary Fibre 0.5 g; Cholesterol 41 mg;
611 kJ (146 cal)

Rub the butter into the flour with your fingertips
until the mixture resembles fine breadcrumbs.

Add the lemon juice and condensed milk to the
filling mixture.

Lightly prick each pastry case three times with a
fork to prevent the pastry rising.

CHOCOLATE-ALMOND TARTS

Preparation time: 40 minutes
Total cooking time: 15 minutes
Makes 18 tarts

1 cup (125 g/4 oz) plain flour
60 g (2 oz) unsalted butter, chilled and
    cubed
1 tablespoon icing sugar
1 tablespoon lemon juice

FILLING
1 egg
1/3 cup (90 g/3 oz) caster sugar
2 tablespoons cocoa powder
1/2 cup (90 g/3 oz) ground almonds
3 tablespoons cream
3 tablespoons apricot jam
18 blanched almonds

1 Preheat the oven to 180°C (350°F/
Gas 4). Lightly grease two 12-cup
shallow patty tins. Mix the flour, butter
and icing sugar in a food processor for
10 seconds, or until fine and crumbly.
Add the juice and process until the
dough forms a ball. Roll out between
two sheets of baking paper to 6 mm
(1/4 inch) thick. Cut rounds with a
7 cm (2³/4 inch) fluted cutter to line
the tins and refrigerate for 20 minutes.
2 Beat the egg and sugar with electric
beaters until thick and pale. Sift the
cocoa over the top. With a flat-bladed
knife, stir in the ground almonds
and cream.
3 Place a dab of jam in the centre
of each pastry base. Spoon the filling
into the bases and place an almond
in the centre of each one. Bake for
15 minutes, or until puffed and set on
top. Leave in the tins for 5 minutes,
then cool on wire racks.

NUTRITION PER TART
Protein 2 g; Fat 8 g; Carbohydrate 15 g;
Dietary Fibre 1 g; Cholesterol 23 mg;
560 kJ (135 cal)

Mix the flour, butter and icing sugar in a food
processor until fine crumbs form.

Use a flat-bladed knife to stir the ground almonds
and cream into the filling.

Spoon the filling into the pastry cases and then
place a blanched almond on top of each one.

DATE AND MASCARPONE TART

Preparation time: 50 minutes +
  25 minutes refrigeration
Total cooking time: 45 minutes
Serves 6–8

1/2 cup (90 g/3 oz) rice flour
1/2 cup (60 g/2 oz) plain flour
2 tablespoons icing sugar
1/4 cup desiccated coconut
100 g (31/2 oz) marzipan, chopped
100 g (31/2 oz) unsalted butter, chilled
  and cubed

FILLING
200 g (61/2 oz) fresh dates, stones
  removed
2 eggs
2 teaspoons custard powder

125 g (4 oz) mascarpone
2 tablespoons caster sugar
1/3 cup (80 ml/23/4 fl oz) cream
2 tablespoons flaked almonds

1 Preheat the oven to 180°C (350°F/ Gas 4). Grease a shallow 10 x 35 cm (4 x 14 inch) fluted loose-based tart tin. Mix the flours, icing sugar, coconut and marzipan in a food processor for 10 seconds. Add the butter and mix for 10–20 seconds, or until the dough just comes together when squeezed. (Do not overprocess.) Turn out onto a lightly floured surface and gather into a ball. Wrap in plastic and refrigerate for 15 minutes.
2 Cut the dates into quarters lengthways. Roll out the pastry between two sheets of baking paper until large enough to line the tin, trimming away the excess. Refrigerate

for another 5–10 minutes. Cover the pastry-lined tin with baking paper and spread with a layer of baking beads or rice. Place the tin on an oven tray and bake for 10 minutes. Remove from the oven and discard the paper and beads. Return to the oven and bake for another 5 minutes or until just golden. Leave to cool.
3 Arrange the dates over the pastry base. Whisk together the eggs, custard powder, mascarpone, sugar and cream until smooth. Pour over the dates and sprinkle with almonds. Bake for 25–30 minutes, or until golden and just set. Serve immediately, while still warm from the oven.

NUTRITION PER SERVE (8)
Protein 7 g; Fat 27 g; Carbohydrate 50 g;
Dietary Fibre 4 g; Cholesterol 106 mg;
1890 kJ (450 cal)

Process the mixture until the dough will just come together when squeezed.

Ease the pastry into the tin and then trim away the excess with a knife or rolling pin.

Arrange the dates in the pastry case and then pour the custard filling over the top.

ORANGE MACADAMIA TARTS

Preparation time: 40 minutes +
    15 minutes refrigeration
Total cooking time: 45 minutes
Makes 6

1¹/₂ cups (185 g/6 oz) plain flour
100 g (3¹/₂ oz) unsalted butter
3–4 tablespoons iced water

FILLING
1¹/₂ cups (240 g/7¹/₂ oz) macadamia
    nuts
3 tablespoons brown sugar
2 tablespoons light corn syrup

20 g (³/₄ oz) unsalted butter, melted
1 egg, lightly beaten
2 teaspoons finely grated orange rind

1 Preheat the oven to 180°C (350°F/Gas 4). Spread the nuts on an oven tray and bake for 8 minutes, or until lightly golden. Leave to cool.
2 Mix the flour and butter in a food processor for 15 seconds, or until fine and crumbly. Add almost all the water and process briefly until the dough just comes together, adding more water if necessary. Turn out onto a lightly floured surface and press together into a smooth ball. Divide into six portions and roll out to line six 8 cm (3 inch) fluted tart tins. Refrigerate the lined

tins for 15 minutes.
3 Line the tins with baking paper and spread with a layer of baking beads or rice. Bake for 15 minutes, then discard the paper and beads. Bake for another 10 minutes, or until the pastry is dry and lightly golden. Cool completely.
4 Divide the nuts among the tarts. With a wire whisk, beat the sugar, syrup, butter, egg, orange rind and a pinch of salt and pour over the nuts. Bake for 20 minutes, until set and lightly browned.

NUTRITION PER TART
Protein 7 g; Fat 43 g; Carbohydrate 40 g;
Dietary Fibre 3 g; Cholesterol 80 mg;
2360 kJ (560 cal)

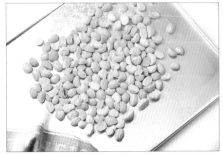

Spread the macadamia nuts on an oven tray and toast until lightly golden.

Divide the dough into six portions and roll out to line the tins.

Divide the nuts among the pastry cases and then pour the filling over the top.

BANANA TART

Preparation time: 40 minutes + chilling
Total cooking time: 35 minutes
Serves 6

1³/4 cups (215 g/7 oz) plain flour
160 g (5¹/2 oz) unsalted butter
  (chill 100 g/3¹/2 oz of it)

FILLING
grated rind and juice of 2 oranges
4 tablespoons soft brown sugar
¹/4 teaspoon cardamom seeds
1 tablespoon rum
3–4 ripe bananas

1 For the pastry, sift the flour into a bowl with a pinch of salt and rub in the unchilled butter. Mix in enough cold water (about 155 ml/5 fl oz) with a flat-bladed knife to make a dough-like consistency. Turn out onto a floured surface and knead until just smooth. Roll into a rectangle 10 x 30 cm (4 x 12 inches). Cut a third of the chilled butter into cubes and dot all over the top two-thirds of the pastry, leaving a little room around the edge. Fold the bottom third of the pastry up and the top third down and press the edges down to seal. Now turn the pastry to your left, so the hinge is on your right, and roll and fold as before. Chill for 20 minutes, then, with the hinge to your right, roll it out again, cover the top two-thirds of the pastry with another third of the butter and roll and fold. Repeat, using the rest of the butter. Roll and fold once more without adding any butter.
2 Roll out the pastry on a floured surface into a rectangle 25 x 30 cm (10 x 12 inches), cut a 2 cm (³/4 inch) strip off each side and use this to make a frame on the pastry by brushing the edges of the pastry with water and sticking the strips onto it. Trim off any excess and put the tart base on a baking tray lined with baking paper, cover with plastic wrap and refrigerate until required.
3 To make the filling, put the orange rind, juice, brown sugar and cardamom seeds in a small pan. Bring to the boil, simmer for 5 minutes, then remove from the heat and add the rum. Set aside to cool. Preheat the oven to 220°C (425°F/Gas 7).
4 Slice the bananas in half length-ways and arrange on the tart in an even layer, cut-side-up. Brush with a little syrup. Bake on the top shelf of the oven for 20–30 minutes, making sure the pastry does not overbrown. Brush with syrup and serve.

NUTRITION PER SERVE
Protein 5 g; Fat 22 g; Carbohydrate 49 g; Dietary Fibre 3 g; Cholesterol 68 mg; 1765 kJ (422 cal)

Roll the dough into a rectangle and dot the top two-thirds with cubes of chilled butter.

Fold the bottom third of the pastry up over the butter and then the top third down.

Turn the pastry over so the hinge is to the right. Press the edges down to seal, then roll and fold.

LEMON BRULEE TARTS

Preparation time: 40 minutes +
  4 hours refrigeration
Total cooking time: 35 minutes
Serves 4

1¼ cups (310 ml/10 fl oz) cream
2 teaspoons grated lemon rind
4 egg yolks
2 tablespoons caster sugar
2 teaspoons cornflour
2 tablespoons lemon juice
2 sheets puff pastry
⅓ cup (90 g/3 oz) sugar

1 Heat the cream in a pan with the lemon rind until almost boiling. Cool slightly. Whisk the egg yolks, sugar, cornflour and lemon juice until thick and pale. Add the cream gradually, whisking constantly. Strain into a clean pan and stir over low heat until thickened enough to coat the back of a wooden spoon. Pour into a heatproof bowl, cover with plastic wrap and refrigerate for at least 4 hours.
2 Preheat the oven to 210°C (415°F/ Gas 6–7). Lightly grease four 12 cm (5 inch) round loose-based tart tins. Cut two rounds of pastry from each sheet to line the tins. Trim the edges and prick the bases. Line with baking paper and spread with a layer of baking beads or rice. Bake for 15 minutes, discard the paper and beads and bake for another 5 minutes, or until lightly golden. Leave to cool.
3 Using a tart tin as a guide, cut four foil rings a little bigger than the tin. These will protect the pastry cases from burning. Spoon lemon custard into the pastry shells. Smooth the tops and do not overfill. Cover the edges with foil rings and sprinkle sugar generously over the custard. Cook under a very hot grill until the sugar begins to colour. Serve immediately.

NUTRITION PER SERVE
Protein 14 g; Fat 66 g; Carbohydrate 41 g;
Dietary Fibre 1 g; Cholesterol 632 mg;
33680 kJ (805 cal)

HINT: Put the tarts close to the grill so they brown quickly without burning.

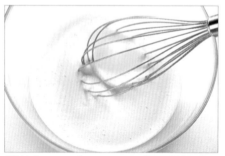
Whisk the egg yolks, sugar, cornflour and lemon juice until thick and pale.

Heat until the mixture thickens enough to coat the back of a spoon.

Spread a layer of baking beads or rice evenly over the paper and blind bake the pastry.

Cover the cooked pastry edges with a ring of foil to stop them burning.

RASPBERRY SHORTCAKE

Preparation time: 30 minutes +
  50 minutes refrigeration
Total cooking time: 20 minutes
Serves 6–8

1 cup (125 g/4 oz) plain flour
4 tablespoons icing sugar
90 g (3 oz) unsalted butter, chilled and
  cubed
1 egg yolk
1/2 teaspoon vanilla essence

TOPPING
750 g (1 1/2 lb) fresh raspberries
3–4 tablespoons icing sugar, to taste
4 tablespoons redcurrant jelly

1 Put the flour and icing sugar in a food processor. Add the butter and process for 15 seconds, or until the mixture is crumbly. Process for 10 seconds, adding the egg yolk, vanilla essence and enough cold water (about 1/2–1 tablespoon) to make the dough just come together. Turn out onto a lightly floured surface and gather together into a ball. Wrap in plastic and refrigerate for 30 minutes.
2 Preheat the oven to 180°C (350°F/ Gas 4). Roll out the pastry to fit a fluted 20 cm (8 inch) loose-based tart tin and trim the edges. Prick all over with a fork and chill for 20 minutes. Bake for 15–20 minutes, or until golden. Cool on a wire rack.
3 To make the topping, set aside 500 g (1 lb) of the best raspberries and mash the rest with the icing sugar. Spread the mashed raspberries over the shortcake just before serving. Cover with the whole raspberries.
4 Melt the redcurrant jelly in a small pan until smooth and brush over the raspberries with a soft pastry brush. Serve in slices with thick cream.

NUTRITION PER SERVE (8)
Protein 4 g; Fat 10 g; Carbohydrate 34 g;
Dietary Fibre 6 g; Cholesterol 50 mg;
1026 kJ (245 cal)

VARIATION: You can use 800 g (1 lb 10 oz) frozen raspberries. Thaw in the packet overnight in the fridge and only use when ready to serve.

Use your fingertips to bring the dough together and form into a smooth ball.

Remove any excess pastry by rolling across the top of the tin.

Use a fork to mash the icing sugar into the raspberries for the filling.

Use a soft pastry brush to heavily coat the raspberries with warm glaze.

PRUNE AND ALMOND CUSTARD TART

Preparation time: 2 hours + 1 hour
    soaking + refrigeration
Total cooking time: 50 minutes
Serves 6–8

375 g (12 oz) pitted prunes
2/3 cup (170 ml/5^{1}/$_{2}$ fl oz) muscat or
    sweet sherry
4 tablespoons redcurrant jelly

ALMOND SHORTCRUST PASTRY
1^{1}/$_{2}$ cups (185 g/6 oz) plain flour
1/3 cup (60 g/2 oz) ground almonds
1/4 cup (60 g/2 oz) caster sugar
125 g (4 oz) unsalted butter, chilled
    and cubed
1 egg yolk
2–3 tablespoons iced water
60 g (2 oz) marzipan, grated

CUSTARD CREAM
3 tablespoons custard powder
1^{2}/$_{3}$ cups (410 ml/13 fl oz) milk
1/2 cup (125 g/4 oz) sour cream
1 tablespoon caster sugar
2 teaspoons vanilla essence

1 Put the prunes in a pan with the muscat or sherry, leave to soak for 1 hour, then simmer over very low heat for 10 minutes, or until the prunes are tender but not mushy. Remove from the liquid with a slotted spoon and leave to cool. Add the redcurrant jelly to the pan and stir over low heat until dissolved. Cover and set aside.
2 To make the pastry, mix the flour, almonds and sugar in a food processor for 15 seconds. Add the butter and process for 15 seconds until crumbly. Add the egg yolk and enough water to make the dough just come together.

Turn out onto a lightly floured surface and gather into a ball. Refrigerate for 15 minutes. Preheat the oven to 180°C (350°F/Gas 4) and heat a baking tray.
3 Roll out the pastry between two sheets of baking paper until large enough to line a lightly greased 23 cm (9 inch) loose-based tart tin, trimming away the excess. (If it is still too soft, the pastry may need to be refrigerated for another 10 minutes.)
4 Cover the pastry with baking paper and spread with a layer of baking beads or rice. Chill for 15 minutes and then bake on the heated baking tray for 15 minutes. Remove the beads and paper, reduce the heat to 160°C (315°F/Gas 2–3) and bake for another 5 minutes. Sprinkle marzipan over the pastry base and bake for a further 5–10 minutes, or until golden. Leave in the tin to cool.
5 To make the custard cream, blend the custard powder with a little milk until smooth. Transfer to a pan and add the remaining milk, sour cream and sugar. Stir over medium heat for 5–7 minutes, or until thickened. Stir in the vanilla essence. (If you aren't using the custard cream immediately, lay plastic wrap on the surface to prevent a skin forming.)
6 Spread the warm custard cream evenly over the pastry case. Cut the prunes in half lengthways and arrange over the custard. Warm the redcurrant and muscat mixture and carefully spoon over the tart to cover it completely. Refrigerate for at least 2 hours to let the custard firm up before serving.

NUTRITION PER SERVE (8)
Protein 7 g; Fat 25 g; Carbohydrate 60 g;
Dietary Fibre 5 g; Cholesterol 88 mg;
2060 kJ (490 cal)

Cook the prunes over low heat until they are tender but not mushy.

Add only enough iced water to make the dough come together.

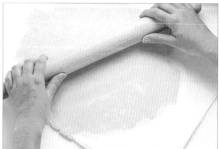

Roll out the pastry between two sheets of baking paper.

Lift the baking paper and beads or rice out of the pastry base.

Blend the custard powder with a little milk until smooth and then transfer to a pan.

Spread the warm custard ceam evenly into the pastry base.

SUMMER BERRY TART

Preparation time: 35 minutes +
  20 minutes refrigeration
Total cooking time: 35 minutes
Serves 4–6

1 cup (125 g/4 oz) plain flour
90 g (3 oz) unsalted butter, chilled and
  cubed
2 tablespoons icing sugar
1–2 tablespoons iced water

FILLING
3 egg yolks
2 tablespoons caster sugar
2 tablespoons cornflour
1 cup (250 ml/8 oz) milk
1 teaspoon vanilla essence
250 g (8 oz) strawberries, halved

125 g (4 oz) blueberries
125 g (4 oz) raspberries
1–2 tablespoons redcurrant jelly

1 Preheat the oven to 180°C (350°F/ Gas 4). Mix the flour, butter and icing sugar in a food processor for 15 seconds or until fine and crumbly. Add enough of the water to make the dough just come together. Turn out onto a lightly floured surface and press together into a ball. Roll out to line a 20 cm (8 inch) fluted tart tin, trimming away the excess. Refrigerate for 20 minutes. Line with baking paper and spread with a layer of baking beads or rice. Bake for 15 minutes, then remove the paper and beads. Bake for another 15 minutes, or until the pastry is dry and lightly golden.
2 Whisk the egg yolks, sugar and cornflour until pale. Heat the milk in a small pan until almost boiling, then add gradually to the egg mixture, beating constantly. Strain into the pan. Stir over low heat for 3 minutes or until the custard boils and thickens. Remove from the heat and add the vanilla. Transfer to a bowl, lay plastic wrap directly on the surface to prevent a skin forming, and leave to cool.
3 Spread the custard in the pastry shell. Top with the strawberries, blueberries and raspberries. Heat the redcurrant jelly until liquid in a small pan or in the microwave and brush over the fruit with a soft pastry brush.

NUTRITION PER SERVE (6)
Protein 6 g; Fat 17 g; Carbohydrate 36 g;
Dietary Fibre 2 g; Cholesterol 133 mg;
1317 kJ (315 cal)

Trim the excess pastry from the tin with a knife or by rolling over it with the rolling pin.

Press plastic wrap onto the surface of the custard to prevent a skin forming.

Warm the redcurrant jelly until it is liquid and brush over the fruit with a soft brush.

GOLDEN PINE NUT TARTS

Preparation time: 25 minutes
Total cooking time: 20 minutes
Makes 24

1/2 cup (60 g/2 oz) plain flour
60 g (2 oz) unsalted butter, chilled and
   cubed
3 tablespoons pine nuts
20 g (3/4 oz) unsalted butter, melted
1/2 cup (180 g/6 oz) golden syrup
2 tablespoons brown sugar

1 Preheat the oven to 180°C (350°F/Gas 4). Brush two 12-hole mini muffin tins with melted butter. Mix the flour and butter in a food processor for 20–30 seconds or until the mixture comes together. Turn out onto a lightly floured surface and press together into a smooth ball.
2 Roll out to a thickness of 3 mm (1/8 inch). Cut out rounds with a 5 cm (2 inch) fluted scone cutter. Lift gently with a flat-bladed knife and line each muffin hole with pastry. Spread the pine nuts on a baking tray and toast in the oven for 1–2 minutes, until just golden. Cool a little, then divide among the pastry cases.
3 Whisk together the butter, syrup and sugar. Pour over the pine nuts. Bake for 15 minutes, until golden. Cool the tarts in the trays for 5 minutes before cooling on a wire rack.

NUTRITION PER TART
Protein 0.5 g; Fat 4 g; Carbohydrate 9 g;
Dietary Fibre 0 g; Cholesterol 9 mg;
297 kJ (71 cal)

VARIATION: You can use chopped walnuts or pecans instead of pine nuts.

Turn the dough out onto a lightly floured surface and gather into a smooth ball.

Toast the pine nuts until lightly golden and then divide among the pastry cases.

Whisk together the butter, syrup and sugar and pour over the pine nuts.

PASSIONFRUIT TART

Preparation time: 30 minutes +
    20 minutes refrigeration
Total cooking time: 45 minutes
Serves 8

1 cup (125 g/4 oz) plain flour
$1/4$ cup (45 g/$1^1/2$ oz) ground almonds
$1/4$ cup (60 g/2 oz) caster sugar
60 g (2 oz) unsalted butter, chilled and
    cubed
2–3 tablespoons iced water

FILLING
6 egg yolks
$1/2$ cup (125 g/4 oz) caster sugar
$3/4$ cup (185 ml/6 fl oz) fresh
    passionfruit pulp
75 g ($2^1/2$ oz) unsalted butter
1 teaspoon gelatine
$1^1/2$ cups (325 ml/12 fl oz) cream,
    whipped

1 Preheat the oven to 180°C (350°F/
Gas 4). Mix the flour, almonds, sugar
and butter in a food processor for
30 seconds or until fine and crumbly.
Add almost all the water and process
for another 30 seconds or until the
dough just comes together (add more
water if necessary). Turn out onto a
lightly floured surface and press
together into a smooth ball.
2 Roll out the pastry to fit a 23 cm
(9 inch) fluted tart tin, trimming away
the excess. Refrigerate for 20 minutes.
Cover with baking paper and spread
with a layer of baking beads or rice.
Bake for 15 minutes, then discard the
paper and beads. Bake for another
15 minutes, or until the pastry is lightly
golden and dry. Cool completely.
3 Whisk the yolks and sugar in a
heatproof bowl for 1 minute or until
slightly thickened and pale. Stir in the
passionfruit pulp. Stand the bowl over
a pan of simmering water and stir
gently but constantly for 15 minutes,
adding the butter gradually until the
mixture thickens. Remove from the
heat and cool slightly.
4 Put the gelatine in a small bowl with
1 tablespoon water. Leave until
spongy, then stir until dissolved. Stir
thoroughly into the passionfruit filling.
Cool to room temperature, stirring
occasionally. Fold in a third of the
whipped cream. Spread into the pastry
shell and smooth the surface. Pipe the
remaining whipped cream around the
edge of the tart and decorate with
mandarin segments and passionfruit.

NUTRITION PER SERVE
Protein 7 g; Fat 40 g; Carbohydrate 40 g;
Dietary Fibre 3 g; Cholesterol 240 mg;
2257 kJ (540 cal)

STORAGE: Keep the tart refrigerated
until you are ready to serve.

Add almost all the iced water and mix until the
dough just starts to come together.

Whisk the egg yolks and sugar until thickened
and pale, then stir in the passionfruit pulp.

Dissolve the gelatine in a little water and then stir
into the passionfruit filling.

FILO PEACH TARTLETS

Preparation time: 40 minutes
Total cooking time: 25 minutes
Makes 8

6 sheets filo pastry
60 g (2 oz) unsalted butter, melted
2/3 cup (90 g/3 oz) slivered almonds
1 1/2 teaspoons ground cinnamon
1/2 cup (100 g/3 1/2 oz) soft brown
   sugar
3/4 cup (185 ml/6 fl oz) orange juice,
   strained
4 peaches

1 Preheat the oven to 180°C (350°F/ Gas 4). Cut each sheet of pastry into eight squares. Line eight large muffin tins with three layers of filo pastry, brushing the pastry with melted butter between layers and overlapping the sheets at angles.
2 Mix together the almonds, cinnamon and half the sugar. Sprinkle into the pastry cases, then cover with the three final squares of filo brushed with butter. Bake for 10–15 minutes.
3 Meanwhile, dissolve the remaining sugar in the orange juice, bring to the boil, reduce the heat and simmer. Halve the peaches and slice thinly.

Add to the syrup and stir gently to coat the fruit. Simmer for 2–3 minutes then lift from the pan with a slotted spoon. Arrange the peaches on the pastries.

NUTRITION PER TARTLET
Protein 2 g; Fat 7 g; Carbohydrate 27 g;
Dietary Fibre 1 g; Cholesterol 20 mg;
750 kJ (180 cal)

VARIATION: You can use tinned peaches if fresh are not available.

Brush the filo squares with melted butter and use three to line each tin.

Sprinkle the combined almonds, cinnamon and half the sugar over the pastry bases.

Remove the peaches from the syrup with a slotted spoon.

BANOFFIE PIE

Preparation time: 35 minutes +
  50 minutes refrigeration
Total cooking time: 40 minutes
Serves 8

1¼ cups (150 g/5 oz) plain flour
2 tablespoons icing sugar
90 g (3 oz) ground walnuts
80 g (2¾ oz) unsalted butter, chilled
  and cubed
2–3 tablespoons iced water

FILLING
400 g (13 oz) condensed milk
30 g (1 oz) unsalted butter
1 tablespoon golden syrup
4 bananas, sliced
1½ cups (375 ml/12 fl oz) cream
50 g (1¾ oz) dark chocolate, melted

1 Sift the flour and icing sugar into a large bowl. Add the walnuts. Rub in the butter until the mixture resembles fine breadcrumbs. Add the water, mixing with a knife until the dough just comes together. Turn out onto a lightly floured surface and press together into a ball. Wrap in plastic and refrigerate for 15 minutes. Roll out until large enough to line a 23 cm (9 inch) tart tin, trimming away the excess. Refrigerate for 20 minutes.
2 Preheat the oven to 180°C (350°F/ Gas 4). Cover the pastry with baking paper and spread with a layer of baking beads or rice. Bake for 15 minutes, then remove the paper and beads. Bake the pastry for another 20 minutes, or until dry and lightly golden. Leave to cool completely.
3 Heat the condensed milk, butter and syrup in a small pan for 5 minutes, stirring constantly until it boils, thickens and turns light caramel. Cool slightly. Arrange half the banana over the pastry and pour the caramel over the top. Refrigerate for 30 minutes.
4 Whip the cream and spoon over the caramel. Top with more banana and drizzle with melted chocolate.

NUTRITION PER SERVE
Protein 10 g; Fat 45 g; Carbohydrate 66 g; Dietary Fibre 3 g; Cholesterol 116 mg; 2940 kJ (700 cal)

Rub in the butter until the mixture forms crumbs, then stir in water until it comes together.

Line the tin with pastry and blind bake until it is dry and lightly golden.

Stir the condensed milk, butter and syrup over the heat until it boils, thickens and turns caramel.

Whip the cream and then spoon over the caramel, before topping with the banana.

LOW-FAT BANANA AND BLUEBERRY TART

Preparation time: 30 minutes
Total cooking time: 25 minutes
Serves 6

1 cup (125 g/4 oz) plain flour
1/2 cup (60 g/2 oz) self-raising flour
1 teaspoon cinnamon
1 teaspoon ground ginger
40 g (1¼ oz) unsalted butter, chilled
    and cubed
1/2 cup (95 g/3 oz) soft brown sugar

1/2 cup (125 ml/4 fl oz) buttermilk
200 g (6½ oz) blueberries
2 bananas
2 teaspoons lemon juice
1 tablespoon demerara sugar

1 Preheat the oven to 200°C (400°F/ Gas 6). Lightly grease a baking tray or pizza tray. Sift the flours and spices into a bowl. Add the butter and sugar and rub in until the mixture resembles fine breadcrumbs. Make a well in the centre and add enough buttermilk to mix to a soft dough.
2 Roll out the dough on a lightly

floured surface into a 23 cm (9 inch) circle. Place on the tray and roll the edge to form a lip to hold in the fruit.
3 Spread the blueberries over the dough. Slice the bananas, toss them in the lemon juice, then arrange over the top. Sprinkle with the sugar, and bake for 25 minutes, until the base is browned. Serve immediately.

NUTRITION PER SERVE
Protein 5 g; Fat 6 g; Carbohydrate 55 g;
Dietary Fibre 3 g; Cholesterol 20 mg;
1215 kJ (290 cal)

Rub the butter into the flour with your fingertips until the mixture resembles fine breadcrumbs.

Pour in the buttermilk, using enough to form a soft dough.

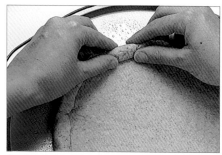
Put the circle of dough on the tray and roll the edge to form a lip.

LOW-FAT FRUIT TARTS

Preparation time: 25 minutes +
  30 minutes refrigeration
Total cooking time: 20 minutes
Makes 8

1 cup (125 g/4 oz) plain flour
1/4 cup (30 g/1 oz) custard powder
1/4 cup (30 g/1 oz) icing sugar
40 g (1 1/4 oz) unsalted butter
2 tablespoons skim milk
2 x 130 g (4 1/2 oz) tubs low-fat
  fromage frais
100 g (3 1/2 oz) ricotta
strawberries, blueberries, kiwi fruit
3–4 tablespoons redcurrant jelly

1 Lightly grease eight 7 cm (2 3/4 inch) loose-based tart tins. Process the flour, custard powder, icing sugar and butter in a food processor until the mixture forms fine crumbs, then add enough of the milk to form a soft dough. Gather together into a ball. Wrap in plastic and refrigerate for 30 minutes.
2 Preheat the oven to 200°C (400°F/ Gas 6). Divide the dough into eight portions and roll out to fit the tins. Cover with baking paper and spread with a layer of baking beads or rice. Bake for 10 minutes, remove the paper and beads and bake for another 10 minutes, or until golden. Allow to cool before removing from the tins.
3 Mix the fromage frais and ricotta until smooth. Spread over the pastry bases and top with fruit. Heat the redcurrant jelly until liquid in a small pan and brush over the fruit.

NUTRITION PER TART
Protein 3.5 g; Fat 8 g; Carbohydrate 20 g; Dietary Fibre 1 g; Cholesterol 20 mg; 690 kJ (165 cal)

Add enough milk to the crumbly mixture to form a soft dough.

Cover the pastry with baking paper and fill with a layer or baking beads or uncooked rice.

Remove the rice or beads and paper and return the pastry to the oven until golden.

LOW-FAT PASSIONFRUIT TART

Preparation time: 25 minutes +
   30 minutes refrigeration
Total cooking time: 1 hour
Serves 8

3/4 cup (90 g/3 oz) plain flour
2 tablespoons icing sugar
2 tablespoons custard powder
30 g (1 oz) unsalted butter, chilled and
   cubed
3 tablespoons light evaporated milk

FILLING
1/2 cup (125 g/4 oz) ricotta
1 teaspoon vanilla essence
1/4 cup (30 g/1 oz) icing sugar
2 eggs, lightly beaten
4 tablespoons passionfruit pulp
   (about 8 passionfruit)
3/4 cup (185 ml/6 fl oz) light
   evaporated milk

1 Preheat the oven to 200°C (400°F/
Gas 6). Lightly grease a 22 cm (9 inch)
loose-based tart tin. Sift the flour, icing
sugar and custard powder into a bowl
and rub in the butter until the mixture
resembles fine breadcrumbs. Add
enough evaporated milk to form a soft
dough. Bring together on a lightly
floured surface until just smooth.
Gather into a ball, wrap in plastic and
refrigerate for 15 minutes.
2 Roll the pastry out on a floured
surface, to fit the tin, then refrigerate
for 15 minutes. Cover with baking
paper and spread with baking beads
or rice. Bake for 10 minutes, remove
the beads and paper and bake for
another 5–8 minutes, or until golden.
Allow to cool. Reduce the oven to
160°C (315°F/Gas 2–3).
3 Beat the ricotta with the vanilla
essence and icing sugar until smooth.
Add the eggs, passionfruit pulp and
milk, then beat well. Put the tin on a
baking tray and gently pour in the
mixture. Bake for 40 minutes, or until
set. Allow to cool in the tin.

NUTRITION PER SERVE
Protein 8 g; Fat 6.5 g; Carbohydrate 25 g;
Dietary Fibre 3 g; Cholesterol 65 mg;
750 kJ (180 cal)

When the ricotta mixture is smooth, add the eggs,
passionfruit pulp and milk.

Put the tin on a baking tray to catch any drips and
gently pour in the filling.

Custards & Creams

Cream, custard or ice cream are all ideal companions for sweet pies and tarts. If you want to be a little more adventurous, try one of these flavoured creams or custards.

LIQUEUR CUSTARD

Using a wire whisk, beat 3 egg yolks and 2 tablespoons of sugar in a bowl for about 3 minutes, or until very light and creamy. Heat 1 1/2 cups (375 ml/ 12 fl oz) milk in a small pan until just boiling, then pour slowly onto the egg mixture, whisking constantly. Return to the pan and stir with a wooden spoon over very low heat for about 5 minutes, until the custard thickens enough to coat the spoon. Do not allow to boil or the custard will curdle. Stir in 1–2 tablespoons of your favourite liqueur to serve.
Serves 6–8

MASCARPONE BRANDY CREAM

Stir together 250 g (8 oz) mascarpone, 1/2 cup (125 ml/4 fl oz) cream and 1 tablespoon caster sugar until thoroughly combined. Beat 2 egg whites into firm peaks and fold through the mascarpone mixture with a metal spoon. Add brandy to taste (about 1–2 tablespoons) and stir to combine. Refrigerate for at least 1 hour before serving.
Serves 8

SABAYON

Place 4 egg yolks and 3 tablespoons caster sugar in a large heatproof bowl. Beat for 1 minute with electric beaters until the mixture is light and creamy. Stand the bowl over a pan of barely simmering water, add 1/2 cup (125 ml/ 4 fl oz) sweet white wine and continue beating for 5 minutes, until the mixture is thick, light and foamy. Serve immediately, as the sabayon will separate if left to stand.
Serves 8

YOGHURT CREAM

Whisk 1 cup (250 g/8 oz) plain yoghurt, 1/2 cup (125 g/4 oz) sour cream, 1 teaspoon of vanilla essence and 2 teaspoons of soft brown sugar together in a glass or ceramic bowl. Refrigerate for at least 8 hours before serving to let the cream thicken. Serves 6

ORANGE RICOTTA CREAM

Place 250 g (8 oz) ricotta cheese, 1/2 cup (125 ml/4 fl oz) cream, 1 teaspoon of finely grated orange rind and 2 tablespoons of caster sugar in a bowl. Beat with electric beaters for a minute until smooth. Add 2 tablespoons of Grand Marnier and beat until just mixed through. Refrigerate for 1 hour before serving. **Serves 6–8**

LEFT TO RIGHT: Liqueur custard, Mascarpone brandy cream, Yoghurt cream, Sabayon, Orange ricotta cream

Index

USEFUL INFORMATION

The recipes in this book were developed using a tablespoon measure of 20 ml. In some other countries the tablespoon is 15 ml. For most recipes this difference will not be noticeable but, for recipes using baking powder, gelatine, bicarbonate of soda, small amounts of flour and cornflour, we suggest that, if you are using the smaller tablespoon, you add an extra teaspoon for each tablespoon.

The recipes in this book are written using convenient cup measurements. You can buy special measuring cups in the supermarket or use an ordinary household cup: first you need to check it holds 250 ml (8 fl oz) by filling it with water and measuring the water (pour it into a measuring jug or a carton that you know holds 250 ml). This cup can then be used for both liquid and dry cup measurements.

Liquid cup measures

$1/4$ cup	60 ml	2 fluid oz
$1/3$ cup	80 ml	$2^3/4$ fluid oz
$1/2$ cup	125 ml	4 fluid oz
$3/4$ cup	180 ml	6 fluid oz
1 cup	250 ml	8 fluid oz

Spoon measures

$1/4$ teaspoon	1.25 ml
$1/2$ teaspoon	2.5 ml
1 teaspoon	5 ml
1 tablespoon	20 ml

Nutritional Information

The nutritional information given for each recipe does not include any garnishes or accompaniments, such as rice or pasta, unless they are included in specific quantities in the ingredients list. The nutritional values are approximations and can be affected by biological and seasonal variations in foods, the unknown composition of some manufactured foods and uncertainty in the dietary database. Nutrient data given are derived primarily from the NUTTAB95 database produced by the Australian and New Zealand Food Authority.

Oven Temperatures

You may find cooking times vary depending on the oven you are using. For fan-forced ovens, as a general rule, set oven temperature to 20°C lower than indicated in the recipe.

Note: Those who might be at risk from the effects of salmonella food poisoning (the elderly, pregnant women, young children and those suffering from immune deficiency diseases) should consult their GP with any concerns about eating raw eggs.

Alternative names (UK/US)

bicarbonate of soda	—	baking soda
besan flour	—	chickpea flour
capsicum	—	red or green bell pepper
chickpeas	—	garbanzo beans
cornflour	—	cornstarch
fresh coriander	—	cilantro
single cream	—	cream
aubergine	—	eggplant
flat-leaf parsley	—	Italian parsley
hazelnut	—	filbert
minced beef	—	ground beef
plain flour	—	all-purpose flour
polenta	—	cornmeal
prawn	—	shrimp
Roma tomato	—	plum or egg tomato
sambal oelek	—	chilli paste
mangetout	—	snow pea
spring onion	—	scallion
thick cream	—	heavy cream
tomato purée	—	tomato paste
courgette	—	zucchini

Weight

10 g	$1/4$ oz	220 g	7 oz	425 g	14 oz
30 g	1 oz	250 g	8 oz	475 g	15 oz
60 g	2 oz	275 g	9 oz	500 g	1 lb
90 g	3 oz	300 g	10 oz	600 g	$1^1/4$ lb
125 g	4 oz	330 g	11 oz	650 g	1 lb 5 oz
150 g	5 oz	375 g	12 oz	750 g	$1^1/2$ lb
185 g	6 oz	400 g	13 oz	1 kg	2 lb

This edition published in 2003 by Bay Books, an imprint of Murdoch Magazines Pty Limited, GPO BOX 1203, Sydney, NSW 1045, AUSTRALIA

Editor: Jane Price **Designer:** Annette Fitzgerald **Chief Executive:** Juliet Rogers **Publisher:** Kay Scarlett

ISBN 1 74045 272 0 Printed by Toppan Printing Hong Kong Co. Ltd. PRINTED IN CHINA.